Machine Learning 101: From Zero to Hero

Gilbert Gutiérrez

Artificial Intelligence is shaping the future of technology, and at the heart of it lies Machine Learning (ML)—the revolutionary field that enables computers to learn from data and make intelligent decisions. Whether you're a complete beginner or someone looking to deepen your understanding, Machine Learning 101: From Zero to Hero is your ultimate step-by-step guide to mastering the core concepts and applications of ML.

This book is the fourth installment in the AI from Scratch series, designed for those who want to build a strong foundation in artificial intelligence without prior experience. Through this structured guide, you will embark on a journey from understanding the basic principles of ML to implementing complex models in real-world scenarios. Each chapter is carefully crafted to provide clear explanations, practical examples, and hands-on projects that bring theoretical concepts to life.

Why This Book?

Unlike other books that overwhelm readers with complex jargon and abstract theories, Machine Learning 101: From Zero to Hero takes a beginner-friendly, step-by-step approach. Whether you are a student, developer, entrepreneur, or enthusiast, this book ensures you grasp the essential concepts before diving into advanced topics. We start with the absolute basics—what machine learning is, how it works, and why it matters—and gradually progress to practical coding implementations using Python, TensorFlow, and Scikit-learn.

By the end of this book, you will not only understand how machine learning models work but also gain hands-on experience in building, training, and optimizing ML models.

What You Will Learn

Part 1: Foundations of Machine Learning

- **Introduction to Machine Learning** – Understand the core idea behind ML, its importance in today's world, and how it differs from traditional programming.
- **Types of Machine Learning** – Explore the three main types: Supervised, Unsupervised, and Reinforcement Learning, along with real-world applications.
- **Mathematical Foundations** – Learn the essential mathematical concepts behind ML, including linear algebra, probability, statistics, and optimization techniques like gradient descent.
- **Understanding Data** – Discover how to collect, clean, preprocess, and engineer features from data to make it usable for ML models.

Part 2: Supervised Learning

- **Regression Models** – Learn about simple and multiple linear regression, polynomial regression, and regularization techniques like Lasso and Ridge.
- **Classification Models** – Understand how classifiers like Logistic Regression, Decision Trees, SVMs, and Naïve Bayes work.
- **Model Evaluation & Optimization** – Master the techniques of evaluating ML models, avoiding overfitting, and tuning hyperparameters using cross-validation and optimization methods.

Part 3: Unsupervised Learning

- **Clustering Algorithms** – Explore different clustering techniques like K-Means, Hierarchical Clustering, and DBSCAN, and learn how they group data.
- **Dimensionality Reduction** – Understand how PCA, t-SNE, and autoencoders help simplify high-dimensional data while retaining essential information.
- **Anomaly Detection & Association Rules** – Learn how ML is used to detect anomalies and find patterns in transactional data through techniques like Apriori and FP-Growth.

Part 4: Advanced Topics & Deep Learning

- **Neural Networks & Deep Learning** – Get an introduction to artificial neural networks, perceptrons, activation functions, and backpropagation.
- **Convolutional Neural Networks (CNNs)** – Learn how CNNs are used for image processing, feature extraction, and deep learning applications in computer vision.
- **Recurrent Neural Networks (RNNs) & LSTMs** – Understand how sequential data is processed in applications like time series forecasting and natural language processing.

Part 5: Practical Implementation & Real-World Applications

- **Machine Learning with Python** – Hands-on tutorials on using Python libraries such as Scikit-learn, TensorFlow, and PyTorch for ML development.
- **Building Your First ML Model** – A step-by-step guide to implementing, training, and optimizing your first machine learning model.
- **ML in the Real World** – Case studies on how ML is applied in industries like finance, healthcare, and e-commerce.

Part 6: Future of Machine Learning & Next Steps

- **Ethics & Bias in AI** – Discussion on fairness, transparency, and ethical concerns in machine learning.
- **The Future of Machine Learning** – Emerging trends like AutoML, federated learning, and quantum machine learning.
- **Becoming an ML Hero** – A roadmap for continuous learning, career paths, and building a portfolio in ML.

Who Is This Book For?

✔ **Beginners & Students** – If you are completely new to machine learning and want a structured, easy-to-follow guide, this book is perfect for you.

✔ **Developers & Engineers** – If you have basic programming knowledge but want to transition into machine learning, this book will provide hands-on experience.

✔ **Entrepreneurs & Business Professionals** – If you are looking to understand how machine learning can be applied in business, this book will give you the foundational knowledge you need.

✔ **AI Enthusiasts & Researchers** – If you are interested in AI but feel overwhelmed by the technical details, this book will simplify complex concepts in an engaging way.

Why Should You Read This Book?

📌 **Step-by-Step Learning** – Concepts are introduced gradually, ensuring a smooth learning curve.

📌 **Real-World Applications** – Includes case studies and examples from industries like healthcare, finance, and e-commerce.

📌 **Hands-On Coding** – Practical implementations using Python, Scikit-learn, TensorFlow, and PyTorch.

📌 **Beginner-Friendly Approach** – No prior experience in AI or ML is required.

Bonus Resources

🎯 Free access to datasets and ML projects for practice.

🎯 Online resources for further learning and career growth.

🎯 Exclusive membership to an AI learning community.

Final Thoughts

Machine Learning is no longer a futuristic technology—it is a present-day reality that is transforming industries and careers. Whether you are looking to start a career in AI, enhance your programming skills, or apply machine learning to your business, Machine Learning 101: From Zero to Hero will provide you with everything you need to succeed.

Join us on this exciting journey and take your first step toward mastering the world of machine learning! 🚀

1. Introduction to Machine Learning

Machine Learning (ML) is transforming industries by enabling computers to learn from data and make intelligent decisions. In this chapter, we introduce the fundamental concepts of ML, explore its real-world applications, and discuss how it differs from traditional programming. By the end, you'll have a solid understanding of why ML is a game-changer in AI.

1.1 What is Machine Learning?

Machine Learning (ML) is one of the most exciting and rapidly growing fields in technology today. It is a subset of Artificial Intelligence (AI) that enables computers to learn from data and make decisions or predictions without being explicitly programmed. From recommendation systems like Netflix and Amazon to self-driving cars and fraud detection in banking, ML is transforming industries and making technology smarter.

This chapter will introduce the fundamental concepts of Machine Learning, explore its real-world applications, and highlight how it differs from traditional programming. By the end of this section, you will have a solid foundation to understand why Machine Learning is considered a game-changer in the world of AI and data science.

Understanding Machine Learning

Definition of Machine Learning

Machine Learning is a field of study that focuses on developing algorithms that allow computers to learn from and make decisions based on data. Instead of being explicitly programmed with a fixed set of instructions, ML systems use data to improve their performance over time. The term "Machine Learning" was coined by Arthur Samuel in 1959, who defined it as:

"The field of study that gives computers the ability to learn without being explicitly programmed."

A more formal definition by Tom Mitchell (1997) states:

"A computer program is said to learn from experience E with respect to some task T and some performance measure P, if its performance on T, as measured by P, improves with experience E."

This means that an ML model improves its accuracy as it processes more data and learns patterns over time.

How Machine Learning Works

Machine Learning operates through a cycle of training and testing. Here's a high-level overview of how an ML model is developed:

Collecting Data: A dataset is gathered from various sources like databases, sensors, web scrapers, or user input.

Data Preprocessing: The collected data is cleaned, formatted, and structured to be usable for the model.

Feature Selection: Important features (variables) are chosen to ensure the model captures meaningful patterns.

Choosing a Model: A suitable algorithm is selected based on the problem (classification, regression, clustering, etc.).

Training the Model: The model is fed historical data so it can learn patterns and relationships.

Evaluating the Model: The model is tested on new, unseen data to assess its accuracy and performance.

Fine-Tuning: Hyperparameters are adjusted to improve model accuracy.

Deployment: The final model is deployed for real-world use, where it continuously improves with new data.

This iterative learning process allows ML models to improve over time without human intervention.

Traditional Programming vs. Machine Learning

In traditional programming, a programmer writes explicit rules and conditions to solve a problem. The logic is hardcoded into the program, and any changes require manual updates. For example, a rule-based spam filter might block emails containing specific words like "lottery" or "free money."

In Machine Learning, the computer learns rules by analyzing large datasets instead of relying on fixed conditions. A spam filter powered by ML will analyze thousands of spam emails, identify patterns, and create a model that predicts whether a new email is spam based on learned characteristics.

Feature	Traditional Programming	Machine Learning
Approach	Rule-based instructions	Data-driven learning
Flexibility	Limited; requires manual updates	High; adapts to new data
Performance	Works well for predictable tasks	Works well for complex tasks with patterns
Example	If-else conditions for fraud detection	Predictive ML model for fraud detection

This shift from rule-based systems to pattern-learning models is what makes ML a revolutionary technology.

Types of Machine Learning

Machine Learning can be broadly classified into three main types:

1. Supervised Learning

Supervised learning involves training a model on labeled data, meaning the input data has corresponding output labels. The model learns by mapping inputs to correct outputs.

Example: Predicting house prices based on features like location, square footage, and number of bedrooms.

Common Algorithms: Linear Regression, Decision Trees, Random Forest, Support Vector Machines (SVMs), Neural Networks.

2. Unsupervised Learning

Unsupervised learning deals with unlabeled data. The model identifies hidden patterns and structures without predefined outputs.

Example: Customer segmentation in marketing, where customers are grouped based on purchasing behavior.

Common Algorithms: K-Means Clustering, Principal Component Analysis (PCA), Autoencoders.

3. Reinforcement Learning

Reinforcement Learning (RL) trains models through a system of rewards and penalties. The model interacts with an environment, makes decisions, and learns by maximizing positive outcomes.

Example: Training AI to play chess or teaching a robot to walk.

Common Algorithms: Q-Learning, Deep Q Networks (DQN), Policy Gradient Methods.

Each type of ML is used for different applications and problem-solving scenarios.

Real-World Applications of Machine Learning

Machine Learning is already a part of our daily lives. Here are some key areas where ML is making a significant impact:

Healthcare: Diagnosing diseases, predicting patient outcomes, and personalizing treatments using ML models.

Finance: Fraud detection, stock market predictions, and credit risk analysis.

E-Commerce: Recommendation engines that suggest products based on user behavior (e.g., Amazon, Netflix).

Autonomous Vehicles: Self-driving cars use ML to recognize objects, predict traffic behavior, and navigate safely.

Natural Language Processing (NLP): Virtual assistants like Siri and Google Assistant, chatbots, and language translation tools.

Cybersecurity: Detecting suspicious activities and preventing cyber threats through anomaly detection.

Manufacturing: Predictive maintenance, quality control, and supply chain optimization.

These real-world applications highlight why Machine Learning is a critical technology shaping the future.

Machine Learning is an exciting and powerful tool that enables computers to learn from data, recognize patterns, and make intelligent decisions. Unlike traditional programming, ML algorithms improve their accuracy over time without needing explicit instructions. With its vast applications in healthcare, finance, marketing, automation, and AI-driven technologies, ML is revolutionizing the way we interact with technology.

This introduction sets the stage for deeper exploration into the types of ML, algorithms, and real-world implementation. As we move forward, you will learn how to apply ML techniques, build models, and harness the power of data to solve complex problems. Welcome to the world of Machine Learning—where the possibilities are endless!

1.2 How ML Differs from Traditional Programming

In the world of software development, programming has always been about providing a clear, step-by-step set of instructions that a computer follows to perform a specific task. This is the traditional way of writing software, where the program is explicitly coded to handle known conditions and predefined scenarios. Machine learning (ML), on the other hand, introduces a paradigm shift in how we build systems that can solve problems by learning from data, rather than being explicitly programmed to follow rigid instructions.

To understand how machine learning differs from traditional programming, let's first establish what each of these approaches entails and then highlight their key distinctions.

Traditional Programming: The Explicit Rule-Based Approach

In traditional programming, the developer writes code with specific rules and logic that the computer follows to solve problems. This approach assumes that the problem is well-defined and the solutions can be articulated using a set of deterministic instructions. For example, if you wanted to write a program to calculate the total price of a shopping cart, you would explicitly tell the program to add up the individual prices of the items in the cart, and multiply it by the appropriate tax rate.

Consider a simple example: you are asked to write a program that identifies whether a number is odd or even. In traditional programming, you would explicitly define a set of rules that tell the program how to check if a number is divisible by two. Here is a simple Python example:

```python
def is_even(number):
    if number % 2 == 0:
        return True
    else:
        return False
```

This solution works because the problem is well understood, and the instructions for determining if a number is even are straightforward. The logic is rigid, and the output will always be the same for the same input.

Machine Learning: The Data-Driven Approach

Machine learning, by contrast, is fundamentally different because it is driven by data rather than fixed instructions. Instead of explicitly programming a computer to perform a task by specifying a set of rules, in machine learning, we build models that learn patterns from data. The computer is given examples of input data and output labels, and it "learns" how to map the inputs to the correct outputs.

In this way, machine learning automates the process of learning from examples, making it particularly useful when explicit rules are difficult to define or when the problem is too complex to describe through simple logic. For instance, let's say you wanted to build a system that classifies emails as spam or not spam. Instead of explicitly defining what makes an email spam, you would gather a dataset of labeled emails (spam or not spam) and train a machine learning model on it.

Here is a simplified process of how this would work:

- **Data Collection**: Gather a large dataset of labeled emails (e.g., "spam" and "not spam").

- **Feature Extraction**: Identify features that might help in classifying an email, such as the frequency of certain words, the sender's email address, and the time of sending.
- **Model Training**: Use a machine learning algorithm (like a decision tree or a neural network) to learn the relationships between the input features (the email's content, metadata, etc.) and the output label (spam or not).
- **Prediction**: Once the model has been trained, it can classify new, unseen emails based on the patterns it learned from the data.

The key difference here is that instead of hardcoding the logic for detecting spam, the system learns from historical data, detecting subtle patterns that may be difficult to articulate manually.

Key Differences Between ML and Traditional Programming

Rule Definition vs. Pattern Recognition

- In traditional programming, you explicitly define a set of rules or instructions to solve a problem. The program follows these rules exactly, regardless of the context or data it encounters.
- In machine learning, the system is designed to recognize patterns from data. Rather than writing explicit instructions, you train the model using examples, and it generalizes those examples to predict outcomes for new, unseen data.

Handling of Uncertainty

- Traditional programming is deterministic, meaning that given the same input, the output will always be the same. The rules and logic don't change unless the developer modifies the code.
- Machine learning models, on the other hand, are probabilistic. They are designed to handle uncertainty and make predictions based on the patterns they have learned. While the model's output is influenced by the data it has seen, it may produce different outputs for the same input if the data changes or if it is uncertain about the correct answer.

Flexibility in Problem Solving

- Traditional programming works well for problems that are well-understood and for which the rules are clear. It excels when there is a straightforward set of operations to perform based on known conditions.

- Machine learning shines in situations where the problem is complex, the rules are not easily defined, or there is a large amount of data that can provide insight. ML can adapt to new, unseen situations by learning from patterns in the data, whereas traditional programming might struggle or require constant updates to handle new conditions.

Human Intervention

- In traditional programming, the developer plays a crucial role in defining the rules and logic. The developer must understand the problem and the required solution, and then translate that knowledge into code.
- In machine learning, the developer's role shifts from explicitly defining rules to curating and preprocessing data, selecting appropriate algorithms, and tuning models. The model takes on a more autonomous role, learning from the data without direct intervention in the specific decision-making process.

Scalability

- Traditional programs are generally built to solve a fixed set of problems. As long as the input data stays consistent with the expectations of the program, it will continue to work effectively.
- Machine learning models, however, are often better suited to scaling. As more data is fed into the system, the model can continue to improve and refine its predictions. Machine learning systems can handle vast amounts of data and complex relationships, whereas traditional programs might require frequent updates as new rules and exceptions arise.

Maintenance and Adaptation

- In traditional programming, once the system is deployed, it may require significant manual updates to accommodate new edge cases, exceptions, or evolving requirements. The logic has to be rewritten, and new rules have to be defined.
- With machine learning, models can often adapt themselves over time. When new data becomes available, the model can be retrained or fine-tuned to reflect changes in the environment or underlying patterns, allowing for continuous improvement without needing to explicitly rewrite code.

Machine learning represents a fundamental shift in how we approach problem-solving in software development. Traditional programming relies on explicit rules and deterministic logic, while machine learning models learn from data and make predictions based on patterns and probabilistic reasoning. While traditional programming excels in well-defined, structured problems, machine learning shines in complex, data-driven environments where rules are not easily defined or understood.

By understanding these differences, developers and engineers can better appreciate where and how machine learning can be applied, enabling them to harness its power to solve complex problems that were once thought too challenging for automated systems. As the field of machine learning continues to evolve, it will increasingly influence how we think about building intelligent systems and software applications.

1.3 The Role of ML in Artificial Intelligence

Artificial Intelligence (AI) is a broad field focused on creating machines that can perform tasks typically requiring human intelligence. These tasks include recognizing speech, understanding natural language, making decisions, and even perceiving and interacting with the world. AI aims to build systems that exhibit cognitive functions such as learning, reasoning, problem-solving, and perception, all of which traditionally required human intervention. Machine learning (ML) is one of the most crucial components that drive AI systems forward, acting as the backbone of many AI applications.

To understand the role of ML in AI, we first need to distinguish between AI, machine learning, and deep learning—the key concepts and subfields within this domain. By doing so, we can better grasp how ML fits into the larger picture of AI and contributes to its evolution.

The Relationship Between AI and Machine Learning

AI is the overarching field that encompasses a variety of approaches to create intelligent systems. These approaches can be rule-based, knowledge-based, or data-driven, and they span everything from traditional computer science algorithms to newer, more flexible models that can adapt over time.

Machine learning is a subset of AI focused on creating systems that can learn from data and improve their performance over time without explicit programming. Instead of being manually programmed to follow specific rules, ML algorithms enable machines to detect patterns in data, make predictions, and even make decisions based on that data. ML allows AI systems to "learn" from examples, improving their functionality as they process more data.

While AI encompasses a range of techniques, ML stands out as one of the most effective and widely used tools in achieving intelligent behavior. In fact, much of today's AI progress, such as image recognition, speech recognition, and natural language processing, has been driven by advances in machine learning.

How Machine Learning Powers AI

Machine learning plays a pivotal role in achieving AI because it enables machines to perform tasks that are not easily solvable through traditional programming. Some of the primary ways that ML contributes to AI include:

Enabling Adaptability

AI systems powered by machine learning are highly adaptable. Unlike traditional AI systems that require explicit programming for each scenario, ML-based AI systems can learn from data, adapting their behavior as they are exposed to more examples. For instance, a machine learning algorithm trained to recognize faces can continuously improve as it is fed more images, allowing it to adapt to changes such as lighting, angles, or different facial expressions.

Automating Complex Decision-Making

AI systems often need to make decisions in complex, uncertain environments. Machine learning provides tools to create models that analyze patterns in large datasets and make decisions based on learned relationships. For example, in self-driving cars, machine learning algorithms analyze sensor data from cameras and LIDAR (Light Detection and Ranging) systems to make real-time driving decisions, such as when to stop, accelerate, or avoid obstacles. These decisions are made without explicit human input, but based on patterns the machine has learned from its training data.

Improving with More Data

One of the defining features of machine learning is its ability to improve as it encounters more data. As the system is exposed to larger and more varied datasets, it refines its predictions, offering better performance over time. In AI applications like recommendation systems (think Netflix or Amazon), ML algorithms use user behavior data to suggest content or products that align with an individual's preferences, improving with each new interaction.

Handling Unstructured Data

AI systems powered by machine learning excel at processing unstructured data—data that doesn't fit neatly into rows and columns, such as text, images, or sound. Many traditional AI systems, such as expert systems, rely on structured data and rules that can be explicitly programmed. In contrast, machine learning allows AI systems to work with unstructured data, making it possible to analyze things like customer feedback (text data), identify objects in images, or transcribe speech to text. These tasks require the AI to learn from patterns within raw data, which ML is particularly adept at doing.

Enhancing Natural Language Processing (NLP)

One of the most exciting areas where ML intersects with AI is in natural language processing (NLP). NLP is the branch of AI that enables machines to understand, interpret, and generate human language. Traditional rule-based NLP systems were limited in their capabilities, often requiring manual programming of grammar rules and language structures. With ML, especially deep learning techniques, AI systems can learn language patterns from vast amounts of text data. This is how voice assistants like Siri, Google Assistant, and Alexa can understand spoken language and respond in a human-like manner.

Optimization and Efficiency

Machine learning algorithms are also used to optimize processes and improve the efficiency of AI systems. For instance, in machine vision, ML algorithms help AI systems interpret visual data more efficiently, making decisions faster than traditional vision systems. In game-playing AI, such as AlphaGo by DeepMind, ML is used to optimize strategies by learning from millions of past moves, allowing the AI to make highly effective decisions that challenge even expert human players.

Types of Machine Learning in AI

Within machine learning, there are various types of algorithms and techniques, each suited to different types of problems. These methods help AI systems perform specific tasks in unique ways. The three main categories of machine learning that are widely used in AI applications are:

Supervised Learning

Supervised learning is the most common form of machine learning and plays a significant role in AI. In supervised learning, the model is trained on labeled data—data that is already categorized or annotated with the correct answers. The model learns from these examples and generalizes patterns to make predictions on new, unseen data. Supervised learning is used in AI for tasks such as image classification (e.g., identifying objects in pictures) and sentiment analysis (e.g., determining if a piece of text is positive or negative).

Unsupervised Learning

Unsupervised learning involves training models on data that has not been labeled. The goal of unsupervised learning is to discover hidden patterns or structures in the data. Clustering and anomaly detection are common applications of unsupervised learning in AI, such as grouping similar customers for targeted marketing or detecting unusual patterns in cybersecurity. This type of learning is used when we don't have explicit labels to guide the model, but still want the AI to make sense of the data.

Reinforcement Learning

Reinforcement learning (RL) is a type of machine learning where an agent learns by interacting with an environment and receiving feedback in the form of rewards or penalties. This feedback guides the agent to take actions that maximize long-term rewards. RL has become the foundation of AI applications like robotics, game playing (e.g., AlphaGo), and autonomous systems, where an AI agent must make a series of decisions to achieve a goal, such as navigating a maze or learning a complex task.

Deep Learning

Deep learning, a subset of machine learning, is a powerful approach that mimics the neural networks of the human brain. By using large, multi-layered neural networks, deep learning enables AI to process complex data like images, speech, and text. Deep learning has contributed significantly to advancements in areas like computer vision, speech recognition, and autonomous vehicles.

Machine learning is not only a key element of AI, but it also drives many of the most impactful developments in the field. By allowing machines to learn from data, adapt to new information, and make decisions autonomously, ML has unlocked new possibilities in automation, efficiency, and intelligence. In applications from self-driving cars to virtual assistants, machine learning enables AI systems to perform tasks that were once considered too complex for machines to handle.

As AI continues to evolve, machine learning will remain at the core of these advancements, empowering AI systems to become even more capable, adaptable, and intelligent. For anyone embarking on the journey of mastering AI, understanding machine learning and its integral role is essential for building the intelligent systems of tomorrow.

1.4 Key Terminologies: Model, Training, Testing, Features

As you begin to explore the world of machine learning (ML), you'll encounter a range of terms that are fundamental to understanding how machine learning systems work. These concepts form the backbone of most ML processes, and having a solid understanding of them will give you the foundation to dive deeper into more complex topics. In this section, we'll break down four key terminologies—model, training, testing, and features—which are essential for building and evaluating machine learning systems.

1.4.1 Model

A model in machine learning refers to the mathematical representation of a process or system that maps input data to output predictions or decisions. The model is the product of the learning process and is what makes the machine "intelligent." Think of the model as the learned version of an algorithm—once it has been trained on data, it can be used to make predictions or classify new, unseen data.

In simple terms, a model is like a "map" that connects inputs (such as images, numbers, or text) to outputs (such as classifications, predictions, or recommendations). For example, in a spam email classifier, the model would take an email's content as input and output whether the email is spam or not.

There are many types of machine learning models, and the choice of model depends on the problem you are trying to solve. Some of the most common models include:

- **Linear Regression**: Used for predicting continuous values (e.g., predicting house prices based on features like square footage and location).
- **Decision Trees**: Used for classification and regression tasks, where the model makes decisions by branching based on features.
- **Neural Networks**: Inspired by the human brain, these are used for complex tasks like image recognition, natural language processing, and deep learning applications.
- **K-Nearest Neighbors (KNN):** A simple model used for classification, where the model predicts the class of an input based on the majority class of its neighbors.

The model itself is not born with any knowledge; it must first learn from the data provided to it.

1.4.2 Training

Training refers to the process of teaching a machine learning model to learn from data. During training, the model is exposed to a large set of input-output pairs (also called the training data), and it attempts to learn patterns and relationships between the input features and the output labels.

In a supervised learning scenario, the training data consists of examples where both the input data (e.g., images or text) and the corresponding labels (e.g., spam or not spam, or the correct category of an image) are provided. The model's task is to learn how to map the input data to the correct output label by adjusting its internal parameters.

To train the model, an algorithm iteratively processes the data, adjusting the parameters or weights within the model. This process continues until the model reaches a point where it can make accurate predictions or classifications on the training data. The main goal during training is to minimize the error between the model's predictions and the actual outcomes, which is often done by using optimization techniques like gradient descent.

Key steps in the training process include:

- **Initialization**: The model's parameters are initialized with random values or heuristics.
- **Learning from Data**: The model uses the input data to predict outputs, comparing the predictions with the actual labels.
- **Error Calculation**: The difference between the predicted output and the actual label (i.e., the error) is computed.
- **Parameter Adjustment**: The model's parameters are updated based on the error to reduce it in future predictions.
- **Iteration**: This process is repeated for many cycles (called epochs) until the model's performance reaches an acceptable level.

The model is considered "trained" once it has learned from the training data and can generalize to new data, meaning it has captured the underlying patterns and is ready to make predictions.

1.4.3 Testing

Testing refers to the process of evaluating a trained machine learning model's performance on a separate set of data that it has never seen before. This data is called the test data or test set, and it is used to measure how well the model generalizes to new, unseen data. The goal is to ensure that the model is not just memorizing the training data (a problem known as overfitting) but can make accurate predictions on data it hasn't encountered during training.

Testing typically involves running the trained model on the test data, calculating its predictions, and comparing them to the true values (labels) in the test set. This comparison generates performance metrics such as:

- **Accuracy**: The percentage of correct predictions out of the total number of predictions.
- **Precision**: The percentage of true positive predictions out of all positive predictions made by the model.
- **Recall**: The percentage of true positive predictions out of all actual positives.
- **F1 Score**: The harmonic mean of precision and recall, which balances both metrics when they are imbalanced.
- **Mean Squared Error (MSE):** A common metric for regression tasks, which measures the average of the squared differences between predicted and actual values.

In addition to testing, the model may also undergo validation, which is similar to testing but is typically done during training to fine-tune model parameters and select the best model. Together, testing and validation help assess how well the model performs in real-world scenarios.

1.4.4 Features

In machine learning, features refer to the individual measurable properties or characteristics of the data used for training the model. Features are the inputs to the machine learning algorithm and play a critical role in determining the model's performance. They represent the information that the model will use to make predictions or classifications.

For example, if you were training a machine learning model to predict house prices, the features might include:

- Square footage of the house

- Number of bedrooms
- Location (e.g., city or neighborhood)
- Year built
- Lot size
- Proximity to public transport

Each of these attributes is a feature that the model can use to learn the relationship between a house's characteristics and its price.

Features can be of various types:

- **Numerical features**: Continuous values, such as the height of a person or the temperature of a location.
- **Categorical features**: Discrete categories, such as color (red, blue, green) or type of fruit (apple, banana, cherry).
- **Textual features**: Words or phrases extracted from documents or conversations, often used in natural language processing tasks.
- **Image features**: Pixel values or more complex representations (like edges, textures, and shapes) extracted from images.

Feature selection is an important part of the machine learning pipeline. Good features can significantly improve the model's performance, while irrelevant or redundant features can introduce noise and lead to worse results. Feature engineering is the process of transforming raw data into a suitable format and selecting the best features to train the model.

In summary, understanding the key terminologies of machine learning—model, training, testing, and features—will help you navigate the process of building and evaluating ML systems. The model is the learned representation that makes predictions, training is the process through which a model learns from data, testing evaluates the model's generalization ability, and features are the input characteristics that allow the model to make decisions. These concepts are the building blocks of any machine learning project and will guide you as you develop your own intelligent systems.

2. Types of Machine Learning

Machine Learning is broadly categorized into Supervised, Unsupervised, and Reinforcement Learning. This chapter breaks down each type, explaining their key differences, how they work, and where they are used. Through practical examples, you'll learn how ML is applied across various industries.

2.1 Supervised Learning: Concept & Examples

Supervised learning is one of the most widely used approaches in machine learning. It is a type of machine learning where the model learns from labeled data to make predictions or decisions. In supervised learning, the algorithm is trained on a dataset that includes both input data (also known as features) and the corresponding correct output (known as the label). The primary goal of supervised learning is for the model to learn a mapping from inputs to outputs, such that when given new, unseen data, it can accurately predict the correct output.

To put it simply, supervised learning works like a teacher-student relationship, where the "teacher" (the labeled dataset) provides the correct answers (the labels), and the "student" (the model) learns to predict those answers based on the input features.

Let's explore the concept of supervised learning, how it works, and some real-world examples to understand how it can be applied.

How Supervised Learning Works

In supervised learning, the process follows a typical workflow:

Data Collection: The first step in supervised learning is gathering a dataset that contains labeled examples. Each example consists of input data (features) and the correct output label. For example, if we are building a model to predict whether an email is spam or not, the features might be the content of the email, the sender, and the subject, while the label would be "spam" or "not spam."

Data Preprocessing: The raw data is cleaned and preprocessed. This might involve handling missing values, normalizing or scaling numerical features, encoding categorical features (such as converting "male" and "female" into numerical values), and splitting the dataset into training and testing sets.

Model Training: The next step is to choose a machine learning algorithm and train a model on the training data. The model is provided with the input features and their corresponding labels. The algorithm learns to find the underlying patterns in the data and adjusts its internal parameters to minimize the error between its predictions and the actual labels.

Model Evaluation: After the model has been trained, it is tested on unseen data (test data) to evaluate its performance. Various performance metrics, such as accuracy, precision, recall, and F1-score, are used to measure how well the model is generalizing to new data.

Prediction: Once the model is trained and validated, it can be used to make predictions on new, unseen data. The model takes in the input features and produces an output, which could be a classification or a continuous value, depending on the problem.

Types of Supervised Learning

Supervised learning is typically divided into two main categories based on the type of output the model is predicting:

Classification

In classification problems, the goal is to predict a discrete label or category. The output variable is categorical, and the task is to assign the input data into one of these predefined classes. Common examples of classification tasks include:

- **Email Spam Detection**: The model is trained to classify emails as either "spam" or "not spam" based on features like the sender's address, subject line, and content.
- **Medical Diagnosis**: A model may be trained to classify patients as either having a certain disease (e.g., cancer) or not, based on features like age, symptoms, and test results.
- **Image Recognition**: A model can be trained to recognize objects in images, such as identifying whether a picture contains a "dog," "cat," or "bird."

Common algorithms used for classification include decision trees, k-nearest neighbors (KNN), logistic regression, and support vector machines (SVM).

Regression

In regression problems, the goal is to predict a continuous value. The output variable is numerical, and the model is trained to find the relationship between the input features and the continuous output. Examples of regression tasks include:

- **House Price Prediction**: Given features like the size of the house, the number of bedrooms, and the location, the model predicts the price of the house.
- **Stock Market Forecasting**: A model might predict the future price of a stock based on features such as past stock prices, trading volume, and market indicators.
- **Weather Prediction**: A model could predict the temperature on a given day based on historical weather data, such as humidity, wind speed, and time of year.

Common algorithms used for regression include linear regression, decision trees, and random forests.

Example 1: Spam Email Detection (Classification)

Let's take the example of a spam email detection system to better understand how supervised learning works in classification.

Problem: You want to build a model that can classify incoming emails as "spam" or "not spam."

Data Collection: You collect a dataset of emails that includes both the text content of the email and the label for each email ("spam" or "not spam"). The dataset might include 10,000 emails with labeled data.

Features: The features could include:

- The frequency of certain words (e.g., "free," "money," "offer").
- The sender's email address.
- Whether the email contains a link or attachment.
- The subject line and body of the email (encoded as numerical vectors, using techniques like bag-of-words or TF-IDF).

Training: You split the dataset into a training set (e.g., 80% of the data) and a testing set (e.g., 20% of the data). The model is then trained on the training set, learning patterns in the data that distinguish spam emails from non-spam emails.

Model Evaluation: Once trained, you evaluate the model on the test set to see how well it generalizes to new, unseen data. You might use performance metrics like accuracy (the proportion of correctly classified emails), precision (how many of the predicted spam emails are actually spam), and recall (how many of the actual spam emails were correctly identified).

Prediction: Once the model is trained and evaluated, you can use it to classify new emails as spam or not spam based on their content.

Example 2: House Price Prediction (Regression)

Let's look at a regression problem, where the goal is to predict a continuous value.

Problem: You want to build a model that predicts the price of a house based on features such as the number of bedrooms, square footage, location, and age of the house.

Data Collection: You collect a dataset containing the prices of homes along with their features. For example, the dataset may contain 1,000 homes, each with features like:

- Number of bedrooms
- Square footage
- Location (represented numerically or as categorical values)
- Age of the house

Features: The features (inputs) might be the number of bedrooms, square footage, location, and the age of the house.

Training: You use this dataset to train the regression model. The model will learn to predict the price of the house based on these features by fitting a mathematical relationship (e.g., a line or a curve) between the input features and the target price.

Model Evaluation: Once trained, the model's predictions are evaluated using metrics such as Mean Squared Error (MSE) or Root Mean Squared Error (RMSE), which measure the difference between the predicted and actual prices.

Prediction: After training and evaluation, the model can be used to predict the price of a new house based on its features.

Common Supervised Learning Algorithms

Here are some of the most common algorithms used in supervised learning:

- **Linear Regression**: Used for regression tasks, it assumes a linear relationship between input features and the target output.
- **Logistic Regression**: Despite its name, it is used for binary classification tasks (e.g., spam vs. not spam).
- **Decision Trees**: These models split the data into subsets based on feature values, making them easy to interpret. They can be used for both classification and regression.
- **Random Forests**: An ensemble method that combines multiple decision trees to improve performance and reduce overfitting.
- **Support Vector Machines (SVM):** A powerful classification algorithm that finds the optimal hyperplane that best separates the classes in the feature space.
- **K-Nearest Neighbors (KNN):** A simple classification algorithm that assigns a class to a sample based on the majority class of its nearest neighbors.

Supervised learning is one of the most essential techniques in machine learning, providing a method for training models using labeled data to make predictions on new, unseen data. Whether you're working on a classification problem (e.g., spam detection) or a regression task (e.g., predicting house prices), supervised learning algorithms are powerful tools for building intelligent systems. By understanding the key concepts and examples outlined in this section, you'll be well on your way to applying supervised learning to real-world problems.

2.2 Unsupervised Learning: Concept & Examples

Unsupervised learning is another foundational approach in machine learning, and it differs from supervised learning in key ways. In unsupervised learning, the algorithm is tasked with finding hidden patterns or structures in a dataset that does not have labeled outputs. Unlike supervised learning, where we provide both the inputs and the corresponding correct outputs (labels), unsupervised learning relies solely on input data with no explicit target labels. The goal is to uncover the underlying structure of the data, whether that's grouping similar data points together, reducing the complexity of the data, or finding anomalies.

Unsupervised learning is often used when the goal is to understand the structure or distribution of data, or when labels are unavailable, costly, or hard to obtain. Let's explore the concept of unsupervised learning, how it works, and some practical examples to illustrate its applications.

How Unsupervised Learning Works

The general process of unsupervised learning involves the following steps:

Data Collection: Just like supervised learning, unsupervised learning begins with gathering data. However, in this case, the dataset lacks labeled output values. The data might consist of a collection of features, such as customer behaviors, product characteristics, or sensor readings, without predefined categories or labels.

Data Preprocessing: Similar to supervised learning, the raw data is preprocessed. This may involve cleaning the data, handling missing values, scaling or normalizing the features, and transforming the data into a format suitable for the machine learning algorithm.

Model Selection: Unlike supervised learning, where you select a model based on the type of output (classification or regression), in unsupervised learning, the model's objective is to find patterns, relationships, or structure within the data. You would select an unsupervised learning algorithm depending on the task at hand, such as clustering or dimensionality reduction.

Model Training: During this phase, the algorithm learns from the features in the dataset without being provided with specific labels or output data. It looks for patterns, similarities, or hidden structures in the data. For example, in clustering, the algorithm groups similar data points together, and in dimensionality reduction, it seeks to represent the data in a simpler form.

Evaluation and Interpretation: After the model has been trained, you evaluate the output (e.g., the clusters formed or the reduced dimensions) and interpret the findings. Evaluation of unsupervised learning models can be more challenging compared to supervised learning, as the "correct answer" isn't always obvious. However, methods like silhouette scores for clustering or visual inspection for dimensionality reduction can help assess the model's performance.

Prediction or Insights: The model's output might be a set of clusters, reduced dimensions, or outliers, which can then be used for analysis, visualization, or further decision-making.

Types of Unsupervised Learning

Unsupervised learning is typically divided into two main categories based on the nature of the output:

Clustering Clustering is one of the most common tasks in unsupervised learning. The goal is to group similar data points together into clusters, where each group contains elements that are more similar to each other than to elements in other groups.

Clustering algorithms try to find the natural structure in data by organizing it into clusters based on the similarity of the data points. Some well-known clustering algorithms include:

- **K-Means**: This is one of the most widely used clustering algorithms, which partitions data into a predefined number of clusters (k) based on the similarity of data points.
- **DBSCAN** (Density-Based Spatial Clustering of Applications with Noise): Unlike K-means, DBSCAN does not require specifying the number of clusters in advance. It works by identifying regions of high density and finding the clusters within these regions.
- **Hierarchical Clustering**: This approach builds a tree-like structure (dendrogram) that shows how data points cluster together. It can be agglomerative (bottom-up) or divisive (top-down).

Example: Customer Segmentation in Marketing

A retail company wants to segment its customers into groups based on purchasing behavior, such as frequent buyers, occasional buyers, and non-buyers. Using clustering techniques like K-Means, the company can group customers with similar buying patterns. These segments could then be used for targeted marketing campaigns.

Dimensionality Reduction Dimensionality reduction refers to techniques that reduce the number of features in a dataset while retaining as much of the important information as possible. These techniques are especially useful when dealing with high-dimensional data, such as images or text, where the number of features can be very large.

The goal of dimensionality reduction is to simplify the dataset, making it easier to analyze or visualize, while still maintaining the core structure of the data. Some popular techniques for dimensionality reduction include:

- **Principal Component Analysis (PCA):** PCA is a widely used technique that transforms the data into a smaller set of uncorrelated variables (called principal components) that retain the most important variance in the data. PCA is commonly used in image compression, facial recognition, and exploratory data analysis.

- t-**Distributed Stochastic Neighbor Embedding (t-SNE):** t-SNE is a technique primarily used for visualizing high-dimensional data in a two- or three-dimensional space. It works by preserving the pairwise similarities between data points and is often used for visualizing complex datasets, such as images or text.

Example: Visualizing High-Dimensional Data with PCA

Imagine a dataset with several features describing the characteristics of flowers, such as petal length, petal width, and sepal length. If there are too many features, PCA could be used to reduce the data to two or three principal components for easier visualization. This reduced representation would allow analysts to visualize the data in a 2D or 3D space, identifying patterns or groups of flowers based on their features.

Anomaly Detection Anomaly detection is another important unsupervised learning task, where the goal is to identify unusual or rare data points that deviate significantly from the norm. This is particularly useful in situations where the majority of the data is normal, but you want to spot unusual instances, such as fraud detection, equipment failure, or network intrusion.

Algorithms used for anomaly detection include:

- **Isolation Forest**: This algorithm isolates anomalies by randomly selecting features and splitting the data points into small, distinct groups. The data points that are isolated quickly are considered anomalies.
- **One-Class SVM**: A variation of Support Vector Machines, One-Class SVM is often used for identifying outliers in data. It works by creating a boundary around the normal data points and flagging any points outside this boundary as anomalies.

Example: Fraud Detection in Credit Card Transactions

A financial institution might want to detect fraudulent credit card transactions. By training an anomaly detection model on a dataset of normal transaction patterns (e.g., location, amount, time), the algorithm can flag transactions that significantly deviate from typical spending patterns as potential frauds.

Key Unsupervised Learning Algorithms

Here are some of the most commonly used algorithms in unsupervised learning:

- **K-Means Clustering**: A widely used clustering algorithm that groups data into k clusters by minimizing the variance within each cluster.
- **DBSCAN**: A density-based clustering algorithm that can find arbitrarily shaped clusters and outliers.
- **PCA (Principal Component Analysis):** A technique for reducing the dimensionality of data while retaining as much variance as possible.
- **t-SNE**: A dimensionality reduction algorithm mainly used for visualizing high-dimensional data in two or three dimensions.
- **Isolation Forest**: An algorithm for detecting anomalies by isolating data points.
- **Autoencoders**: Neural networks used for unsupervised learning, particularly for anomaly detection and dimensionality reduction.

Unsupervised learning is a powerful approach in machine learning that helps uncover hidden patterns or structures in data without the need for labeled outputs. Whether it's grouping similar data points through clustering, reducing data complexity with dimensionality reduction, or detecting anomalies, unsupervised learning is widely used in various fields, from marketing to fraud detection. By understanding the core concepts and algorithms of unsupervised learning, you can harness its power to gain valuable insights from complex, unstructured data.

2.3 Reinforcement Learning: Concept & Examples

Reinforcement Learning (RL) is a type of machine learning that enables an agent to learn how to make decisions by interacting with an environment in order to achieve a goal. Unlike supervised learning, where the model learns from labeled data, or unsupervised learning, where the model tries to find hidden structures in the data, reinforcement learning focuses on learning through trial and error. The model (or agent) learns to take actions in an environment that maximize some notion of cumulative reward over time.

RL is inspired by behavioral psychology, where an agent learns behaviors through rewards and punishments. Think of how a child learns to solve a puzzle: they try different strategies, receive feedback (either positive or negative), and adjust their behavior based on that feedback to eventually complete the puzzle. This process of learning from experience is the foundation of reinforcement learning.

Let's dive deeper into the concept of reinforcement learning, its components, and how it works, along with some real-world examples to illustrate its applications.

Key Components of Reinforcement Learning

Reinforcement learning involves a few key components that interact in a cycle:

Agent: The learner or decision-maker. The agent is responsible for taking actions in an environment to achieve a goal.

Environment: The external system or world with which the agent interacts. The environment provides feedback based on the agent's actions.

State: A snapshot of the environment at a given time. The state represents all the relevant information about the environment that the agent needs in order to make decisions. For example, in a chess game, the state could represent the current configuration of pieces on the board.

Action: The set of all possible moves or decisions the agent can make. In the chess example, actions would include moving a piece, castling, or resigning the game.

Reward: The feedback signal from the environment. After taking an action, the agent receives a reward or penalty (which could be positive or negative). The goal of the agent is to maximize its total reward over time. In chess, a win could yield a high positive reward, while a loss would result in a negative reward.

Policy: A strategy or a mapping from states to actions. The policy defines what action the agent should take in any given state. The policy can be deterministic (a specific action is chosen for each state) or stochastic (there's a probability distribution over possible actions).

Value Function: A measure of the long-term reward an agent can expect to receive from a given state. It evaluates how good it is for the agent to be in a particular state, considering future rewards. The value function helps the agent to make decisions that lead to the most rewarding outcomes over time.

Q-Function (Action-Value Function): A function that provides the expected reward for a given state-action pair. It helps the agent understand how much reward it can expect for taking a specific action in a specific state, considering the future states that will follow.

How Reinforcement Learning Works

The process of reinforcement learning can be described in terms of an iterative loop:

Initialization: The agent starts by exploring the environment. Initially, it may not know the best actions to take, so it tries a variety of actions and observes the results.

Interaction: At each step, the agent observes the current state of the environment, takes an action based on its current policy (or random exploration), and receives feedback in the form of a reward from the environment. The agent also moves to a new state based on its action.

Learning: Based on the reward received and the next state, the agent updates its policy. The agent uses algorithms to adjust its behavior over time, seeking to maximize cumulative reward. This could involve learning an optimal policy, where it takes actions that maximize its expected future rewards.

Iteration: The agent continues to interact with the environment, continually refining its policy to improve its performance and achieve better rewards.

The learning process is often modeled as a Markov Decision Process (MDP), where the outcome of an action depends only on the current state, not on previous states. The goal is for the agent to learn a policy that maximizes the expected sum of rewards over time, often called the return.

Types of Reinforcement Learning Algorithms

Reinforcement learning algorithms can be categorized into three main types:

Value-Based Methods

These methods focus on estimating the value of each state or state-action pair and using that information to make decisions. The goal is to learn a value function that helps determine which actions to take. One common value-based algorithm is Q-Learning, where the agent learns a Q-function that estimates the expected return for each action in each state. Over time, the agent converges to the optimal policy.

Policy-Based Methods

In policy-based methods, the agent directly learns a policy (a mapping from states to actions), rather than learning the value of states or actions. The policy is usually represented as a neural network or some other function approximator. A popular policy-based algorithm is REINFORCE, which uses gradient ascent to update the policy in the direction of higher rewards.

Actor-Critic Methods

These methods combine both value-based and policy-based approaches. An actor component chooses actions based on the policy, while a critic evaluates how good the chosen actions are by estimating the value function. The critic provides feedback to the actor to improve the policy. The A3C (Asynchronous Advantage Actor-Critic) algorithm is an example of this type.

Exploration vs. Exploitation

One of the key challenges in reinforcement learning is balancing exploration and exploitation:

- Exploration refers to trying new actions to discover more about the environment and possibly find better long-term rewards.
- Exploitation refers to using the current knowledge (the learned policy) to choose actions that maximize immediate rewards.

An agent needs to strike a balance between exploring new actions (which may lead to higher long-term rewards) and exploiting the best-known actions (which yield immediate rewards). Too much exploration can result in slow learning, while too much exploitation can lead to suboptimal solutions.

Examples of Reinforcement Learning in the Real World

Reinforcement learning is increasingly being applied to a wide variety of domains. Here are a few real-world examples:

Game Playing (Chess, Go, Video Games)

- One of the most famous applications of reinforcement learning is in game playing. For example, DeepMind's AlphaGo used reinforcement learning to master the game of Go. AlphaGo learned by playing millions of games against itself, using RL to improve its strategies. It eventually defeated some of the world's best Go players.

- In chess, RL-based agents like AlphaZero have outperformed traditional chess engines by learning the game entirely through self-play, without human intervention.

Robotics

- In robotics, RL is used to train robots to perform complex tasks such as walking, grasping objects, or assembling products. For example, Boston Dynamics uses RL to teach robots like Spot and Atlas to navigate diverse environments and perform tasks in dynamic settings.
- Autonomous robots or drones can use RL to learn how to interact with their environment and adapt to new obstacles or challenges, improving over time.

Autonomous Vehicles

Self-driving cars use reinforcement learning to learn how to navigate roads, avoid obstacles, and make decisions in traffic. The car interacts with its environment (the road and other vehicles), learns from feedback (rewards for successful maneuvers, penalties for collisions), and gradually becomes better at driving autonomously.

Finance and Trading

RL is used in algorithmic trading, where an agent learns to buy and sell stocks in order to maximize profit. The agent interacts with the stock market environment, receiving feedback based on its trades (such as profit or loss), and improves its decision-making strategies over time.

Healthcare and Personalized Treatment

RL can be used in personalized medicine, where an agent learns the best course of treatment for a patient based on their medical history, genetic information, and responses to previous treatments. It can adjust treatment plans in real-time, optimizing outcomes and minimizing side effects.

Reinforcement learning is a powerful and versatile approach to machine learning that enables agents to learn through interaction with their environment. By exploring different actions and receiving feedback in the form of rewards, agents gradually learn to make better decisions over time. RL has proven particularly successful in areas like game playing, robotics, autonomous vehicles, finance, and healthcare, where the decision-making process is complex and dynamic. Understanding the core concepts of RL, such as exploration vs. exploitation, the agent-environment interaction, and the different types of algorithms, is key to applying reinforcement learning to real-world problems.

2.4 Hybrid Learning Methods

Hybrid learning methods are a powerful approach that combines multiple machine learning techniques to leverage the strengths of each individual method. In machine learning, each type of learning — whether supervised, unsupervised, or reinforcement learning — has its own advantages and challenges. By integrating different methods, hybrid learning aims to create models that are more robust, efficient, and accurate in solving complex tasks. These hybrid approaches often outperform models that rely on a single learning paradigm, making them particularly useful in real-world applications.

In this section, we'll explore the concept of hybrid learning methods, how they work, and provide examples of how they are applied in practice.

What are Hybrid Learning Methods?

Hybrid learning methods involve the combination of two or more machine learning paradigms or algorithms to address a problem more effectively. These combinations can be structured in various ways depending on the task, the data at hand, and the desired outcomes. The main goal of hybrid methods is to take advantage of the complementary strengths of different techniques to improve overall performance.

There are several types of hybrid learning, and they generally fall into one of the following categories:

Combining Different Learning Paradigms

- This involves integrating various types of learning, such as supervised learning with unsupervised learning or combining supervised learning with reinforcement learning.
- For example, a hybrid model may use unsupervised learning for feature extraction or data preprocessing and then apply supervised learning for classification or regression.

Combining Different Algorithms Within the Same Paradigm

- In this case, different algorithms within the same learning paradigm are combined to improve performance.
- For example, combining decision trees with neural networks, or using ensemble methods like bagging, boosting, or stacking to combine multiple models to make better predictions.

Ensemble Learning

- Ensemble methods are a specific type of hybrid learning where multiple models are combined to produce a final prediction. The idea behind ensemble learning is that a group of diverse models can collectively perform better than any single model alone.
- Each hybrid approach seeks to address the weaknesses of individual methods while enhancing their strengths. Let's take a closer look at some common hybrid learning methods and how they work.

Key Hybrid Learning Approaches

Ensemble Learning Ensemble learning is one of the most common hybrid methods used in machine learning. It involves combining multiple models to achieve a more accurate prediction or decision than any single model could on its own. There are several types of ensemble learning methods, including:

Bagging (Bootstrap Aggregating): In bagging, multiple models (usually of the same type) are trained independently on different subsets of the data, generated through bootstrapping (sampling with replacement). The final prediction is made by aggregating the predictions from all the models, usually through voting or averaging. One popular bagging algorithm is Random Forest, where multiple decision trees are built and their predictions are aggregated.

Example: In a classification problem, the Random Forest model might take the majority vote from all the decision trees to determine the most likely class for an input sample.

Boosting: Boosting involves training a sequence of models where each model corrects the errors of the previous one. The models are built sequentially, and each new model gives more weight to the data points that were misclassified by previous models. AdaBoost and Gradient Boosting (including XGBoost and LightGBM) are popular boosting techniques.

Example: Boosting can be used to improve the accuracy of a simple model, like a decision tree, by focusing on the mistakes made by the previous trees and correcting them.

Stacking: Stacking combines multiple different types of models (e.g., decision trees, support vector machines, and neural networks) and trains a final model (called a meta-model) to make the final prediction based on the outputs of the individual models. The goal is to combine the strengths of different models to create a more accurate overall prediction.

Example: In a regression task, different models might predict the target value, and a meta-model (e.g., a logistic regression model) would take these predictions as input to generate the final result.

Advantages of Ensemble Methods:

- Better generalization to new data, especially when individual models are prone to overfitting.
- Higher accuracy compared to individual models, as errors from different models tend to cancel each other out.

Hybrid Supervised and Unsupervised Learning In some cases, unsupervised learning can be used for pre-processing or feature extraction before applying supervised learning for the final prediction. This hybrid method is particularly useful when the data is unlabeled or when you need to reduce the dimensionality of a dataset.

- **Unsupervised Preprocessing for Supervised Learning**: In this approach, unsupervised techniques like clustering, principal component analysis (PCA), or autoencoders are used to find patterns or reduce the complexity of data before applying supervised learning techniques (e.g., classification or regression).
- **Example**: In text classification, unsupervised techniques like topic modeling (e.g., Latent Dirichlet Allocation or LDA) might be used to extract topics from text data. The topics can then be used as features for a supervised classification model, such as a support vector machine (SVM).

- **Semi-supervised Learning**: A hybrid approach that combines both labeled and unlabeled data for training. Semi-supervised learning methods assume that while labels may be scarce or expensive to obtain, there is abundant unlabeled data that can still be used to improve learning.

- **Example**: In medical image analysis, only a few images may be labeled with diagnoses, but a large number of images are unlabeled. Semi-supervised learning techniques can leverage both labeled and unlabeled data to build a more accurate model for diagnosing medical conditions.

Hybrid Supervised and Reinforcement Learning Hybridizing supervised learning with reinforcement learning can be particularly useful in environments where the agent needs to learn from both labeled data and its own interactions with the environment. Supervised learning can help the agent initially learn some basic knowledge, while reinforcement learning allows the agent to improve its decision-making through feedback and exploration.

Example: In robotics, a robot can initially be trained with supervised learning to recognize objects and their attributes (such as shape, color, or location) using labeled data. Once the robot has learned basic object recognition, it can then be trained using reinforcement learning to navigate and interact with the objects to achieve specific goals (e.g., pick up an object or sort items).

Neuro-Inspired Hybrid Methods Another type of hybrid approach is the combination of neural networks with other machine learning models or algorithms. For example, neural networks can be combined with evolutionary algorithms, swarm intelligence, or decision trees to optimize model performance. This is useful in situations where the problem requires both high-level pattern recognition and optimization.

Example: Genetic algorithms are often used alongside neural networks to optimize the weights or architecture of a neural network. By evolving the architecture over generations, this hybrid method can produce more efficient or accurate networks for tasks like image classification.

Real-World Applications of Hybrid Learning Methods

Hybrid learning methods are widely used across various industries, where complex problems require a combination of different learning strategies. Some examples include:

Healthcare: In personalized medicine, hybrid methods are used to combine supervised learning (for classification of diseases) with reinforcement learning (for treatment optimization). This can help design personalized treatment plans that adapt to individual patient responses.

Autonomous Vehicles: Self-driving cars use a hybrid of supervised learning (for object detection and classification) and reinforcement learning (for decision-making and navigation) to safely and efficiently navigate through complex environments.

Finance: Hybrid models combining supervised learning (for predicting market trends based on historical data) with reinforcement learning (for portfolio optimization or algorithmic trading) can help investors make better decisions and maximize returns.

Recommendation Systems: Hybrid recommendation systems often use both collaborative filtering (an unsupervised learning method) and content-based filtering (a supervised learning method) to provide more accurate and personalized recommendations. For example, Netflix uses hybrid methods to recommend movies based on both user behavior and content features.

Hybrid learning methods are an essential and powerful tool in the machine learning toolkit, combining different algorithms and paradigms to solve complex problems more effectively. Whether it's through ensemble learning, integrating supervised and unsupervised learning, or combining reinforcement learning with other techniques, hybrid methods enable models to achieve better accuracy, generalization, and robustness. In practice, these methods are used across various industries, from healthcare and finance to autonomous systems and recommendation engines, highlighting their versatility and importance in real-world applications.

3. Mathematical Foundations

Understanding ML requires a grasp of basic mathematical concepts such as linear algebra, probability, and statistics. This chapter simplifies these topics, explaining matrices, vectors, probability distributions, and optimization techniques like gradient descent—key tools for building ML models.

3.1 Linear Algebra for ML (Vectors, Matrices, Eigenvalues)

Linear algebra is a fundamental branch of mathematics that deals with vector spaces and the linear mappings between these spaces. It forms the backbone of many machine learning algorithms and models, as it provides the tools necessary to represent and manipulate data efficiently. From basic operations like addition and multiplication to more advanced concepts like eigenvalues and eigenvectors, linear algebra is crucial for understanding how machine learning works under the hood.

In this section, we will break down the key concepts of linear algebra—vectors, matrices, and eigenvalues—and discuss how they are applied in machine learning.

1. Vectors

A vector is a one-dimensional array of numbers, which can represent anything from a simple list of numbers to more complex data like the features of an object in a dataset. Vectors are fundamental in machine learning, as they are used to represent data points, weights, and many other quantities.

Key Concepts Related to Vectors:

Vector Notation: A vector is typically represented as a column or row of numbers:

$$\mathbf{v} = \begin{bmatrix} v_1 \\ v_2 \\ v_3 \\ \vdots \\ v_n \end{bmatrix}$$

Dot Product: The dot product (or scalar product) of two vectors is a fundamental operation in linear algebra and is used in many machine learning algorithms, such as in computing the similarity between two vectors. If you have two vectors a and b, their dot product is calculated as:

$$\mathbf{a} \cdot \mathbf{b} = a_1 b_1 + a_2 b_2 + \cdots + a_n b_n$$

In machine learning, this operation is often used in models like linear regression and neural networks.

Norm (Magnitude): The magnitude or norm of a vector measures its length. The most common norm is the Euclidean norm, defined as:

$$\|\mathbf{v}\| = \sqrt{v_1^2 + v_2^2 + \cdots + v_n^2}$$

The norm is important in machine learning algorithms like k-nearest neighbors (KNN), where distances between vectors (representing data points) are measured using the norm.

Unit Vector: A unit vector is a vector with a magnitude of 1. It is often used to represent direction in machine learning, particularly in optimization algorithms, where it is important to normalize vectors to avoid numerical issues.

Applications in Machine Learning:

- **Data Representation**: In machine learning, a data point is often represented as a vector. For example, in image classification, an image can be flattened into a vector where each element represents a pixel's intensity.
- **Model Weights**: In linear regression or neural networks, model parameters (weights) are represented as vectors, and their updates during training involve operations like dot products.

2. Matrices

A matrix is a two-dimensional array of numbers arranged in rows and columns. Matrices are incredibly powerful in machine learning, as they can represent datasets, transformations, and more complex structures. Each row or column of a matrix can represent a feature vector, and operations on matrices are used to perform computations on large datasets.

Key Concepts Related to Matrices:

Matrix Notation: A matrix A is typically written as:

$$A = \begin{bmatrix} a_{11} & a_{12} & \cdots & a_{1n} \\ a_{21} & a_{22} & \cdots & a_{2n} \\ \vdots & \vdots & \ddots & \vdots \\ a_{m1} & a_{m2} & \cdots & a_{mn} \end{bmatrix}$$

Matrix Operations:

- **Matrix Addition**: Two matrices of the same dimension can be added together by adding their corresponding elements:

$$C = A + B \quad \text{where} \quad c_{ij} = a_{ij} + b_{ij}$$

- **Matrix Multiplication**: The product of two matrices A (of dimension $m \times n$) and B (of dimension $n \times p$) results in a new matrix C (of dimension $m \times p$), calculated as:

$$C = A \cdot B \quad \text{where} \quad c_{ij} = \sum_{k=1}^{n} a_{ik} \cdot b_{kj}$$

  Matrix multiplication is used in many machine learning algorithms, such as in the **forward pass** of neural networks, where matrices represent layers of neurons and their connections.

- **Transpose**: The transpose of a matrix A is obtained by flipping it over its diagonal, swapping its rows and columns. The transpose is denoted as A^T.

$$A^T = \begin{bmatrix} a_{11} & a_{21} & \cdots \\ a_{12} & a_{22} & \cdots \\ \vdots & \vdots & \ddots \\ a_{1n} & a_{2n} & \cdots \end{bmatrix}$$

  The transpose is used in optimization, especially in gradient descent algorithms, where the gradient of the loss function is computed with respect to the parameters of the model.

Applications in Machine Learning:

- **Data Representation**: In machine learning, datasets are often represented as matrices, where each row is a data point and each column is a feature.
- **Transformation**: Matrices are used to represent linear transformations. For example, in Principal Component Analysis (PCA), the covariance matrix of the data is used to find the directions (principal components) that maximize the variance in the data.
- **Neural Networks**: Neural networks use matrices to represent the weights and activations of neurons. The process of computing the outputs of layers in a neural network can be efficiently done using matrix multiplication.

3. Eigenvalues and Eigenvectors

Eigenvalues and eigenvectors are concepts that arise from linear transformations and are crucial in many areas of machine learning, including dimensionality reduction, data compression, and optimization.

Key Concepts Related to Eigenvalues and Eigenvectors:

- Eigenvectors: An eigenvector of a matrix A is a non-zero vector $\mathbf{v}$ that, when the matrix is applied to it, results in a scaled version of the same vector. Mathematically, this can be expressed as:

$$Av - \lambda v$$

  where λ is the eigenvalue corresponding to the eigenvector $\mathbf{v}$.

- Eigenvalues: The eigenvalue λ represents the scaling factor by which the eigenvector $\mathbf{v}$ is stretched or compressed during the transformation. Eigenvalues give insight into the behavior of the system represented by the matrix.

- Diagonalization: If a matrix A has a full set of eigenvectors, it can be diagonalized, which means that the matrix can be expressed in terms of its eigenvalues. This is useful for simplifying matrix computations.

Applications in Machine Learning:

Principal Component Analysis (PCA): PCA is a popular dimensionality reduction technique that uses eigenvectors and eigenvalues. It involves finding the eigenvectors (principal components) of the covariance matrix of the data, which represent the directions of maximum variance. The eigenvalues determine the importance of each principal component, allowing you to reduce the dimensionality by retaining only the most important components.

Example: In face recognition, PCA is used to reduce the dimensionality of facial images, focusing on the most significant features (eigenfaces) that capture the most variation in the data.

Spectral Clustering: This method uses the eigenvalues and eigenvectors of a similarity matrix to cluster data points into groups. By analyzing the eigenvectors corresponding to the smallest eigenvalues, you can uncover the intrinsic structure of the data.

Linear algebra provides the foundation for understanding and implementing many machine learning algorithms. Vectors and matrices are used to represent data and operations on data, while eigenvalues and eigenvectors help to uncover important structures within the data. Mastery of these concepts is crucial for building more efficient and effective machine learning models. Whether you're implementing algorithms like PCA, training neural networks, or optimizing a machine learning model, linear algebra plays a central role in processing and manipulating data to extract valuable insights.

3.2 Probability and Statistics Basics

Probability and statistics are essential tools in the machine learning (ML) toolkit. Machine learning algorithms frequently work with uncertain or incomplete data, and probability and statistics help quantify this uncertainty and make informed predictions. Understanding the basics of probability and statistics allows practitioners to build better models, evaluate their performance, and interpret results in meaningful ways.

In this section, we will cover key concepts in probability and statistics that form the foundation for understanding and working with machine learning algorithms.

1. Probability Fundamentals

Probability is the branch of mathematics that deals with quantifying uncertainty. In the context of machine learning, probability helps in making predictions about unknown data based on known data. It enables us to express the likelihood of different outcomes.

Key Concepts Related to Probability:

- **Random Experiment**: A random experiment is an action or process that leads to one of several possible outcomes, where the outcome cannot be predicted with certainty. For example, rolling a die or drawing a card from a deck are random experiments.

- **Sample Space**: The sample space is the set of all possible outcomes of a random experiment. For a die roll, the sample space is $\{1, 2, 3, 4, 5, 6\}$.

- **Event**: An event is a subset of the sample space, representing one or more outcomes. For example, in a die roll, the event "rolling an even number" is $\{2, 4, 6\}$.

- **Probability of an Event**: The probability of an event is a number between 0 and 1 that expresses how likely the event is to occur. The sum of the probabilities of all possible events in the sample space must equal 1. For an event A in a sample space S, the probability $P(A)$ is given by:

$$P(A) = \frac{\text{Number of favorable outcomes}}{\text{Total number of outcomes in the sample space}}$$

In the case of a fair six-sided die, the probability of rolling a 4 is:

$$P(4) = \frac{1}{6}$$

- **Conditional Probability**: Conditional probability is the probability of an event occurring given that another event has occurred. It is denoted as $P(A|B)$, which represents the probability of event A occurring given that event B has already occurred. It is calculated using Bayes' theorem:

$$P(A|B) = \frac{P(A \cap B)}{P(B)}$$

Conditional probability is important in machine learning when we want to predict one variable given another (e.g., predicting a label given a feature).

- **Bayes' Theorem**: Bayes' Theorem relates the conditional probabilities of events and is widely used in machine learning algorithms like **Naive Bayes classifiers**. It allows us to update our beliefs about a hypothesis based on new evidence. Bayes' theorem is expressed as:

$$P(A|B) = \frac{P(B|A)P(A)}{P(B)}$$

where:

- $P(A|B)$ is the probability of A given B (posterior probability),
- $P(B|A)$ is the probability of B given A (likelihood),
- $P(A)$ is the prior probability of A,
- $P(B)$ is the total probability of B.

Applications in Machine Learning:

- **Classification**: In supervised learning, particularly in classification problems, probability is used to predict the likelihood of different classes. For example, in logistic regression, a model estimates the probability of each class, and the class with the highest probability is chosen as the prediction.
- **Naive Bayes Classifier**: This probabilistic classifier uses Bayes' theorem and the assumption of independence between features to classify data.

2. Descriptive Statistics

Descriptive statistics are used to summarize and describe the features of a dataset. This includes measures of central tendency, variability, and distribution shape, all of which help in understanding the structure of the data.

Key Concepts Related to Descriptive Statistics:

Mean (Average): The mean is the sum of all data points divided by the number of data points. It is a measure of the central location of the data.

$$\mu = \frac{1}{n} \sum_{i=1}^{n} x_i$$

where x_i are the individual data points and n is the number of data points.

Median: The median is the middle value of the data when it is sorted in ascending or descending order. If there are an even number of data points, the median is the average of the two middle values. The median is a better measure of central tendency than the mean when the data contains outliers.

Mode: The mode is the value that appears most frequently in the dataset. A dataset can have one mode (unimodal), more than one mode (multimodal), or no mode at all.

Variance and Standard Deviation: Variance measures the spread of data points around the mean. The standard deviation is the square root of the variance and is used to quantify the amount of variation in a dataset.

$$\text{Variance} = \frac{1}{n} \sum_{i=1}^{n} (x_i - \mu)^2$$

Range: The range is the difference between the maximum and minimum values in a dataset, providing a simple measure of the spread of the data.

Skewness and Kurtosis: Skewness describes the asymmetry of the data distribution, while kurtosis measures the "tailedness" of the distribution. A highly skewed distribution can affect the performance of certain machine learning models, so it is important to understand the shape of the data.

Applications in Machine Learning:

- **Data Exploration**: Descriptive statistics are used during the exploratory data analysis (EDA) phase of a machine learning project to understand the dataset, identify outliers, and determine the distribution of features.
- **Feature Scaling**: Understanding the mean, variance, and range of features is essential for feature scaling (e.g., normalization or standardization), which is crucial for algorithms that are sensitive to the scale of the input data, such as k-nearest neighbors or gradient descent optimization.

3. Inferential Statistics

Inferential statistics involve making predictions or inferences about a population based on a sample of data. In machine learning, inferential statistics help us estimate parameters, make predictions, and evaluate models.

Key Concepts Related to Inferential Statistics:

Population vs. Sample: A population is the entire group being studied, while a sample is a subset of the population. Machine learning models typically work with samples of data, and inferential statistics help generalize findings from the sample to the population.

Hypothesis Testing: Hypothesis testing involves making an assumption about a population and using sample data to test the validity of that assumption. The results of hypothesis tests are often expressed in terms of p-values, which represent the probability of observing the data if the null hypothesis is true.

Confidence Intervals: A confidence interval provides a range of values within which we expect a population parameter to lie, with a certain level of confidence (e.g., 95%). Confidence intervals are important when assessing the uncertainty in model predictions.

p-value: The p-value is used to determine the statistical significance of a hypothesis test. A p-value lower than a predefined threshold (e.g., 0.05) indicates that the null hypothesis can be rejected, suggesting that the result is statistically significant.

Applications in Machine Learning:

- **Model Evaluation**: In machine learning, inferential statistics are used to assess the performance of models. For instance, when performing A/B testing to compare different algorithms or hyperparameters, hypothesis tests can help determine whether the differences in performance are statistically significant.

- **Parameter Estimation**: In algorithms like linear regression, inferential statistics can be used to estimate the parameters (e.g., slope and intercept) and evaluate their statistical significance.

4. Probability Distributions

Probability distributions describe the likelihood of various outcomes in a random experiment. In machine learning, probability distributions are used to model uncertainties in data and predictions.

Key Concepts Related to Probability Distributions:

Normal Distribution: The normal distribution (or Gaussian distribution) is one of the most important probability distributions in machine learning. It is symmetric and characterized by the mean and standard deviation. Many machine learning algorithms assume that the data follows a normal distribution, or they use it as an approximation.

Binomial Distribution: The binomial distribution models the number of successes in a fixed number of independent binary trials (e.g., coin flips). It is used in classification tasks and when working with discrete data.

Poisson Distribution: The Poisson distribution models the number of events occurring within a fixed interval of time or space. It is often used in machine learning when modeling rare events.

Applications in Machine Learning:

- **Model Assumptions**: Many machine learning algorithms make assumptions about the underlying distribution of the data. For example, Gaussian Naive Bayes assumes that the features follow a normal distribution.
- **Probabilistic Models**: Probabilistic models like Hidden Markov Models (HMMs) or Gaussian Mixture Models (GMMs) use probability distributions to model data.

Probability and statistics are essential concepts for understanding and working with machine learning algorithms. Probability helps model uncertainty and make predictions based on data, while descriptive and inferential statistics provide the tools to summarize, analyze, and evaluate data. By mastering these concepts, machine learning practitioners can build more robust models, interpret results effectively, and make decisions based on data-driven insights.

3.3 Gradient Descent and Optimization

In machine learning, optimization is the process of adjusting the parameters of a model to minimize or maximize a function, usually a loss or cost function. The goal is to find the optimal parameters that allow the model to make accurate predictions or classifications. Gradient Descent is one of the most popular optimization algorithms used in machine learning for this purpose. It is particularly effective for problems where the solution involves minimizing a continuous function, such as the loss function in supervised learning.

This section will explore the concept of gradient descent, how it works, and its application in machine learning optimization.

1. Optimization in Machine Learning

Optimization in machine learning refers to the process of adjusting the model's parameters (e.g., weights in a neural network, coefficients in linear regression) to minimize (or sometimes maximize) a function. The function that is minimized or maximized is typically called the cost function or loss function. For supervised learning, the goal is usually to minimize the difference between the model's predictions and the actual values in the dataset.

Key Concepts in Optimization:

Objective Function: The function that we are trying to minimize (or maximize). In machine learning, the objective function is typically the loss function that quantifies the difference between the predicted values and the true values in the training dataset.

Parameters: The variables that define the model and are optimized during training. These parameters include the weights and biases in models like linear regression and neural networks.

Global Minimum vs. Local Minimum: When optimizing a function, the "minimum" refers to the lowest point on the function's graph. The global minimum is the lowest point across the entire function, while a local minimum is a lower point in a small region of the function. Optimization algorithms aim to find the global minimum, though in many cases, they may get stuck in local minima.

Convex vs. Non-Convex Functions: A convex function has a single global minimum, and the optimization problem is easier to solve. A non-convex function, on the other hand, has multiple local minima, making the optimization more challenging.

2. Gradient Descent: Concept and Intuition

Gradient Descent is an iterative optimization algorithm used to minimize a loss function by updating the model parameters in the opposite direction of the gradient of the function. The gradient of a function at a specific point gives the direction and rate of the steepest ascent. In gradient descent, we take steps in the direction that decreases the function's value.

How Gradient Descent Works:

Start with Initial Parameters: The process begins with random or predefined initial values for the model parameters. These values do not need to be optimal initially.

Compute the Gradient: The gradient (or derivative) of the cost function is computed with respect to each model parameter. The gradient tells you how the loss function changes with respect to a small change in each parameter.

Update the Parameters: The model parameters are updated in the opposite direction of the gradient to minimize the cost function. This is done by subtracting a small fraction of the gradient (called the learning rate) from each parameter.

Repeat the Process: The process of calculating the gradient and updating the parameters is repeated iteratively until the model parameters converge to the optimal values (i.e., when the loss function stops improving or reaches a minimum threshold).

The update rule for each parameter θ_j (where j refers to a specific parameter) can be written as:

$$\theta_j \leftarrow \theta_j - \eta \cdot \frac{\partial J(\theta)}{\partial \theta_j}$$

Where:

- θ_j is the parameter,

- η is the learning rate,

- $\frac{\partial J(\theta)}{\partial \theta_j}$ is the partial derivative of the cost function $J(\theta)$ with respect to θ_j (the gradient).

Visualizing Gradient Descent:

Imagine a hiker standing on a mountain and wanting to reach the lowest point in a valley (the minimum of the loss function). The hiker doesn't know the lowest point in advance, so they begin at some random point and start walking downhill. The steepest slope at their current location determines which direction they should walk, and the size of their steps depends on the learning rate. Over time, the hiker takes smaller steps as they approach the bottom of the valley.

3. Types of Gradient Descent

There are different variations of gradient descent, depending on how much data is used to compute the gradient and how the parameters are updated:

Batch Gradient Descent: In batch gradient descent, the gradient is computed using the entire dataset. While this method is computationally expensive, it guarantees convergence to the global minimum (in the case of convex functions). It is ideal for small to medium-sized datasets where computing the gradient over the entire dataset is feasible.

- Advantages: Guarantees convergence to the global minimum for convex functions, stable and deterministic.
- Disadvantages: Computationally expensive for large datasets, as the entire dataset needs to be processed in every iteration.

Stochastic Gradient Descent (SGD): In stochastic gradient descent, the gradient is computed using only one random data point at a time. This method makes frequent updates and allows the algorithm to escape local minima by introducing randomness into the optimization process. It converges faster but may have more variance in its updates.

- **Advantages**: Faster updates, can handle large datasets, more efficient.
- **Disadvantages**: Can result in noisy updates, leading to oscillation and slow convergence near the optimal point.

Mini-Batch Gradient Descent: Mini-batch gradient descent strikes a balance between batch gradient descent and stochastic gradient descent by using a small batch of data points (e.g., 32 or 64 samples) to compute the gradient. This method is faster and more stable than pure stochastic gradient descent while benefiting from the computational efficiency of vectorized operations.

- **Advantages**: More efficient than batch gradient descent, less noisy than SGD, faster convergence.
- **Disadvantages**: Requires tuning of batch size, still can be computationally expensive for very large datasets.

4. Learning Rate and Convergence

One of the most important hyperparameters in gradient descent is the learning rate. The learning rate controls how big a step the algorithm takes in the direction of the gradient. A learning rate that is too small will result in slow convergence, while a learning rate that is too large can cause the algorithm to overshoot the minimum or even diverge.

Learning Rate Schedules:

- **Constant Learning Rate**: The learning rate remains fixed throughout the training process. While simple, this can be inefficient if the learning rate is not well-tuned.
- **Decay Learning Rate**: The learning rate decreases over time as the algorithm converges, allowing for more fine-tuned updates as it gets closer to the optimal solution.
- **Adaptive Learning Rates**: Techniques like Adam and Adagrad automatically adjust the learning rate for each parameter based on its gradient history, helping the algorithm converge more efficiently.

Convergence:

The goal of gradient descent is to minimize the cost function, but it is essential to monitor the convergence behavior to ensure the algorithm is finding the optimal solution. Convergence occurs when the change in the cost function between iterations is small enough, or when the gradients become negligible (i.e., the loss function is flat).

5. Challenges and Solutions

Local Minima: In non-convex functions, gradient descent can get stuck in local minima. This is common in complex models such as neural networks. To mitigate this, techniques like momentum (which uses previous gradients to smooth updates) and random restarts can be employed.

Exploding/Vanishing Gradients: When training deep networks, gradients can sometimes become too large (exploding gradients) or too small (vanishing gradients), which causes instability or slow convergence. This is often addressed by using techniques like gradient clipping (for exploding gradients) or normalization layers (e.g., batch normalization) to stabilize the gradient.

6. Applications in Machine Learning

Linear Regression: Gradient descent is often used to find the optimal weights for linear regression models, where the objective is to minimize the mean squared error (MSE) loss function.

Logistic Regression: Gradient descent is used to minimize the cross-entropy loss function in logistic regression, which is used for classification tasks.

Neural Networks: Deep learning models, especially neural networks, rely heavily on gradient descent (and its variants) to optimize weights and biases across many layers during training.

Support Vector Machines (SVMs): In training support vector machines, gradient-based optimization methods can be used to find the optimal hyperplane that separates different classes.

Gradient descent is a fundamental optimization algorithm in machine learning, allowing algorithms to learn from data and improve their performance. Understanding the mechanics of gradient descent, its variations, and the importance of the learning rate helps machine learning practitioners optimize models effectively. Whether working with simple linear models or complex deep learning networks, optimization through gradient descent plays a central role in training accurate and efficient machine learning models.

3.4 Cost Functions and Loss Functions

In machine learning, cost functions and loss functions are crucial concepts that help us quantify the difference between the model's predictions and the actual values from the data. These functions serve as a guide during the training process, helping optimization algorithms like gradient descent adjust the model parameters to minimize errors and improve prediction accuracy. While the terms "cost function" and "loss function" are often used interchangeably, there are subtle differences between the two, which we will discuss in this section.

1. What Are Cost Functions and Loss Functions?

Loss Function: A loss function measures the error between the predicted value and the actual target value for a single data point. It quantifies how far off the model's prediction is from the true value.

Cost Function: The cost function is the average of the loss function over the entire dataset. It provides a global measure of how well the model is performing on all the data points.

In simpler terms:

- A loss function tells you how good or bad your model's prediction is for a single data point.
- A cost function provides a summary of how good or bad the model is for the entire dataset by averaging the individual losses.

During training, the goal is to minimize the cost function, which corresponds to reducing the average error across all data points. The cost function is used to guide the optimization process, typically through gradient descent or other optimization algorithms.

2. Types of Loss Functions

There are several different loss functions used in machine learning, each suited for specific types of tasks (e.g., regression, classification, etc.). The most common ones are:

A. Mean Squared Error (MSE) – Common for Regression

For regression tasks, the Mean Squared Error is the most widely used loss function. It calculates the squared difference between the predicted value and the actual target value for each data point, then averages these squared errors.

The formula for MSE is:

$$MSE = \frac{1}{n} \sum_{i=1}^{n} (y_i - \hat{y}_i)^2$$

Where:

- y_i is the actual value,

- $\hat{y}_i$ is the predicted value,

- n is the number of data points.

Why is MSE popular?

- It punishes larger errors more than smaller ones because the errors are squared, making it sensitive to outliers.
- It is differentiable, making it suitable for optimization methods like gradient descent.

B. Mean Absolute Error (MAE) – Another Option for Regression

The Mean Absolute Error (MAE) is another loss function for regression problems. Unlike MSE, which squares the errors, MAE calculates the absolute difference between the predicted value and the actual value. MAE is less sensitive to outliers, as it treats all errors equally.

The formula for MAE is:

$$MAE = \frac{1}{n} \sum_{i=1}^{n} |y_i - \hat{y}_i|$$

Why use MAE?

- It is more robust to outliers compared to MSE.
- It results in linear penalties for errors, meaning large and small errors contribute equally.

C. Log Loss (Cross-Entropy Loss) – Common for Classification

In classification tasks, especially binary classification (i.e., two classes), the log loss or cross-entropy loss is frequently used. This loss function measures the performance of classification models whose output is a probability value between 0 and 1 (typically produced by a sigmoid or softmax function).

The formula for binary cross-entropy loss is:

$$\text{Log Loss} = -\frac{1}{n} \sum_{i=1}^{n} \left(y_i \log(\hat{y}_i) + (1 - y_i) \log(1 - \hat{y}_i) \right)$$

Where:

- y_i is the actual class label (0 or 1),

- $\hat{y}_i$ is the predicted probability that the instance belongs to class 1.

Why use log loss?

- It directly deals with probabilities, and is well-suited for models like logistic regression and neural networks.
- It penalizes confident but incorrect predictions heavily, making it a good choice for classification tasks where false positives and false negatives are costly.

D. Hinge Loss – Common for Support Vector Machines (SVMs)

The hinge loss is typically used for training support vector machines (SVMs), particularly for binary classification tasks. It is designed to ensure that not only are the predictions correct, but that they are made with a margin, which is especially useful in SVMs.

The formula for hinge loss is:

$$\text{Hinge Loss} = \frac{1}{n} \sum_{i=1}^{n} \max(0, 1 - y_i \cdot \hat{y}_i)$$

Where:

- y_i is the actual class label (-1 or 1),
- $\hat{y}_i$ is the predicted value (typically a signed score).

Why use hinge loss?

- It encourages the model to not only predict the correct class, but also make predictions with a certain margin of confidence.
- It works well in situations where you want to enforce a large margin between classes, which is the basis of SVMs.

E. Categorical Cross-Entropy – Multi-class Classification

For multi-class classification problems, where there are more than two classes, the categorical cross-entropy loss is used. It extends the binary cross-entropy loss to multiple classes.

The formula for categorical cross-entropy is:

$$\text{Categorical Cross-Entropy} = - \sum_{i=1}^{n} y_i \log(\hat{y}_i)$$

Where:

- y_i is the one-hot encoded true label (0 or 1 for each class),
- $\hat{y}_i$ is the predicted probability of class i.

Why use categorical cross-entropy?

- It is well-suited for problems where there are more than two classes.
- It makes the model learn to output probability distributions over multiple classes and minimizes the difference between the predicted and true distributions.

3. The Relationship Between Loss and Cost Functions

As previously discussed, the loss function calculates the error for a single data point, while the cost function calculates the average error across all data points. In many cases, minimizing the cost function is the primary goal of training a machine learning model, as it provides a measure of how well the model is performing over the entire dataset.

In other words:

$$\text{Cost Function} = \frac{1}{n} \sum_{i=1}^{n} \text{Loss Function for each data point}$$

Where n is the number of data points in the training set. By minimizing the cost function, the model learns to make accurate predictions for all data points in the dataset.

4. Choosing the Right Loss Function

Choosing the right loss function is crucial for the success of the machine learning model. The choice depends on the type of machine learning task (regression, binary classification, multi-class classification, etc.) and the nature of the data.

- For regression tasks, mean squared error or mean absolute error are commonly used.
- For binary classification, log loss (cross-entropy loss) is widely used.
- For multi-class classification, categorical cross-entropy is typically employed.
- For SVMs, hinge loss is often the choice.

Cost functions and loss functions are the backbone of machine learning optimization. By quantifying the error between predictions and true values, they guide the optimization process, helping the model improve its accuracy over time. Choosing the appropriate loss function based on the task and the characteristics of the data is essential for successful model training and performance. Understanding these concepts will enable you to make better decisions when designing and training machine learning models.

4. Understanding Data

Data is the backbone of ML. This chapter teaches you how to collect, clean, preprocess, and visualize data for machine learning models. You'll learn about handling missing values, feature engineering, and how to prepare high-quality datasets for effective model training.

4.1 Data Collection & Cleaning

Data is the lifeblood of machine learning models. No matter how sophisticated your algorithms or models are, they rely heavily on the quality of the data they are trained on. Data collection and cleaning are foundational steps in the machine learning pipeline, directly impacting the performance and accuracy of the model. In this section, we'll explore how to collect high-quality data and clean it effectively to ensure the best possible results from your machine learning projects.

1. The Importance of Data in Machine Learning

Machine learning models are only as good as the data they are trained on. Data serves as the input for the model and is used to learn patterns, make predictions, or classify information. Having the right data in the right format is critical for training an accurate and robust model. Poor quality data—whether due to missing values, outliers, or noise—can lead to poor performance, overfitting, or underfitting, thereby limiting the model's ability to generalize to new, unseen data.

The two essential steps in preparing your data for machine learning are data collection and data cleaning.

2. Data Collection: Gathering the Raw Data

Data collection is the first step in any machine learning project. The quality of your data directly impacts the accuracy and reliability of your machine learning models. There are several ways to collect data depending on the project and the resources available:

A. Types of Data Sources

Existing Datasets: Many machine learning practitioners and researchers use publicly available datasets for their projects. These datasets can come from various domains, including healthcare, finance, image recognition, natural language processing, and more. Some popular sources for open datasets include:

- **Kaggle**: A platform for machine learning competitions that also hosts datasets for practice.
- **UCI Machine Learning Repository**: A collection of datasets from various domains used for machine learning research.
- **Google Dataset Search**: A search engine for finding datasets hosted on the web.

Web Scraping: Sometimes, the data you need might not be readily available, but can be scraped from websites. Web scraping involves extracting data from web pages by writing scripts that parse HTML content. This method requires some programming skills, often using libraries like BeautifulSoup (Python) or Scrapy.

APIs: Many platforms, such as Twitter, Google, and Facebook, provide public APIs that allow you to collect data programmatically. APIs are an efficient way to pull real-time or large amounts of data directly from the source.

Surveys and Questionnaires: For certain projects, especially in areas like marketing, social sciences, or healthcare, you may need to collect primary data from respondents. Surveys or questionnaires can be distributed to gather data directly from users.

Sensors and IoT Devices: In industries such as manufacturing or agriculture, sensors can be used to collect real-time data on environmental conditions, machinery performance, or crop health.

Internal Databases: Many organizations already have vast amounts of data stored in internal databases. This data can be accessed via database queries to retrieve the relevant data for analysis and model training.

B. Data Collection Best Practices

Understand the Problem: Before collecting data, ensure that you clearly understand the problem you're solving and the type of data that will be useful. For example, in a classification problem, labeled data is needed; for a regression task, you'll need continuous numerical data.

Data Quantity: Ensure you collect enough data to train your model effectively. Machine learning algorithms perform better with larger and diverse datasets, as they are better able to detect patterns and generalize.

Data Variety: Your data should reflect the diversity of real-world scenarios. Inadequate or biased data can lead to overfitting, where the model performs well on the training data but poorly on new data.

3. Data Cleaning: Preparing the Data for Analysis

Once you have collected your data, the next step is data cleaning. This is often the most time-consuming and complex part of the data preparation process. Data cleaning involves handling missing values, eliminating duplicates, identifying outliers, and transforming data into a format suitable for analysis. Here's an overview of the key tasks involved in data cleaning:

A. Handling Missing Data

In real-world datasets, missing data is quite common. It's essential to handle missing values properly to avoid bias or errors during model training. There are several approaches to dealing with missing data:

Removing Missing Data: If the number of missing values is small or inessential for the analysis, it may be acceptable to remove the rows or columns that contain them. However, this could result in losing valuable information, so it should be done cautiously.

Imputation: Imputation involves filling in missing values with a reasonable estimate. Common imputation techniques include:

- **For numerical data**: Using the mean, median, or mode of the column, or employing more advanced techniques such as regression imputation.
- **For categorical data**: Using the mode (most frequent category) or filling with a new category such as "Unknown."

Using Algorithms That Handle Missing Data: Some machine learning algorithms, such as XGBoost and Random Forests, can handle missing data by incorporating it into the model's structure during training.

B. Removing Duplicates

Sometimes datasets include duplicate rows or entries, which can distort the model's learning process. Identifying and removing duplicate records is an essential part of data cleaning. Duplicates can occur due to errors during data entry or improper merging of datasets. It's important to identify duplicate entries and decide whether to drop them or aggregate the data in some way.

C. Handling Outliers

Outliers are data points that significantly differ from other observations in the dataset. While outliers might represent valid but rare cases, they can also skew statistical analysis or interfere with model training.

Visualizing the Data: Use methods such as box plots, scatter plots, or histograms to identify outliers visually.

Removing or Transforming Outliers: If an outlier is determined to be a result of an error or anomaly in the data, it may be appropriate to remove it. Alternatively, you can transform the data using techniques such as log transformation to reduce the effect of outliers.

Use Robust Models: Some machine learning algorithms are more resistant to outliers, such as Robust Regression or Tree-based models like Random Forests.

D. Standardizing and Normalizing Data

Many machine learning algorithms, especially those that rely on distance metrics like k-NN, support vector machines, and gradient descent, require the input data to be on a similar scale. This is because features with larger numeric ranges can dominate the learning process.

Normalization: This technique scales the data to a fixed range, typically between 0 and 1. It is useful when the data does not follow a Gaussian distribution.

- Formula: $X_{\text{norm}} = \frac{X - \min(X)}{\max(X) - \min(X)}$

Standardization: This involves rescaling the data so that it has a mean of 0 and a standard deviation of 1. It's particularly useful when the data follows a Gaussian distribution and is typically used in algorithms like logistic regression or SVM.

- Formula: $X_{\text{std}} = \frac{X - \mu}{\sigma}$

E. Encoding Categorical Data

Most machine learning algorithms require numerical inputs, but data is often in the form of categorical variables (e.g., gender, country, product type). To convert categorical data into numerical values, you can use encoding techniques such as:

- **Label Encoding**: Assign a unique integer to each category.
- **One-Hot Encoding**: Create a binary column for each category (suitable for nominal categorical variables).

F. Feature Engineering and Transformation

Feature engineering is the process of creating new features or modifying existing features to improve the model's predictive power. This may involve:

- Combining or transforming features (e.g., extracting day of the week from a timestamp).
- Creating interaction terms between features.
- Handling skewed distributions (e.g., applying logarithmic transformations).

4. Data Cleaning Tools and Techniques

Various tools and libraries can assist with data collection and cleaning:

- **Pandas (Python):** Provides comprehensive functionality for cleaning and manipulating datasets, such as handling missing data, filtering, and transforming data.
- **NumPy (Python):** Useful for numerical operations, especially when performing mathematical operations or transformations on datasets.
- **OpenRefine**: An open-source tool for working with messy data, allowing users to clean and transform data without writing code.
- **SQL**: If your data is stored in a relational database, SQL can be used to clean data by filtering, aggregating, and transforming datasets.

Data collection and cleaning are critical steps in the machine learning pipeline that directly influence the quality of the resulting models. Collecting diverse, high-quality data and ensuring it is clean and formatted properly is essential for effective machine learning. By addressing missing values, outliers, duplicates, and other issues, and by transforming the data into a suitable format for modeling, you provide your machine learning algorithms with the best foundation for learning and making predictions. Proper data collection and cleaning can be time-consuming but are indispensable for developing successful machine learning models.

4.2 Handling Missing Data & Outliers

In machine learning, the quality of the data plays a critical role in the performance and accuracy of models. Often, raw data is incomplete, noisy, or includes anomalies. Missing data and outliers are two common issues that can adversely affect machine learning algorithms. In this section, we will explore methods and techniques to handle both missing data and outliers effectively, ensuring that your dataset is clean and ready for model training.

1. Handling Missing Data

Missing data is a common challenge in real-world datasets. Data can be missing for various reasons, such as errors in data collection, problems with data entry, or system failures. When data is missing, it can lead to biased or inaccurate model predictions if not addressed properly. Here are some strategies for handling missing data:

A. Identify Missing Data

The first step in handling missing data is identifying where and how much data is missing. In many datasets, missing values are represented as NaN (Not a Number), null, or NA (Not Available). You can inspect the dataset to find missing values using summary statistics or visualizations.

For example:

In Python, using the Pandas library, you can check for missing data with the .isnull() or .isna() functions:

```
import pandas as pd
df.isnull().sum()  # Get the count of missing values per column
```

B. Methods for Handling Missing Data

Once you've identified missing data, there are several approaches to handle it, depending on the nature of the data and how much is missing.

Removing Missing Data:

If the amount of missing data is small and removing those rows or columns won't significantly impact your analysis, you can simply drop them.
In Pandas, this can be done using:

```
df.dropna()  # Drop rows with missing data
df.dropna(axis=1)  # Drop columns with missing data
```

Imputation:

Imputation involves filling in missing values with an estimated or calculated value based on the existing data. The choice of imputation method depends on the data type and context.

For numerical data:

Mean/Median Imputation: Replace missing values with the mean or median of the column. Use the mean when the data is approximately normally distributed and the median when it is skewed.

```
df['column_name'].fillna(df['column_name'].mean(), inplace=True)
```

Forward/Backward Fill: Fill missing values with the last valid observation or the next valid observation. This is useful when data is time-series.

```
df.fillna(method='ffill')  # Forward fill
df.fillna(method='bfill')  # Backward fill
```

Interpolation: Use interpolation methods to estimate missing values based on other data points.

```
df['column_name'].interpolate(method='linear', inplace=True)
```

For categorical data:

Mode Imputation: Replace missing values with the most frequent category (mode).

```
df['category_column'].fillna(df['category_column'].mode()[0], inplace=True)
```

Advanced Imputation: More sophisticated techniques such as K-Nearest Neighbors (KNN) or Multiple Imputation can be used to predict missing values based on the relationships between features in the dataset.

Using Algorithms That Handle Missing Data:

Some machine learning algorithms, such as Random Forests and XGBoost, can handle missing data internally by making use of the available information during training. However, relying on these algorithms to handle missing data should only be done after a careful evaluation of their behavior.

C. When to Impute vs. Remove Data

- Imputation is typically used when a significant portion of the data is missing, and removing it would reduce the dataset size significantly or lead to biased results.
- Removing data is appropriate when the proportion of missing data is small, or when missingness itself could indicate an important pattern (e.g., a specific group of patients in a healthcare dataset might be missing due to a unique characteristic that is worth exploring).

2. Handling Outliers

Outliers are data points that deviate significantly from the other observations in a dataset. They can occur due to errors in data collection, recording issues, or naturally occurring rare events. While outliers may sometimes represent important data points, they can also distort statistical analyses and model training, leading to biased results. Here are strategies to deal with outliers:

A. Identifying Outliers

The first step in handling outliers is detecting them. Several techniques can be used to identify outliers in both numerical and categorical data:

Visual Inspection:

- **Box Plots**: Box plots are useful for visualizing the distribution of numerical data and identifying outliers. Outliers typically appear as points outside the "whiskers" of the box plot.

- **Scatter Plots**: Scatter plots are useful when checking for outliers in two-dimensional data, as points that fall far from the general cluster of data can be considered outliers.

Statistical Methods:

Z-Score: The Z-score represents how many standard deviations a data point is from the mean. A Z-score greater than 3 (or less than -3) typically indicates an outlier.

```
from scipy import stats
z_scores = stats.zscore(df['column_name'])
outliers = df[abs(z_scores) > 3]
```

- **Interquartile Range (IQR)**: IQR is the range between the first quartile (Q1) and third quartile (Q3) of the data. Outliers are defined as data points that fall outside the range of $Q1 - 1.5 \times IQR$ and $Q3 + 1.5 \times IQR$.

```
Q1 = df['column_name'].quantile(0.25)
Q3 = df['column_name'].quantile(0.75)
IQR = Q3 - Q1
lower_bound = Q1 - 1.5 * IQR
upper_bound = Q3 + 1.5 * IQR
outliers = df[(df['column_name'] < lower_bound) | (df['column_name'] > upper_bound)]
```

B. Methods for Handling Outliers

Once outliers are identified, you need to decide how to handle them. The appropriate approach depends on whether the outliers are valid data points or errors.

Removing Outliers:

If the outliers are likely to be errors or if they represent less than 1% of the dataset, removing them might be the best option. However, be cautious, as removing too many data points can result in biased models.

Example:

```
df = df[(df['column_name'] > lower_bound) & (df['column_name'] < upper_bound)]
```

Transforming Data:

Sometimes, transforming the data can reduce the effect of outliers. For example, applying a log transformation or a square root transformation can make the data more normally distributed and less sensitive to extreme values.
Capping or Winsorizing:

Another approach is to cap the outliers by setting them to a predefined threshold. This process is known as winsorizing. For example, you can replace all values greater than a certain threshold with the threshold value itself, or all values below a certain threshold with that threshold.

Imputing Outliers:

In some cases, instead of removing or transforming outliers, you may choose to replace them with more reasonable values, such as the mean, median, or a value based on predictive models.

C. When to Keep Outliers

Outliers might represent important information, especially in certain applications:

- In fraud detection, disease outbreaks, or extreme weather events, outliers could indicate valuable rare occurrences that are highly relevant to the task at hand.
- In such cases, removing outliers may lead to losing important patterns, so it's crucial to analyze whether outliers are genuinely errors or part of the signal.

Handling missing data and outliers is a vital part of the data preprocessing phase in any machine learning project. The methods for dealing with these issues depend on the nature of the data and the context of the problem you're solving. Imputation and removal of missing data should be done thoughtfully to avoid bias, while outliers should be carefully considered, as they may represent rare but important events. By appropriately addressing missing data and outliers, you ensure that your machine learning models are trained on high-quality data, leading to more accurate and reliable predictions.

4.3 Feature Engineering & Selection

Feature engineering and feature selection are two crucial steps in the data preparation phase of machine learning that can significantly influence model performance. Properly engineered features allow the model to capture important patterns and relationships in the data, while feature selection ensures that only the most relevant features are used for model training. In this section, we'll explore what feature engineering and selection are, why they are important, and various techniques to apply in both processes.

1. What is Feature Engineering?

Feature engineering is the process of transforming raw data into meaningful features that better represent the underlying patterns in the data. The goal is to create features that help machine learning algorithms identify important signals, ultimately improving the model's performance.

Good feature engineering is crucial because the performance of a model often hinges on the quality and relevance of the input features. Raw data, especially from real-world sources, often contains noise, irrelevant variables, or relationships that the model can't easily capture unless properly transformed. Therefore, feature engineering often requires domain knowledge, creativity, and understanding of the model's behavior.

A. Common Techniques in Feature Engineering

Handling Categorical Data:

Label Encoding: Converts each unique category in a feature into a numerical value. For example, a "Color" feature with categories "Red," "Blue," and "Green" would be encoded as 0, 1, and 2 respectively.

```
from sklearn.preprocessing import LabelEncoder
le = LabelEncoder()
df['color_encoded'] = le.fit_transform(df['color'])
```

One-Hot Encoding: Converts each category in a feature into a new binary feature, where each feature represents a category. This method avoids ordinal relationships, which might be mistakenly inferred from label encoding.

```
df = pd.get_dummies(df, columns=['color'])
```

Creating Interaction Features:

Interaction features involve combining two or more existing features to form a new feature that might reveal a relationship not captured by individual features. For example, in a dataset involving "height" and "weight," a new feature like "body mass index" (BMI) could be created to better capture the relationship between the two variables.

```
df['bmi'] = df['weight'] / (df['height'] ** 2)
```

Time-based Features:

For time-series data, extracting time-based features can reveal seasonal patterns, trends, or cyclical behavior. For example, extracting the "day of the week," "month," or "quarter" from a timestamp can help the model recognize weekly or yearly patterns.

```
df['day_of_week'] = df['timestamp'].dt.dayofweek
df['month'] = df['timestamp'].dt.month
```

Binning:

Binning (also known as discretization) involves transforming continuous numerical variables into categorical bins. For example, "age" can be divided into bins like "child," "teenager," "adult," and "senior."

```
bins = [0, 18, 35, 50, 100]
labels = ['child', 'teenager', 'adult', 'senior']
df['age_group'] = pd.cut(df['age'], bins=bins, labels=labels)
```

Feature Scaling:

Feature scaling ensures that all features have the same scale, especially when using algorithms that are sensitive to scale (like K-Nearest Neighbors, Support Vector Machines, and Gradient Descent). Scaling is important for numerical data with vastly different ranges.

Standardization: Rescaling the data to have a mean of 0 and a standard deviation of 1.

```
from sklearn.preprocessing import StandardScaler
scaler = StandardScaler()
df[['feature1', 'feature2']] = scaler.fit_transform(df[['feature1', 'feature2']])
```

Normalization: Rescaling the data to a fixed range, typically between 0 and 1.

```
from sklearn.preprocessing import MinMaxScaler
scaler = MinMaxScaler()
df[['feature1', 'feature2']] = scaler.fit_transform(df[['feature1', 'feature2']])
```

Polynomial Features:

Polynomial features involve creating higher-degree combinations of existing features. This can be useful for capturing non-linear relationships between features.

```
from sklearn.preprocessing import PolynomialFeatures
poly = PolynomialFeatures(degree=2)
df_poly = poly.fit_transform(df[['feature1', 'feature2']])
```

Text-Based Features:

- For text data, converting text into numerical features can be done using techniques like Bag of Words, TF-IDF, or Word Embeddings. For example, in Natural Language Processing (NLP), converting the text of a sentence into a vector representation allows the model to process it effectively.
- TF-IDF is a common technique to extract features from text data, which gives higher weights to words that are more relevant to a document but appear less frequently across the corpus.

2. What is Feature Selection?

Feature selection is the process of choosing the most relevant features to use in model training while discarding irrelevant, redundant, or noisy features. The goal is to improve the model's performance by reducing overfitting, speeding up training, and increasing interpretability.

Feature selection helps in preventing the model from becoming too complex by removing irrelevant or redundant features. This not only helps the model generalize better but also reduces the risk of overfitting by simplifying the model's decision-making process.

A. Why Feature Selection is Important

- **Reducing Overfitting**: Including too many irrelevant features increases the likelihood that the model will capture noise in the data, leading to poor generalization on unseen data.
- **Improving Model Accuracy**: Redundant or irrelevant features can decrease the predictive power of the model.
- **Decreasing Training Time**: Fewer features lead to a simpler model, which requires less computational power and time to train.
- **Improving Interpretability**: Fewer features make the model easier to interpret and visualize, especially in cases where model explainability is important.

B. Techniques for Feature Selection

Filter Methods:

Filter methods evaluate each feature independently based on its correlation with the target variable. Features with low correlation or predictive power are discarded.

Correlation Matrix: A simple way to check for features that are highly correlated with the target variable. Features with very low correlation can be dropped.

```
df.corr()  # Shows the correlation matrix for numerical features
```

Chi-Square Test: A statistical test used to determine whether a categorical feature is significantly related to the target variable.

```
from sklearn.feature_selection import SelectKBest
from sklearn.feature_selection import chi2
chi2_selector = SelectKBest(chi2, k=10)
df_selected = chi2_selector.fit_transform(X, y)
```

Wrapper Methods:

Wrapper methods evaluate feature subsets by training a model using different feature combinations and selecting the best-performing set. These methods are more computationally expensive but tend to provide better results.

Recursive Feature Elimination (RFE): This method recursively removes the least important features based on model performance, starting with all features and eliminating one feature at a time.

```
from sklearn.feature_selection import RFE
model = LogisticRegression()
selector = RFE(model, n_features_to_select=5)
X_selected = selector.fit_transform(X, y)
```

Embedded Methods:

Embedded methods perform feature selection during model training. These methods are usually more efficient than wrapper methods since they combine the learning process with feature selection.

L1 Regularization (Lasso): Lasso regression applies L1 regularization, which can shrink some feature coefficients to zero, effectively performing feature selection.

```
from sklearn.linear_model import Lasso
model = Lasso(alpha=0.1)
model.fit(X, y)
selected_features = X.columns[model.coef_ != 0]
```

Tree-based Methods:

Decision tree-based algorithms, such as Random Forests and Gradient Boosting Machines (GBMs), have built-in feature importance scores that help identify the most relevant features.

```
from sklearn.ensemble import RandomForestClassifier
model = RandomForestClassifier()
model.fit(X, y)
feature_importances = model.feature_importances_
```

Principal Component Analysis (PCA):

PCA is a dimensionality reduction technique that transforms the feature space into a set of orthogonal components that capture the maximum variance in the data. It can help reduce the number of features while maintaining the most important information.

```
from sklearn.decomposition import PCA
pca = PCA(n_components=5)
X_pca = pca.fit_transform(X)
```

Feature engineering and feature selection are integral parts of the machine learning pipeline. Feature engineering allows us to create new and meaningful representations of the data, while feature selection ensures that only the most relevant features are used in model training. Both processes help in improving model accuracy, reducing overfitting, and optimizing computational resources. By applying the right techniques for feature engineering and selection, you can significantly enhance the performance of your machine learning models and ensure that they are well-suited to the problem you're trying to solve.

4.4 Data Normalization and Encoding Techniques

In machine learning, data preprocessing plays a crucial role in ensuring that algorithms can learn patterns effectively from the data. Two essential aspects of preprocessing are data normalization and data encoding. Both processes help in transforming data into formats that machine learning models can use efficiently. In this section, we will dive into normalization and encoding techniques, their importance, and how to apply them in practice.

1. What is Data Normalization?

Data normalization is the process of scaling numerical features so that they are on a similar scale, typically within a specific range. Normalization ensures that no single feature dominates others due to its larger magnitude, which is especially important for algorithms that are sensitive to the scale of the data.

When data features are on different scales, algorithms that rely on distance measurements, like K-Nearest Neighbors (KNN) and Support Vector Machines (SVM), may be biased towards features with larger ranges. By normalizing the data, each feature contributes equally to the model, leading to better performance.

A. Why is Normalization Important?

Improves Convergence in Optimization Algorithms:

Many machine learning algorithms, like Gradient Descent, benefit from normalization because it helps them converge more quickly to an optimal solution. Large feature values can slow down the convergence, while normalized features allow faster and more stable learning.

Prevents Feature Dominance:

Features with large numeric values may dominate the model, overshadowing features with smaller numeric values. Normalization ensures that each feature is treated with equal importance.

Essential for Distance-Based Algorithms:

Algorithms like KNN, k-Means clustering, and Principal Component Analysis (PCA) rely on the concept of distance (e.g., Euclidean distance), so it's crucial that all features are on the same scale to avoid skewed distance calculations.

B. Common Normalization Techniques

Min-Max Scaling (Rescaling):

Min-Max scaling transforms features by scaling them to a fixed range, usually between 0 and 1. This is done by subtracting the minimum value of the feature and dividing by the range (max - min).

Formula:

$$X_{scaled} = \frac{X - \min(X)}{\max(X) - \min(X)}$$

Example using Scikit-learn in Python:

```
from sklearn.preprocessing import MinMaxScaler
scaler = MinMaxScaler()
df[['feature1', 'feature2']] = scaler.fit_transform(df[['feature1', 'feature2']])
```

Z-Score Standardization (Standard Scaling):

Z-score standardization transforms features by scaling them to have a mean of 0 and a standard deviation of 1. This method is useful when the data is approximately normally distributed.

Formula:

$$X_{scaled} = \frac{X - \mu}{\sigma}$$

Example using Scikit-learn in Python:

```
from sklearn.preprocessing import StandardScaler
scaler = StandardScaler()
df[['feature1', 'feature2']] = scaler.fit_transform(df[['feature1', 'feature2']])
```

Robust Scaling:

Robust scaling is similar to standard scaling but uses the median and the interquartile range (IQR) instead of the mean and standard deviation. This is helpful when the data contains outliers, as it is less sensitive to extreme values.

Formula:

$$X_{scaled} = \frac{X - \text{median}(X)}{\text{IQR}(X)}$$

Example using Scikit-learn in Python:

```
from sklearn.preprocessing import RobustScaler
scaler = RobustScaler()
```

```
df[['feature1', 'feature2']] = scaler.fit_transform(df[['feature1', 'feature2']])
```

Unit Vector Scaling (Normalization to Unit Length):

This method scales the feature values so that the sum of the squares of all the values equals 1, making the vector a unit vector. It's commonly used in text classification tasks, where features are represented as vectors.

Example using Scikit-learn in Python:

```
from sklearn.preprocessing import Normalizer
normalizer = Normalizer()
df[['feature1', 'feature2']] = normalizer.fit_transform(df[['feature1', 'feature2']])
```

2. What is Data Encoding?

Data encoding refers to the transformation of categorical data into numerical format so that it can be understood and processed by machine learning algorithms. Since most machine learning models require numerical input, encoding categorical variables becomes a critical step in preparing data for training.

There are various encoding methods based on the type of categorical data and the problem being solved. Proper encoding helps retain meaningful relationships within categorical variables while making the data suitable for machine learning models.

A. Why is Encoding Important?

Handling Non-Numerical Data:

Machine learning algorithms generally don't work with non-numeric data. Encoding is required to convert categorical variables into a numeric format that models can understand.

Capturing Relationships:

The choice of encoding method can help preserve and capture relationships within the categorical features. For example, some encoding methods maintain the inherent ordinal relationship in the data, while others treat categories as completely independent.

Improves Model Performance:

Proper encoding ensures that categorical data doesn't mislead the model and helps improve its predictive power.

B. Common Encoding Techniques

Label Encoding:

Label encoding transforms categorical variables into integer labels. Each unique category is assigned a unique integer, which might introduce an ordinal relationship (i.e., the model could assume that one category is "greater" than another, which might not always be the case).

Example using Scikit-learn in Python:

```
from sklearn.preprocessing import LabelEncoder
le = LabelEncoder()
df['encoded_column'] = le.fit_transform(df['categorical_column'])
```

One-Hot Encoding:

One-Hot Encoding creates a binary column for each category in the categorical feature. Each column corresponds to one possible category, and for each row, only the column corresponding to the category is set to 1, while all others are set to 0. This method eliminates any ordinal relationship between categories and ensures that each category is treated independently.

Example using Pandas in Python:

```
df = pd.get_dummies(df, columns=['categorical_column'])
```

Ordinal Encoding:

Ordinal encoding is used when the categorical variable has a natural, ordered relationship (e.g., "low," "medium," "high"). Each category is mapped to an integer based on its rank.

Example in Python:

```
from sklearn.preprocessing import OrdinalEncoder
enc = OrdinalEncoder(categories=[['low', 'medium', 'high']])
df['encoded_column'] = enc.fit_transform(df[['categorical_column']])
```

Binary Encoding:

Binary encoding is a hybrid technique that combines the properties of Label Encoding and One-Hot Encoding. It converts each category into a binary number and then splits the number into individual bits. This can be more efficient than one-hot encoding, especially when there are many categories.

Example using category_encoders in Python:

```
import category_encoders as ce
encoder = ce.BinaryEncoder(cols=['categorical_column'])
df = encoder.fit_transform(df)
```

Frequency Encoding:

Frequency encoding replaces each category with the frequency (count) of its occurrence in the dataset. This method can be useful when there are too many categories, but the frequencies themselves may carry useful information.

Example in Python:

```
freq_map = df['categorical_column'].value_counts().to_dict()
df['encoded_column'] = df['categorical_column'].map(freq_map)
```

Target Encoding (Mean Encoding):

Target encoding replaces each category with the mean of the target variable for that category. This technique is often used for high-cardinality categorical variables, but it needs to be used carefully to avoid data leakage (i.e., using information from the target variable during training).

Example using category_encoders in Python:

```
encoder = ce.TargetEncoder(cols=['categorical_column'])
df['encoded_column'] = encoder.fit_transform(df['categorical_column'], df['target'])
```

3. When to Use Each Encoding or Normalization Method?

Normalization: When your data has numerical features with different scales, especially for distance-based models (KNN, SVM), or algorithms like Gradient Descent-based models. Use Min-Max scaling for bounded features (e.g., between 0 and 1) or Z-score scaling for features with a Gaussian distribution.

Label Encoding: Use when the categorical variable is ordinal (i.e., the categories have an inherent order, like "low," "medium," "high").

One-Hot Encoding: Use when the categorical variable is nominal (i.e., the categories don't have any inherent order, like "red," "blue," "green").

Target Encoding: Use for high-cardinality categorical variables when there are too many categories for one-hot encoding to be efficient.

Data normalization and encoding are essential preprocessing steps for preparing data for machine learning algorithms. Normalization ensures that numerical features are on a similar scale, making the model training more efficient, while encoding transforms categorical data into a numeric format that models can understand. Selecting the appropriate normalization and encoding techniques can have a significant impact on the performance and effectiveness of machine learning models. Understanding when and how to apply these techniques is crucial to achieving optimal results.

5. Regression Models

Regression is a fundamental ML technique used for predicting numerical values. Here, we explore Linear Regression, Polynomial Regression, and advanced methods like Ridge and Lasso regression, using Python to build practical models for real-world scenarios.

5.1 Introduction to Regression

Regression is one of the fundamental techniques in machine learning and statistics, primarily used to model relationships between a dependent variable (or target) and one or more independent variables (or features). Unlike classification tasks, where the goal is to predict a categorical outcome, regression is focused on predicting continuous numerical values. This makes it a core method for tasks such as predicting house prices, forecasting sales, or estimating the future value of stocks.

In this section, we will cover the core concepts of regression, the different types of regression models, and their applications in machine learning.

1. What is Regression?

Regression is a predictive modeling technique that estimates the relationship between variables. The primary aim is to model how a dependent variable changes when one or more independent variables change. In simpler terms, regression helps answer questions like, "How does the price of a house change with respect to the number of bedrooms, square footage, and location?"

In mathematical terms, regression tries to find the best-fitting curve (or line, in simple cases) that minimizes the difference between predicted values and actual values of the dependent variable.

A. Regression Equation:

For simple linear regression, the relationship between a dependent variable y and an independent variable x can be expressed by the equation of a straight line:

$$y = \beta_0 + \beta_1 x + \epsilon$$

Where:

- y is the dependent variable (target),
- x is the independent variable (feature),
- β_0 is the y-intercept (constant term),
- β_1 is the coefficient of the independent variable, representing the slope of the line,
- ϵ is the error term, which accounts for the variability in the data that can't be explained by the model.

For multiple regression, where there are multiple features $x_1, x_2, ..., x_n$, the equation becomes:

$$y = \beta_0 + \beta_1 x_1 + \beta_2 x_2 + ... + \beta_n x_n + \epsilon$$

B. Objective of Regression:

The goal of regression is to estimate the coefficients $\beta_0, \beta_1, ..., \beta_n$ that minimize the error term ϵ and thus improve the model's predictive accuracy. The error term is the difference between the predicted value and the actual value.

2. Types of Regression

There are several types of regression models, each suited for different types of data and problem scenarios. Some common regression models include:

A. Linear Regression

Linear regression is the simplest and most commonly used regression model. It assumes that the relationship between the dependent variable and independent variables is linear, meaning that the dependent variable changes proportionally with the independent variables.

- **Simple Linear Regression**: Involves a single independent variable.

- **Multiple Linear Regression**: Involves multiple independent variables, allowing the model to capture more complex relationships.

Example: Predicting a person's salary based on years of experience using a single feature (years of experience).

B. Polynomial Regression

Polynomial regression is an extension of linear regression. It is used when the relationship between the dependent and independent variables is not linear but can be modeled as a polynomial of degree n. By adding higher-degree terms of the features, this model can capture more complex, non-linear relationships.

Example: Predicting the growth of a plant where the relationship between time and height may not be linear.

The equation for polynomial regression can be written as:

$$y = \beta_0 + \beta_1 x + \beta_2 x^2 + \beta_3 x^3 + \dots + \beta_n x^n$$

C. Ridge Regression (L2 Regularization)

Ridge regression is a variation of linear regression that adds a penalty term to the model to avoid overfitting, especially when the number of features is large. This penalty term is proportional to the square of the coefficients of the features.

Ridge regression solves the following equation:

$$\hat{\beta} = \arg \min_{\beta} \left(\sum_{i=1}^{n} (y_i - \beta_0 - \sum_{j=1}^{p} \beta_j x_{ij})^2 + \lambda \sum_{j=1}^{p} \beta_j^2 \right)$$

Where:

- λ is a hyperparameter that controls the strength of the regularization.

Ridge regression is effective when there is multicollinearity (high correlation between features) in the data.

D. Lasso Regression (L1 Regularization)

Lasso regression is another variation of linear regression that also adds a penalty term but uses the absolute values of the coefficients. Lasso (Least Absolute Shrinkage and Selection Operator) regression has the ability to shrink some coefficients to exactly zero, effectively performing feature selection.

The equation for lasso regression is similar to ridge regression, but the penalty term is based on the absolute values of the coefficients:

$$\hat{\beta} = \arg\min_{\beta} \left(\sum_{i=1}^{n} (y_i - \beta_0 - \sum_{j=1}^{p} \beta_j x_{ij})^2 + \lambda \sum_{j=1}^{p} |\beta_j| \right)$$

Lasso is particularly useful when we want a sparse model with fewer features.

E. Elastic Net Regression

Elastic Net regression combines the penalties of both ridge and lasso regression. It is useful when there are multiple correlated features, as it provides a balance between ridge and lasso, benefiting from both types of regularization.

The Elastic Net objective function is:

$$\hat{\beta} = \arg\min_{\beta} \left(\sum_{i=1}^{n} (y_i - \beta_0 - \sum_{j=1}^{p} \beta_j x_{ij})^2 + \lambda_1 \sum_{j=1}^{p} |\beta_j| + \lambda_2 \sum_{j=1}^{p} \beta_j^2 \right)$$

F. Logistic Regression (For Classification)

Though its name suggests it is a regression algorithm, logistic regression is used for binary classification tasks. It models the probability that a given input belongs to a particular class. The output is a probability value between 0 and 1, which can be mapped to a class label.

The logistic regression model is expressed as:

$$P(y = 1|X) = \frac{1}{1 + e^{-(\beta_0 + \beta_1 X)}}$$

3. Applications of Regression

Regression techniques are widely used across various industries and domains. Some common applications of regression models include:

- **Real Estate**: Predicting house prices based on features such as location, number of rooms, and square footage.
- **Finance**: Forecasting stock prices or predicting the future value of investments.
- **Healthcare**: Estimating patient outcomes based on factors like age, medical history, and lifestyle.
- **Sales and Marketing**: Forecasting sales based on factors like marketing spend, seasonality, and consumer behavior.
- **Economics**: Modeling economic indicators like inflation, GDP growth, and unemployment rates.

4. Evaluation Metrics for Regression Models

To evaluate the performance of a regression model, we use several metrics that measure how well the model's predictions match the actual outcomes:

Mean Absolute Error (MAE): The average of the absolute differences between the predicted and actual values.

$$\text{MAE} = \frac{1}{n} \sum_{i=1}^{n} |y_i - \hat{y}_i|$$

Mean Squared Error (MSE): The average of the squared differences between the predicted and actual values. It penalizes larger errors more heavily.

$$\text{MSE} = \frac{1}{n} \sum_{i=1}^{n} (y_i - \hat{y}_i)^2$$

Root Mean Squared Error (RMSE): The square root of the MSE, which brings the error back to the same units as the target variable.

$$RMSE - \sqrt{MSE}$$

4. **R-Squared** (R^2): A measure of how well the regression model explains the variance in the data. It is the proportion of variance in the dependent variable that is predictable from the independent variables.

$$R^2 - 1 - \frac{\sum_{i-1}^{n}(y_i - \hat{y}_i)^2}{\sum_{i-1}^{n}(y_i - \bar{y})^2}$$

Regression is a fundamental concept in machine learning and statistics, allowing us to predict continuous outcomes based on input features. Understanding different types of regression models and knowing when to use each one is key to building effective predictive models. Whether you are working on a real estate pricing model, forecasting sales, or estimating risk, mastering regression techniques will provide you with a valuable tool for making accurate predictions in various domains.

5.2 Linear Regression with One and Multiple Variables

Linear regression is one of the simplest and most widely used algorithms in machine learning, especially for predicting a continuous target variable based on one or more independent features. In this section, we will dive deeper into linear regression and explore how it works with one variable (simple linear regression) as well as multiple variables (multiple linear regression).

1. Simple Linear Regression (One Variable)

Simple linear regression is used when there is only one independent variable (feature) to predict the dependent variable (target). The relationship between the independent and dependent variables is assumed to be linear, which means that changes in the independent variable result in proportional changes in the dependent variable.

A. Equation of Simple Linear Regression

In simple linear regression, the model tries to fit a line to the data, which can be represented by the equation:

$$y = \beta_0 + \beta_1 x + \epsilon$$

Where:

- y is the dependent variable (target),
- x is the independent variable (feature),
- β_0 is the y-intercept (constant),
- β_1 is the slope of the line, which indicates how much y changes when x changes by one unit,
- ϵ is the error term, which accounts for the residuals or deviations of actual values from the predicted values.

The goal of simple linear regression is to determine the values of β_0 and β_1 that minimize the error term ϵ.

B. Fitting the Line (Finding β_0 and β_1)

The process of fitting the line involves determining the best values for β_0 and β_1. The most common way to find these values is by minimizing the **sum of squared errors** (SSE), which is the difference between the predicted values and the actual values.

The objective is to minimize:

$$SSE - \sum_{i=1}^{n}(y_i - (\beta_0 + \beta_1 x_i))^2$$

Where:

- y_i is the actual value,
- $\hat{y}_i = \beta_0 + \beta_1 x_i$ is the predicted value.

To find the optimal β_0 and β_1, we use **ordinary least squares (OLS)** estimation, which gives us the following formulas for the coefficients:

- Slope β_1:

$$\beta_1 = \frac{\sum_{i=1}^{n}(x_i - \bar{x})(y_i - \bar{y})}{\sum_{i=1}^{n}(x_i - \bar{x})^2}$$

- Intercept β_0:

$$\beta_0 = \bar{y} - \beta_1\bar{x}$$

Where:

- $\bar{x}$ is the mean of the independent variable,

- $\bar{y}$ is the mean of the dependent variable.

C. Example of Simple Linear Regression

Let's consider a real-world example where we want to predict a person's salary based on their years of experience. Here, years of experience is the independent variable, and salary is the dependent variable.

Given the following data:

Years of Experience (x)	Salary (y)
1	40,000
2	50,000
3	60,000
4	70,000
5	80,000

To predict the salary, we would apply the formulas above to calculate the best-fit line.

Once we have the coefficients β_0 and β_1, we can use the equation of the line to predict the salary for any given number of years of experience.

2. Multiple Linear Regression (Multiple Variables)

Multiple linear regression extends simple linear regression to predict the dependent variable using more than one independent variable. This is useful when the relationship between the target and independent variables is influenced by several features. The basic idea remains the same, but we now have more than one feature to predict the target.

A. Equation of Multiple Linear Regression

In multiple linear regression, the equation of the model becomes:

$$y = \beta_0 + \beta_1 x_1 + \beta_2 x_2 + ... + \beta_n x_n + \epsilon$$

Where:

- y is the dependent variable (target),

- $x_1, x_2, ..., x_n$ are the independent variables (features),

- β_0 is the intercept (constant term),

- $\beta_1, \beta_2, ..., \beta_n$ are the coefficients associated with each feature,

- ϵ is the error term.

B. Fitting the Model (Finding Coefficients)

The objective of multiple linear regression is to find the values of $\beta_0, \beta_1, \beta_2, ..., \beta_n$ that minimize the **sum of squared errors** (SSE), just as we did in simple linear regression.

The formula for calculating the coefficients $\beta_0, \beta_1, ..., \beta_n$ is derived through the method of **ordinary least squares (OLS)**. This process is computationally more complex than simple linear regression but follows the same principle of minimizing the error term.

To solve for the coefficients, we can use matrix operations and the following formula:

$$\beta = (X^T X)^{-1} X^T y$$

Where:

- X is the matrix of features (including a column of ones for the intercept),

- X^T is the transpose of X,

- y is the vector of observed values of the target variable,

- β is the vector of coefficients $\beta_0, \beta_1, ..., \beta_n$.

C. Example of Multiple Linear Regression

Suppose we want to predict the price of a house based on two features: **square footage** and **number of bedrooms**. Here, we have two independent variables x_1 (square footage) and x_2 (number of bedrooms), and the dependent variable y is the house price.

Let's consider the following dataset:

Square Footage (x_1)	Number of Bedrooms (x_2)	Price (y)
1,000	2	200,000
1,200	3	250,000
1,500	3	300,000
1,800	4	350,000
2,000	4	400,000

We want to fit a model that predicts the price based on the square footage and number of bedrooms. The model would look something like this:

$$\text{Price} = \beta_0 + \beta_1 \times \text{Square Footage} + \beta_2 \times \text{Number of Bedrooms}$$

Using the method of least squares, we would calculate the coefficients $\beta_0, \beta_1, \beta_2$, and use this model to predict house prices for new data points.

3. Assumptions of Linear Regression

For linear regression to be valid, several assumptions must be met:

- **Linearity**: The relationship between the dependent and independent variables should be linear.
- **Independence**: The residuals (errors) should be independent of each other.
- **Homoscedasticity**: The variance of the residuals should be constant across all levels of the independent variables.
- **Normality of Errors**: The residuals should be approximately normally distributed.
- **No multicollinearity**: The independent variables should not be highly correlated with each other.

4. Evaluating Linear Regression Models

To assess the performance of a linear regression model, we use the following metrics:

R-squared (R^2): Measures the proportion of the variance in the dependent variable that is predictable from the independent variables. A higher R^2 indicates a better fit.

Mean Squared Error (MSE): Measures the average of the squared differences between the predicted and actual values. A lower MSE indicates a better model.

Root Mean Squared Error (RMSE): The square root of MSE, which brings the error back to the original units of the target variable.

Mean Absolute Error (MAE): Measures the average of the absolute differences between the predicted and actual values.

Linear regression, both simple and multiple, is a powerful and interpretable technique used for predicting continuous variables. In simple linear regression, we model the relationship between one independent variable and the dependent variable, while in multiple linear regression, we extend this idea to handle multiple features. Understanding how to implement, interpret, and evaluate linear regression models is essential for any machine learning practitioner working with regression tasks. By carefully selecting the right model and ensuring assumptions are met, linear regression can provide valuable insights into the relationships within the data and enable effective predictions.

5.3 Polynomial Regression

Polynomial regression is an extension of linear regression that allows us to model non-linear relationships between the dependent variable and independent variable(s). While simple linear regression assumes a straight-line relationship, polynomial regression can fit a curved line by adding higher-degree terms of the independent variable(s) to the model. This ability to model non-linearity makes polynomial regression a powerful tool for capturing complex patterns in data.

In this section, we will explore how polynomial regression works, how it differs from linear regression, and how to implement it effectively.

1. What is Polynomial Regression?

Polynomial regression is a type of regression where the relationship between the independent variable x and the dependent variable y is modeled as an n-th degree polynomial. In other words, instead of fitting a straight line to the data, polynomial regression fits a curve.

$$y = \beta_0 + \beta_1 x + \beta_2 x^2 + \beta_3 x^3 + \dots + \beta_n x^n + \epsilon$$

Where:

- y is the dependent variable (target),

- x is the independent variable (feature),

- $\beta_0, \beta_1, \dots, \beta_n$ are the coefficients to be learned by the model,

- $x^2, x^3, \dots, x^n$ are the higher-degree terms that allow the model to capture non-linear relationships,

- ϵ is the error term (residuals).

Polynomial regression allows the model to create curves that fit the data better than a straight line, which is especially useful when the relationship between x and y is not linear.

2. Why Use Polynomial Regression?

Linear regression works well when the data exhibits a straight-line relationship between the target variable and the features. However, in many real-world scenarios, the relationship may be non-linear, and polynomial regression can help capture this complexity.

Polynomial regression can be particularly useful in the following cases:

- **Curved patterns**: When the data exhibits curves rather than a straight-line trend, polynomial regression can capture the shape of the data more effectively.
- **Data with higher-order relationships**: If the relationship between the dependent and independent variables is influenced by quadratic, cubic, or higher-order effects, polynomial regression is a good option.

For example, if you're modeling the relationship between the number of hours studied and exam performance, you may observe diminishing returns — after a certain point, additional study hours might have a less significant impact on performance. This kind of pattern may be better captured by a polynomial regression model.

3. Fitting a Polynomial Regression Model

In polynomial regression, the process is similar to linear regression, except that we add polynomial terms of the independent variable to the model. Let's break this down step by step.

A. Transforming the Features

The first step is to transform the original features by raising them to higher powers. For example, if we have a feature x, we create new features $x^2, x^3, ..., x^n$.

If we want to fit a quadratic (second-degree) polynomial, we add the x^2 term to the dataset:

- Original feature: x
- Transformed feature: x^2

If we want to fit a cubic (third-degree) polynomial, we add the x^2 and x^3 terms:

- Original feature: x
- Transformed features: x^2, x^3

By transforming the features, the model can now capture the curvature in the data.

B. Constructing the Polynomial Regression Model

Once the features are transformed, the polynomial regression model takes the following form:

$$y = \beta_0 + \beta_1 x + \beta_2 x^2 + \beta_3 x^3 + \ldots + \beta_n x^n + \epsilon$$

Here, the model will learn the best values for $\beta_0, \beta_1, \ldots, \beta_n$ using the least squares method (just like in linear regression). These coefficients are found by minimizing the sum of squared errors (SSE):

$$SSE = \sum_{i=1}^{n} (y_i - (\beta_0 + \beta_1 x_i + \beta_2 x_i^2 + \ldots + \beta_n x_i^n))^2$$

C. Choosing the Degree of the Polynomial

Choosing the degree n of the polynomial is an important decision when using polynomial regression. A higher-degree polynomial can fit the data more closely, but it may also lead to overfitting, where the model becomes too complex and captures noise in the data rather than the true underlying pattern. On the other hand, a lower-degree polynomial may underfit the data, failing to capture important patterns.

To avoid overfitting and underfitting, you should:

- Start with a lower-degree polynomial (such as quadratic or cubic).
- Experiment with different degrees and evaluate model performance using metrics like cross-validation and mean squared error (MSE) to find the optimal degree.

4. Example of Polynomial Regression

Let's walk through an example where we predict the price of a car based on its age, but the relationship between the two is non-linear.

Consider the following dataset:

Car Age (x)	Price (y)
1	30,000
2	28,000
3	25,000
4	22,000
5	19,000
6	18,000
7	17,000

The relationship between the car age and price may not be linear — the price may drop rapidly in the first few years and then level off. A linear regression model may not capture this relationship well. We can use polynomial regression to fit a curve that better reflects the data.

1. **Transform the feature**: Add the square of the car age as a new feature (x^2).

   - Age: x

   - Transformed feature: x^2

2. **Fit the polynomial regression model**: Use both x and x^2 in the model:

$$\text{Price} = \beta_0 + \beta_1 \times \text{Car Age} + \beta_2 \times (\text{Car Age})^2$$

By fitting this model, the curve can better match the data, especially if the relationship is quadratic (or even cubic).

5. Overfitting and Underfitting in Polynomial Regression

One of the challenges with polynomial regression is determining the degree of the polynomial. As we increase the degree of the polynomial, the model becomes more flexible and can fit the data more closely. However, this flexibility can lead to overfitting, where the model learns not only the true pattern but also the noise in the data, resulting in poor generalization to new data.

- **Overfitting**: Happens when the model is too complex (too high a degree), capturing noise in the training data and failing to generalize to new data.
- **Underfitting**: Occurs when the model is too simple (too low a degree), failing to capture the underlying patterns in the data.

To avoid overfitting and underfitting, it's crucial to:

- Evaluate the model's performance on a validation dataset or using cross-validation techniques.
- Experiment with different polynomial degrees and select the one that minimizes error without overfitting.

6. Evaluating Polynomial Regression Models

Polynomial regression models are evaluated using the same metrics as linear regression models, including:

R-squared (R^2): Measures how much of the variance in the target variable is explained by the model. A higher R^2 indicates a better fit.

Mean Squared Error (MSE): The average of the squared differences between the predicted and actual values. A lower MSE indicates better model performance.

Cross-Validation: This technique involves splitting the data into multiple subsets (folds) and testing the model's performance on each fold to ensure it generalizes well.

Polynomial regression is a powerful extension of linear regression that allows us to model non-linear relationships between the independent and dependent variables. By introducing higher-degree terms (e.g., x^2, x^3), polynomial regression can fit curved lines that capture more complex patterns in the data. However, it is important to choose the correct degree for the polynomial to avoid overfitting and underfitting. Polynomial regression can be applied in a wide range of fields where the relationship between variables is non-linear, including economics, biology, engineering, and finance. By carefully tuning the model and evaluating its performance, you can use polynomial regression to make accurate predictions in scenarios with non-linear patterns.

5.4 Regularization: Lasso and Ridge Regression

In machine learning, regularization refers to techniques that are used to prevent overfitting by adding a penalty term to the model. Overfitting occurs when a model learns the noise or fluctuations in the training data rather than capturing the true underlying relationship. Regularization helps to ensure that the model generalizes well to unseen data, thus improving its performance.

In this section, we will discuss two popular regularization techniques used with linear regression models: Lasso Regression and Ridge Regression. Both of these methods add a penalty term to the loss function to prevent the model from becoming too complex, but they do so in slightly different ways.

1. Overfitting and the Need for Regularization

Before diving into Lasso and Ridge regression, let's first understand why regularization is necessary.

In linear regression, we try to minimize the sum of squared errors (SSE) between the predicted values and the actual values. While this approach works well when there is a clear linear relationship, it can lead to overfitting if the model becomes too complex or learns patterns that don't generalize well. This is particularly problematic when we have a large number of features or when the features are highly correlated.

Regularization helps solve this issue by adding a penalty to the loss function, discouraging the model from fitting overly complex patterns. By doing so, regularization forces the model to be simpler, reducing its variance and improving its ability to generalize to new data.

2. Ridge Regression (L2 Regularization)

Ridge regression, also known as L2 regularization, is a regularization technique that penalizes large coefficients in the model. The penalty term added to the linear regression cost function is proportional to the sum of the squared values of the coefficients. The goal is to shrink the coefficients, but not necessarily to make them exactly zero.

A. Ridge Regression Equation

The cost function for Ridge regression is:

$$J(\beta) = \sum_{i=1}^{n} (y_i - (\beta_0 + \beta_1 x_1 + \beta_2 x_2 + ... + \beta_p x_p))^2 + \lambda \sum_{j=1}^{p} \beta_j^2$$

Where:

- y_i is the observed value,

- $x_1, x_2, ..., x_p$ are the features (independent variables),

- $\beta_0, \beta_1, ..., \beta_p$ are the model coefficients,

- λ is the regularization parameter (also called the penalty term or hyperparameter).

The second term, $\lambda \sum_{j=1}^{p} \beta_j^2$, is the penalty term added to the ordinary least squares cost function. This term discourages large values for the coefficients $\beta_1, \beta_2, ..., \beta_p$, helping to prevent overfitting.

B. Effect of the Regularization Parameter

The regularization parameter λ controls the strength of the penalty:

- When $\lambda = 0$, Ridge regression becomes equivalent to ordinary linear regression, without any penalty.

- As λ increases, the model coefficients $\beta_1, \beta_2, ..., \beta_p$ are shrunk toward zero. A very large value of λ can result in a model where the coefficients are almost zero, making the model overly simple and underfitting the data.

The optimal value of λ can be determined using techniques like **cross-validation** or **grid search**, which help find the best balance between bias and variance.

C. Benefits of Ridge Regression

- **Prevents overfitting**: By shrinking the coefficients, Ridge regression helps reduce the variance of the model, making it less likely to overfit.
- **Handles multicollinearity**: When features are highly correlated with one another, Ridge regression can reduce the impact of collinearity by shrinking the coefficients of correlated features.
- **Retains all features**: Unlike Lasso, Ridge regression will not set coefficients to exactly zero. It will shrink them, but all features will remain in the model, making it useful when all features are believed to have some importance.

3. Lasso Regression (L1 Regularization)

Lasso regression, or L1 regularization, is another regularization technique, but with a key difference. Instead of penalizing the sum of squared coefficients (like Ridge), Lasso adds a penalty proportional to the sum of the absolute values of the coefficients. This type of regularization can drive some of the coefficients to exactly zero, effectively performing feature selection by excluding less important features from the model.

A. Lasso Regression Equation

The cost function for Lasso regression is:

$$J(\beta) = \sum_{i=1}^{n} (y_i - (\beta_0 + \beta_1 x_1 + \beta_2 x_2 + ... + \beta_p x_p))^2 + \lambda \sum_{j=1}^{p} |\beta_j|$$

Where:

- y_i is the observed value,

- $x_1, x_2, ..., x_p$ are the features,

- $\beta_0, \beta_1, ..., \beta_p$ are the model coefficients,

- λ is the regularization parameter.

The second term, $\lambda \sum_{j=1}^{p} |\beta_j|$, is the L1 penalty term. The difference from Ridge regression is that Lasso penalizes the absolute values of the coefficients, which allows it to set some coefficients exactly to zero, effectively excluding the corresponding features from the model.

B. Effect of the Regularization Parameter

Similar to Ridge regression, the regularization parameter λ controls the strength of the penalty:

- **When $\lambda = 0$**, Lasso regression is equivalent to ordinary linear regression with no regularization.

- **As λ increases**, the coefficients of less important features are driven to zero, and the model becomes simpler. If λ is very large, only a small subset of features may remain in the model, potentially leading to underfitting.

By selecting the appropriate value for λ, Lasso regression can automatically perform feature selection, which is particularly useful in models with many features.

C. Benefits of Lasso Regression

- **Feature selection**: Lasso regression can eliminate irrelevant or redundant features by setting their coefficients to zero, helping to improve model interpretability.
- **Prevents overfitting**: Like Ridge regression, Lasso reduces the complexity of the model and helps to prevent overfitting.
- **Sparse solutions**: By forcing some coefficients to zero, Lasso regression provides sparse solutions, making it ideal for models with many variables.

4. Comparing Lasso and Ridge Regression

While both Ridge and Lasso regression are regularization techniques designed to improve model generalization, they have different characteristics:

Feature	Ridge Regression (L2)	Lasso Regression (L1)
Penalty term	Sum of squared coefficients $\sum \beta_j^2$	Sum of absolute values (\sum
Impact on coefficients	Shrinks coefficients, but doesn't set them to zero	Shrinks some coefficients to zero (feature selection)
Use case	Useful when all features are expected to contribute to the prediction	Useful when some features are irrelevant or redundant
Handling multicollinearity	Handles multicollinearity well by shrinking correlated features	May not handle multicollinearity as well since it can set correlated coefficients to zero
Feature selection	Does not perform feature selection (all features remain)	Performs feature selection by eliminating some features entirely
Computation	Typically more stable and easier to compute	Can be computationally more expensive due to non-differentiability at zero

In practice, Ridge regression is preferred when most or all features are expected to contribute to the model, while Lasso is useful when we suspect that some features may be irrelevant or redundant.

5. Elastic Net: Combining Lasso and Ridge

In some cases, neither Lasso nor Ridge regression alone is sufficient. This is where Elastic Net comes into play. Elastic Net combines both L1 and L2 penalties, allowing it to benefit from the strengths of both Lasso and Ridge.

The Elastic Net cost function is:

$$J(\beta) = \sum_{i=1}^{n}(y_i - (\beta_0 + \beta_1 x_1 + ... + \beta_p x_p))^2 + \lambda_1 \sum_{j=1}^{p} |\beta_j| + \lambda_2 \sum_{j=1}^{p} \beta_j^2$$

Elastic Net is especially useful when:

There are many correlated features.

The number of predictors is greater than the number of observations.

Regularization techniques like Lasso and Ridge regression are essential tools in the machine learning toolkit, especially when dealing with overfitting and multicollinearity. Ridge regression shrinks the coefficients but does not set them to zero, making it ideal for situations where we believe all features are important. Lasso regression, on the other hand, can eliminate irrelevant features entirely by driving their coefficients to zero, making it useful for feature selection. Elastic Net combines the benefits of both techniques and can be especially helpful when dealing with complex datasets.

By carefully selecting the appropriate regularization technique and tuning the regularization parameter, you can create more robust models that generalize better to unseen data and make more accurate predictions.

6. Classification Models

Classification is key to decision-making systems, from spam filters to medical diagnoses. This chapter covers Logistic Regression, Decision Trees, Naïve Bayes, and Support Vector Machines (SVMs), equipping you with the skills to build robust classification models.

6.1 Logistic Regression

Logistic regression is a fundamental algorithm in machine learning, used primarily for classification problems. Unlike linear regression, which is used for predicting continuous values, logistic regression is designed for predicting the probability of a binary outcome, i.e., whether an event happens or not. It is commonly applied in scenarios such as:

- Email spam classification (spam vs. not spam),
- Medical diagnostics (disease vs. no disease),
- Customer churn prediction (will a customer leave or stay?).

In this section, we will explore the underlying concepts, the mechanics of logistic regression, its mathematical formulation, and how it can be used for classification tasks.

1. Why Logistic Regression?

At its core, logistic regression is used when the dependent variable is categorical and binary (i.e., it can only take two values). These two values could represent anything from true/false, success/failure, or yes/no decisions. The goal of logistic regression is to model the probability that a given input point belongs to a particular class.

For example:

If we're trying to predict whether a customer will purchase a product (yes or no), logistic regression will estimate the probability of a customer buying the product based on certain input features (e.g., age, income, browsing history).

The reason for using logistic regression is that it provides a method to classify instances based on probabilities, which is a more useful output in many cases compared to just classifying them as either "class 0" or "class 1".

2. Understanding the Logistic Function

To understand logistic regression, we first need to understand the logistic function (also called the sigmoid function). This function maps any real-valued number into a value between 0 and 1, which is ideal for probability estimation.

The sigmoid function is given by the following equation:

$$\sigma(z) = \frac{1}{1 + e^{-z}}$$

Where:

- $\sigma(z)$ is the output of the sigmoid function (a value between 0 and 1),
- z is the linear combination of the input features (i.e., $z = \beta_0 + \beta_1 x_1 + \beta_2 x_2 + \ldots + \beta_p x_p$),
- e is the base of the natural logarithm.

The output of the sigmoid function represents the probability that the input x belongs to the positive class (class 1). The closer the value of $\sigma(z)$ is to 1, the more likely the instance belongs to class 1, and conversely, the closer it is to 0, the more likely it belongs to class 0.

For example:

- If $\sigma(z) = 0.8$, the model predicts that the input instance has an 80% chance of belonging to class 1.
- If $\sigma(z) = 0.2$, the model predicts that the input instance has a 20% chance of belonging to class 1.

A. The Logistic Regression Equation

The equation for logistic regression is:

$$P(y = 1|X) = \sigma(\beta_0 + \beta_1 x_1 + \beta_2 x_2 + \dots + \beta_p x_p)$$

Where:

- $P(y = 1|X)$ is the probability that the outcome is class 1, given the features X (the input vector),
- σ is the sigmoid function,
- $\beta_0, \beta_1, \beta_2, \dots, \beta_p$ are the coefficients (parameters) that the model learns from the training data,
- $x_1, x_2, \dots, x_p$ are the features of the input.

This equation provides the predicted probability that an observation belongs to class 1. If you wanted to classify the observation into class 1 or class 0, you would choose a threshold (e.g., 0.5) and:

- If $P(y = 1|X) > 0.5$, classify the observation as class 1.
- If $P(y = 1|X) \leq 0.5$, classify the observation as class 0.

B. Decision Boundary

The decision boundary in logistic regression is determined by the threshold value you choose for $\sigma(z)$. If we use a threshold of 0.5, the decision boundary is defined by the following:

$$\beta_0 + \beta_1 x_1 + \beta_2 x_2 + \dots + \beta_p x_p = 0$$

This boundary separates the feature space into two regions: one where the model predicts class 1 and another where it predicts class 0. For values of z greater than 0, the prediction will be class 1, and for values of z less than or equal to 0, the prediction will be class 0.

4. Model Fitting: Maximum Likelihood Estimation (MLE)

In linear regression, we use least squares to minimize the difference between predicted and actual values. In logistic regression, since the output is probabilistic, we need a different method to estimate the parameters (coefficients) of the model. This is done using Maximum Likelihood Estimation (MLE).

The likelihood function represents the probability of observing the given data as a function of the model parameters. For logistic regression, the likelihood function is derived from the Bernoulli distribution, as we're predicting binary outcomes.

The likelihood function $L(\beta)$ is:

$$L(\beta) = \prod_{i=1}^{n} P(y_i|x_i)$$

Where y_i is the true outcome for observation i, and $P(y_i|x_i)$ is the predicted probability from the logistic model.

Logistic regression attempts to find the values of the model parameters $\beta_0, \beta_1, ..., \beta_p$ that **maximize the likelihood function**. In practice, this is often done by maximizing the **log-likelihood function**, which is easier to handle mathematically.

A. Log-Likelihood Function

The log-likelihood function for logistic regression is:

$$\ell(\beta) = \sum_{i=1}^{n} [y_i \log(P(y_i = 1|x_i)) + (1 - y_i) \log(1 - P(y_i = 0|x_i))]$$

Maximizing the log-likelihood will give us the optimal parameters that best fit the data.

5. Training the Model

Training a logistic regression model involves the following steps:

1. **Input Data**: Collect the data with known features and target labels (class 0 or 1).

2. **Model Initialization**: Initialize the model's parameters (coefficients $\beta_0, \beta_1, ..., \beta_p$).

1. **Optimization**: Use an optimization algorithm like Gradient Descent to minimize the cost function (log-likelihood function) and find the optimal values for the parameters.
2. **Model Evaluation**: After training the model, evaluate its performance using metrics such as accuracy, precision, recall, and F1 score.

6. Advantages of Logistic Regression

Simplicity: Logistic regression is easy to understand and implement, making it a good starting point for classification problems.

Interpretability: The coefficients of the model ($\beta_1, \beta_2, ..., \beta_p$) can be interpreted as the log-odds of the outcome, which gives valuable insights into how each feature contributes to the prediction.

Probabilistic Output: Logistic regression provides probabilities for predictions, which can be useful in many applications, such as determining the likelihood of an event occurring.

Efficiency: Logistic regression is computationally efficient, making it suitable for large datasets.

7. Limitations of Logistic Regression

- **Linearity Assumption**: Logistic regression assumes a linear relationship between the log-odds of the outcome and the input features. If the true relationship is non-linear, logistic regression may not perform well unless feature engineering or transformations are applied.
- **Binary Outcomes**: Logistic regression is primarily designed for binary classification. While it can be extended to multi-class classification using techniques like One-vs-Rest or Softmax regression, other algorithms (like decision trees or random forests) may be better suited for multi-class problems.
- **Outliers**: Logistic regression is sensitive to outliers, as it aims to fit a model that explains the majority of the data, which can be skewed by extreme values.

Logistic regression is one of the most commonly used algorithms for binary classification tasks. It models the probability that a given input belongs to a particular class using a logistic (sigmoid) function. By learning the optimal coefficients using Maximum Likelihood Estimation (MLE), logistic regression can make probabilistic predictions that are useful in a wide range of applications. While it is simple and interpretable, it does have limitations, such as its assumption of linearity and its sensitivity to outliers. Despite these limitations, logistic regression remains a go-to algorithm for many classification tasks due to its ease of use, efficiency, and interpretability.

6.2 Decision Trees and Random Forest

In machine learning, decision trees and random forests are powerful algorithms used for both classification and regression tasks. These models are highly interpretable, non-linear, and can handle both numerical and categorical data. While decision trees are easy to understand and implement, they can suffer from overfitting if not properly regulated. Random forests, on the other hand, provide a solution to this problem by combining multiple decision trees to create a more robust and generalized model.

In this section, we will explore both decision trees and random forests, how they work, their strengths and weaknesses, and how they are applied in real-world machine learning problems.

1. Decision Trees

A decision tree is a supervised machine learning algorithm that works by splitting the data into subsets based on the feature values. The tree structure consists of nodes and branches, where each internal node represents a decision based on a feature, and each leaf node represents a predicted outcome.

A. How Decision Trees Work

- **Root Node**: The root node represents the entire dataset. The algorithm will choose a feature that best splits the data into two or more homogeneous subsets based on some criteria, usually a measure of impurity.
- **Splitting**: The dataset is split into subsets by choosing the best feature at each step. The splitting process continues recursively until some stopping criterion is met (e.g., a predefined maximum depth or minimum samples per leaf).
- **Leaf Nodes**: These are the terminal nodes of the tree, where the final decision or prediction is made. In classification tasks, the leaf node contains the most common class for the data points that reach that node. In regression tasks, the leaf node contains the average value of the target variable.

B. Choosing the Best Split

To split the data at each node, a decision tree uses an impurity measure to evaluate how well a feature separates the data. The most commonly used impurity measures are:

Gini Impurity (used in CART — Classification and Regression Trees):

- Gini impurity measures the degree of impurity in a node. The formula for Gini impurity is:

$$Gini - 1 - \sum_{i-1}^{k} p_i^2$$

Where p_i is the probability of class i at the node. A Gini impurity of 0 means that all elements at the node belong to the same class.

Entropy (used in ID3 — Iterative Dichotomiser 3, and C4.5 algorithms):

Entropy measures the uncertainty or disorder in the data. It is defined as:

$$Entropy = -\sum_{i-1}^{k} p_i \log_2(p_i)$$

Where p_i is the probability of class i at the node. A lower entropy value indicates that the node is pure (i.e., the data points are mostly of the same class).

The tree-building process continues until the impurity measure (Gini or entropy) is minimized, i.e., the algorithm chooses the feature and threshold that results in the purest subsets.

C. Pruning

A major challenge with decision trees is overfitting. If a tree is allowed to grow too deep, it may fit the noise in the training data rather than capturing the general patterns. To address this, decision trees are often pruned by:

- Limiting the maximum depth of the tree,
- Setting a minimum number of samples required to split a node,
- Limiting the minimum number of samples required at a leaf node.

These parameters help prevent the tree from becoming overly complex and overfitting the data.

2. Random Forests

A random forest is an ensemble learning technique that combines the predictions of multiple decision trees to produce a more accurate and robust model. Random forests improve upon decision trees by reducing the variance, preventing overfitting, and increasing the generalizability of the model.

A. How Random Forests Work

Bootstrap Aggregating (Bagging): Random forests are built using a technique called bagging, where multiple decision trees are trained on different subsets of the data. These subsets are created by random sampling with replacement from the original training data (i.e., bootstrap sampling). This means that each tree is trained on a slightly different set of data points, which helps to reduce the variance and prevent overfitting.

Random Feature Selection: At each node of a decision tree, random forests choose a random subset of features to split on. This introduces additional randomness and ensures that individual trees do not become overly correlated with each other. By diversifying the trees in the forest, random forests reduce the risk of overfitting compared to a single decision tree.

Ensemble Prediction: Once multiple decision trees are trained, the random forest makes a final prediction by aggregating the predictions from each individual tree:

- **For classification tasks**, the final prediction is determined by majority voting, where the class predicted by most trees is chosen.
- **For regression tasks**, the final prediction is the average of the predictions made by all the trees.

B. Advantages of Random Forests

- **Reduced Overfitting**: By training multiple decision trees on different subsets of the data and using random feature selection, random forests are less likely to overfit the data compared to a single decision tree.
- **Improved Accuracy**: Random forests combine the predictions of multiple trees, which often results in higher accuracy than individual decision trees.
- **Handles Missing Data**: Random forests can handle missing data well by using surrogate splits, where the algorithm will use the next best feature when a value is missing for a particular data point.
- **Feature Importance**: Random forests can provide insights into which features are most important for making predictions, which is valuable in feature selection tasks.

C. Disadvantages of Random Forests

- **Interpretability**: While individual decision trees are easy to interpret, random forests are more like "black-box" models due to the complexity of combining many trees. It can be difficult to explain the reasoning behind a specific prediction made by the forest.
- **Computational Complexity**: Random forests require training multiple decision trees, which can be computationally expensive, especially when working with large datasets.
- **Memory Usage**: Random forests tend to use more memory, as they need to store multiple trees.

3. Applications of Decision Trees and Random Forests

- **Medical Diagnosis**: Both decision trees and random forests are widely used in healthcare for diagnosing diseases. For example, decision trees can help predict whether a patient has a particular disease based on their symptoms and medical history.
- **Customer Segmentation**: Businesses use decision trees and random forests for customer segmentation, grouping customers based on their characteristics (e.g., purchase behavior, demographics) to target specific marketing campaigns.
- **Credit Scoring**: Random forests can be used to predict whether a customer will default on a loan, based on various financial and behavioral features.
- **Image Classification**: In computer vision, decision trees and random forests can be used for classifying images into different categories based on their pixel features.

Both decision trees and random forests are versatile machine learning algorithms that are widely used for classification and regression tasks. While decision trees are simple to understand and interpret, they can easily overfit if not properly pruned. Random forests address this issue by combining multiple decision trees, using techniques like bootstrapping and random feature selection to increase accuracy and robustness.

Random forests are powerful models that offer improved performance over single decision trees, especially in complex tasks. However, their complexity and lack of interpretability make them less suited for problems where model transparency is crucial. Despite this, they remain one of the most popular machine learning algorithms, due to their effectiveness and ability to handle large, high-dimensional datasets.

6.3 Support Vector Machines (SVM)

Support Vector Machines (SVMs) are a class of supervised learning algorithms that are commonly used for classification and regression tasks. Known for their effectiveness in high-dimensional spaces and their ability to handle both linear and non-linear data, SVMs are widely used in a variety of machine learning applications, such as text classification, image recognition, and bioinformatics.

In this section, we will explore the core concepts of SVMs, how they work, the idea behind their use of hyperplanes, and their mathematical foundations.

1. What is Support Vector Machine?

At a high level, an SVM is a machine learning model that finds the best possible boundary (or hyperplane) that separates data points of one class from another in a high-dimensional space. The goal of SVM is to find a hyperplane that maximizes the margin, which is the distance between the closest points of both classes to the hyperplane. These closest points are known as support vectors, and they are crucial to the model's decision-making process.

SVMs are primarily known for their classification capabilities, where they classify data points into distinct classes. They are also used for regression tasks, which we will touch upon later.

2. The Concept of Hyperplanes

A hyperplane in a machine learning context is a flat affine subspace that separates the feature space into two halves. In 2D space, the hyperplane is simply a line, while in 3D space, it is a plane. In higher dimensions (which is typical for most machine learning problems), the hyperplane is a multi-dimensional object that separates the data points into two groups.

The core idea behind SVM is to find a hyperplane that divides the data in such a way that the margin (the space between the nearest data points of either class) is maximized. Maximizing the margin helps ensure that the classifier generalizes well to new, unseen data.

A. Linear SVM for Linearly Separable Data

For linearly separable data, where the two classes can be perfectly separated by a straight line (in 2D) or a plane (in 3D), SVM works as follows:

- Given a dataset of points belonging to two classes, an SVM algorithm identifies a hyperplane that divides the data into two halves, each containing data points from one class.
- The SVM aims to find the hyperplane that maximizes the margin, which is the distance between the hyperplane and the closest data points from each class. These closest data points are called support vectors.
- The idea is that the wider the margin, the better the generalization ability of the classifier, leading to fewer misclassifications on new data.

The equation of a hyperplane in the simplest form is:

$$w \cdot x + b = 0$$

Where:

- w is the normal vector to the hyperplane (defining its orientation),

- x is the vector representing a data point,

- b is the bias term, which shifts the hyperplane.

The goal of the SVM is to maximize the margin, which can be achieved by optimizing the following objective function:

$$\text{maximize } \frac{2}{\|w\|}$$

Under the constraint that all data points are correctly classified:

$$y_i(w \cdot x_i + b) \geq 1, \quad \text{for all } i$$

Where:

- y_i is the class label for data point x_i (either +1 or -1),

- $\|w\|$ represents the magnitude of the normal vector (essentially the width of the margin).

B. Support Vectors

The support vectors are the data points that are closest to the hyperplane and are critical for determining the optimal separating boundary. These points are important because they are the only data points that affect the position and orientation of the hyperplane. All other data points do not influence the decision boundary once the support vectors are identified.

3. Non-Linear SVM: The Kernel Trick

In many real-world problems, data is not linearly separable. That is, no straight line (or hyperplane in higher dimensions) can perfectly separate the two classes. In such cases, SVM uses a technique called the kernel trick to handle non-linearly separable data.

A. What is a Kernel?

A kernel is a function that maps the input data into a higher-dimensional space (possibly infinite dimensions) where it is easier to separate the data with a hyperplane. This transformation allows SVM to classify data that is not linearly separable in the original space.

In practice, SVMs use kernel functions to perform this transformation implicitly, without actually computing the coordinates of the transformed data. Instead, the kernel function computes the dot product of the transformed vectors directly. Some commonly used kernels are:

Linear Kernel: This is simply the dot product between two vectors and is used when the data is already linearly separable.

$$K(x, x') = x \cdot x'$$

Polynomial Kernel: This kernel computes a polynomial dot product of the input data points. It is effective in cases where the decision boundary is not a straight line but can be represented by a polynomial function.

$$K(x, x') = (x \cdot x' + c)^d$$

Radial Basis Function (RBF) Kernel: Also known as the Gaussian kernel, this kernel maps the input data into a much higher-dimensional space, making it effective in handling complex, non-linear relationships.

$$K(x, x') = \exp(-\gamma \|x - x'\|^2)$$

Where γ is a parameter that controls the width of the Gaussian function.

Sigmoid Kernel: This kernel is based on the sigmoid function, which is similar to the activation function used in neural networks.

$$K(x, x') = \tanh(\alpha x \cdot x' + c)$$

B. Using Kernels in SVM

Once the kernel function is chosen, the SVM algorithm proceeds similarly to the linear case but in the higher-dimensional feature space where the data is now linearly separable. The decision boundary is still a hyperplane, but in the transformed space. The kernel trick allows the SVM to efficiently compute the decision boundary in the higher-dimensional space without ever explicitly mapping the data to that space.

4. Soft Margin SVM

In real-world data, perfect separation may not always be possible, and a model that attempts to perfectly separate the data can result in overfitting. To address this, SVM introduces the concept of a soft margin, which allows some data points to be misclassified but still strives to maximize the margin.

The soft margin SVM adds a penalty term to the optimization problem, allowing some data points to be within the margin or even misclassified. The optimization problem becomes:

$$\text{minimize } \frac{1}{2}\|w\|^2 + C \sum_{i=1}^{n} \xi_i$$

Where:

- ξ_i are slack variables that represent the degree of misclassification of the data points,
- C is a regularization parameter that controls the trade-off between maximizing the margin and minimizing classification errors. A large C penalizes misclassification heavily, while a smaller C allows more misclassification but increases the margin.

5. SVM for Regression: Support Vector Regression (SVR)

While SVM is predominantly known for classification, it can also be used for regression tasks. In Support Vector Regression (SVR), the goal is to predict a continuous output rather than a class label. The SVR algorithm tries to find a function that approximates the data points while keeping the model as flat (simple) as possible.

SVR introduces a margin of tolerance around the predicted values, allowing some deviation from the true values but penalizing large deviations. The objective is to minimize the error while keeping the model complexity low.

6. Advantages of SVM

- **Effective in High-Dimensional Spaces**: SVM is particularly powerful when dealing with high-dimensional data, making it well-suited for text classification and bioinformatics applications.
- **Robust to Overfitting**: The concept of maximizing the margin helps SVM generalize well, even when the data is noisy.
- **Works Well for Non-Linearly Separable Data**: With the use of kernel functions, SVM can efficiently classify data that is not linearly separable in the original feature space.

7. Disadvantages of SVM

- **Computational Complexity**: SVMs can be computationally expensive, especially when the dataset is large or when using complex kernel functions.
- **Parameter Tuning**: SVMs require careful tuning of parameters, such as the kernel function and regularization parameter C, to achieve optimal performance.

- **Poor Performance on Large Datasets**: Due to the complexity of the optimization problem, SVMs can become slow when handling very large datasets.

Support Vector Machines (SVM) are powerful and versatile algorithms that are widely used for classification and regression tasks. By focusing on finding the optimal hyperplane that separates the data, SVMs are highly effective in high-dimensional spaces and can handle both linear and non-linear data using the kernel trick. Although they can be computationally expensive and require careful tuning, SVMs remain a strong choice for many machine learning applications where high accuracy and robustness are required.

6.4 Naïve Bayes Classifier

The Naïve Bayes classifier is a probabilistic machine learning model based on Bayes' Theorem. It is widely used for classification tasks, particularly in scenarios where the data can be assumed to belong to independent classes given certain features. Despite its simplicity, the Naïve Bayes classifier has proven to be highly effective in various applications, including spam email detection, sentiment analysis, and document classification.

In this section, we will explore the key concepts of the Naïve Bayes classifier, its working principles, types, and the reasons behind its effectiveness in certain machine learning problems.

1. What is Naïve Bayes Classifier?

The Naïve Bayes classifier is a supervised learning algorithm based on probability theory. It uses Bayes' Theorem to predict the probability of different classes based on the input features. The "naïve" assumption in Naïve Bayes refers to the assumption that all features are independent of each other given the class label, which simplifies the computation of the conditional probability.

The general idea behind Naïve Bayes is to classify a data point by calculating the probability that it belongs to each class, and then selecting the class with the highest probability.

The core of Naïve Bayes relies on Bayes' Theorem, which provides a way to update the probability estimate for a hypothesis (class label) based on new evidence (features).

Bayes' Theorem is given by:

$$P(C|X) = \frac{P(X|C) \cdot P(C)}{P(X)}$$

Where:

- $P(C|X)$ is the **posterior probability**, the probability of the class C given the features X.
- $P(X|C)$ is the **likelihood**, the probability of observing the features X given the class C.
- $P(C)$ is the **prior probability** of the class C, i.e., how likely class C is before observing any data.
- $P(X)$ is the **evidence**, the total probability of the features X across all classes. This acts as a normalizing constant.

The Naïve Bayes classifier computes $P(C|X)$ for each class and chooses the class with the highest probability as the predicted label.

2. The Naïve Assumption

The key feature of the Naïve Bayes classifier is the naïve assumption that the features are conditionally independent given the class. In other words, the algorithm assumes that the presence or absence of a particular feature does not depend on other features, making the computation of the likelihood much easier.

Mathematically, this assumption can be expressed as:

$$P(X|C) = P(x_1|C) \cdot P(x_2|C) \cdots \cdots P(x_n|C)$$

Where $X = (x_1, x_2, \ldots, x_n)$ are the features, and the product of the individual feature probabilities simplifies the calculation of the likelihood. This assumption allows the model to work efficiently even with a large number of features, but it can be a limitation if the features are highly correlated in real-world data.

3. Types of Naïve Bayes Classifiers

There are three main types of Naïve Bayes classifiers, each suitable for different types of data:

A. Gaussian Naïve Bayes

Use case: Continuous data where the features follow a normal (Gaussian) distribution.

Assumption: The features for each class are assumed to follow a normal distribution. The likelihood of a feature given a class is modeled using the Gaussian (normal) distribution formula:

$$P(x_i|C) = \frac{1}{\sqrt{2\pi\sigma^2}} \exp\left(-\frac{(x_i - \mu)^2}{2\sigma^2}\right)$$

Example: In applications such as predicting the height of a person based on weight or predicting the price of a house based on features like square footage, Gaussian Naïve Bayes is used.

B. Multinomial Naïve Bayes

Use case: Discrete data where the features represent counts or frequencies.

Assumption: The features are discrete and represent counts or frequencies, and the probability distribution for each class is assumed to follow a multinomial distribution.

The likelihood for each feature is computed as:

$$P(x_i|C) = \frac{(n_{i,C} + \alpha)}{(N_C + \alpha n)}$$

Where $n_{i,C}$ is the number of times feature x_i appears in class C, N_C is the total number of features in class C, and α is a smoothing parameter (usually set to 1 for Laplace smoothing).

Example: This type is commonly used in text classification tasks such as spam detection and document classification, where each feature represents the frequency of a word in the document.

C. Bernoulli Naïve Bayes

Use case: Binary or Boolean features, where the features take on values of 0 or 1 (representing absence or presence of a characteristic).

Assumption: The features follow a Bernoulli distribution, where each feature is treated as a binary value (presence or absence of a characteristic).

The likelihood for each feature is computed as:

$$P(x_i|C) = P(x_i = 1|C)^{x_i} \cdot P(x_i = 0|C)^{(1-x_i)}$$

Example: It is commonly used in tasks like binary text classification (e.g., whether a word is present or absent in a document) and medical diagnoses (e.g., presence or absence of symptoms).

4. Advantages of Naïve Bayes

- **Simple and Efficient**: Naïve Bayes is easy to implement, computationally efficient, and often works well with large datasets.
- **Fast Training and Prediction**: Naïve Bayes classifiers train quickly since they require minimal computation, making them ideal for real-time or large-scale applications.
- **Works Well with High Dimensional Data**: Due to its reliance on conditional independence, Naïve Bayes is particularly suited for high-dimensional data, such as text data with many features (e.g., words in a document).
- **Good Performance with Small Datasets**: Naïve Bayes tends to perform well even with relatively small datasets, especially when compared to more complex models that require larger datasets to avoid overfitting.

5. Disadvantages of Naïve Bayes

- **Strong Independence Assumption**: The assumption that all features are conditionally independent given the class often does not hold in real-world data, leading to less accurate results when features are highly correlated.
- **Limited Flexibility**: Naïve Bayes can struggle with complex relationships between features, as it assumes independence. In cases where features interact in non-trivial ways, more complex models might perform better.
- **Sensitive to Imbalanced Data**: Like many machine learning algorithms, Naïve Bayes can be sensitive to imbalanced classes, as it may assign the majority class disproportionately high probabilities.

6. Applications of Naïve Bayes

Naïve Bayes classifiers are widely used in a variety of real-world applications:

- **Spam Filtering**: Naïve Bayes is particularly popular for spam email classification, where the presence of certain keywords or phrases can indicate whether an email is spam or not.
- **Sentiment Analysis**: In social media and customer reviews, Naïve Bayes can be used to classify text data into positive, negative, or neutral sentiments based on the words in the text.
- **Document Classification**: Naïve Bayes is widely used in document categorization tasks, such as news categorization, where the classifier assigns documents to predefined categories based on their content.
- **Medical Diagnosis**: Naïve Bayes can be applied to predict disease or conditions based on patient symptoms and medical history.

The Naïve Bayes classifier is a simple yet powerful probabilistic model that is especially useful in scenarios with high-dimensional or discrete data. Its reliance on Bayes' Theorem and the assumption of conditional independence between features allows it to perform well in many classification tasks, particularly in text classification, spam filtering, and medical diagnosis.

While its naïve assumption of feature independence may not always hold in practice, the algorithm can still perform surprisingly well in a wide range of problems. Its simplicity, speed, and effectiveness make it a popular choice for many machine learning tasks, particularly when interpretability and quick training are important.

7. Model Evaluation & Optimization

Building an ML model is just the beginning—evaluating and optimizing it is crucial. In this chapter, you'll learn how to measure accuracy, precision, recall, and F1-score, while also exploring techniques like cross-validation and hyperparameter tuning to improve model performance.

7.1 Train-Test Split and Cross-Validation

In machine learning, evaluating the performance of a model is a critical part of the workflow. When developing a model, you need to assess how well it will generalize to unseen data—this is crucial for ensuring that the model performs well in real-world applications, not just on the data it was trained on. Two common techniques for model evaluation are train-test split and cross-validation. These techniques allow us to gauge the effectiveness of our model by partitioning the data into training and testing sets, ensuring that our model does not overfit or underperform.

In this section, we will dive into the concepts of train-test split and cross-validation, understand their purposes, and explore their differences.

1. Train-Test Split

The train-test split is one of the simplest and most widely used techniques for evaluating machine learning models. It involves splitting the available data into two distinct subsets: one for training the model and one for testing it. The model is trained on the training data, and its performance is evaluated on the test data. This allows you to see how well the model generalizes to data it has not seen before.

A. How Train-Test Split Works

The process of train-test splitting involves the following steps:

Data Split: Divide the dataset into two subsets:

Training Set: This subset is used to train the model. Typically, about 70% to 80% of the data is allocated to the training set.

Test Set: This subset is used to evaluate the model's performance. It typically comprises 20% to 30% of the data.

Model Training: Use the training data to train your machine learning model. The model learns patterns, relationships, and features from this data.

Model Testing: After training, evaluate the model's performance on the test data. The model does not have access to this test set during training, which allows you to assess its ability to generalize to unseen data.

Performance Evaluation: Based on the predictions made on the test set, you can evaluate the model using various performance metrics, such as accuracy, precision, recall, F1 score, and more.

B. Advantages of Train-Test Split

- **Simplicity**: Train-test split is straightforward to implement, and it doesn't require complex procedures or computational overhead.
- **Quick Evaluation**: It allows for quick evaluation of the model, especially when you have a large dataset.

C. Disadvantages of Train-Test Split

- **Data Partitioning**: The primary disadvantage is that the performance of the model can depend heavily on how the data is split. If the training and test sets are not representative of the overall data distribution, the evaluation may be biased.
- **Potential Overfitting or Underfitting**: Since the model is evaluated only once, there's a risk of overfitting to the training data or underfitting if the test set is too small or not representative.

2. Cross-Validation

Cross-validation is a more robust method for model evaluation compared to the train-test split. It is particularly useful when you have limited data and want to maximize the information available for training and testing the model. Cross-validation helps to mitigate the risk of bias introduced by a single train-test split and provides a more accurate estimate of model performance.

A. How Cross-Validation Works

Cross-validation involves splitting the data into multiple subsets, called folds, and using each fold as a test set while the remaining folds are used for training. The model is trained and evaluated multiple times, and the results are averaged to provide a more reliable estimate of its performance.

One of the most commonly used types of cross-validation is k-fold cross-validation.

1. **Split the Data**: Divide the dataset into k equal-sized subsets, called **folds**. A common choice is $k = 5$ or $k = 10$, though other values may be used based on the dataset size.

2. **Training and Testing**: For each fold, the model is trained on $k - 1$ folds (i.e., the data from all but one fold) and evaluated on the remaining fold. This process is repeated k times, with each fold being used as the test set exactly once.

3. **Performance Evaluation**: After all k iterations, the performance scores are averaged to produce a final evaluation of the model's generalization ability. This provides a more reliable estimate of model performance than the single test set evaluation from a train-test split.

B. Types of Cross-Validation

1. **k-Fold Cross-Validation:**

   - The dataset is divided into k folds.
   - For each fold, the model is trained on $k - 1$ folds and tested on the remaining fold.
   - This process repeats k times, with each fold being used as the test set once.

   The advantage of k-fold cross-validation is that it helps ensure that each data point gets used for both training and testing, providing a more robust estimate of the model's performance.

2. Stratified k-Fold Cross-Validation:

   - This is a variant of k-fold cross-validation where the class distribution in each fold is made similar to the overall dataset. This is particularly useful in classification tasks with imbalanced classes.
   - For example, if your dataset has 80% positive class and 20% negative class, each fold will try to maintain this same distribution, reducing bias in the evaluation.

3. Leave-One-Out Cross-Validation (LOOCV):

- This is an extreme case of k-fold cross-validation where k is set to the number of data points. Essentially, each data point serves as a test set while the model is trained on all other data points.
- LOOCV is computationally expensive but can be very useful when the dataset is small.

4. Leave-P-Out Cross-Validation (LPOCV):

Similar to LOOCV, except that p data points are held out for testing at each iteration. This is another approach that can be useful for small datasets, though it can also be computationally intensive.

C. Advantages of Cross-Validation

- **More Reliable Estimate**: Cross-validation provides a more accurate estimate of a model's generalization ability, as the model is evaluated on multiple different subsets of the data.
- **Better Utilization of Data**: Unlike train-test split, where some data points are not used in testing, cross-validation ensures that each data point gets used for both training and testing.
- **Reduced Risk of Overfitting**: Since the model is tested on multiple different subsets, cross-validation helps to ensure that the model is not overfitting to a particular portion of the data.

D. Disadvantages of Cross-Validation

- **Computational Cost**: Cross-validation requires training the model k times, which can be computationally expensive, especially for large datasets or complex models.
- **Complexity**: Cross-validation can be more difficult to implement compared to a simple train-test split, especially when dealing with multiple models or hyperparameter tuning.

3. Choosing Between Train-Test Split and Cross-Validation

While both train-test split and cross-validation are useful for evaluating models, there are a few factors to consider when choosing between the two:

Dataset Size:

- If you have a small dataset, cross-validation is generally preferred, as it makes better use of the available data and provides more reliable performance estimates.
- If you have a large dataset, a simple train-test split might be sufficient, as you can afford to set aside a portion of the data for testing without losing too much training data.

Computational Resources:

- Train-test split is computationally cheaper since the model is trained only once.
- Cross-validation, especially k-fold cross-validation, can be computationally intensive since the model must be trained multiple times. This may not be ideal for large datasets or models with long training times.

Model Tuning:

- When tuning hyperparameters (e.g., learning rate, regularization strength), cross-validation is typically preferred, as it provides more robust performance estimates and helps avoid overfitting to a single validation set.

Both train-test split and cross-validation are essential techniques in the machine learning workflow, helping evaluate the performance of models and ensuring they generalize well to unseen data. While train-test split is a simple and fast approach, cross-validation provides a more thorough evaluation, especially useful in cases of small datasets or when high accuracy is needed. By understanding when and how to use these techniques, you can make more informed decisions about the evaluation and optimization of machine learning models.

7.2 Performance Metrics (Accuracy, Precision, Recall, F1-Score)

When building a machine learning model, evaluating its performance is a critical step. The effectiveness of a model can be assessed using various performance metrics that help determine how well the model is making predictions. The most commonly used metrics are accuracy, precision, recall, and F1-score. These metrics provide insights into different aspects of a model's performance, especially in classification tasks.

In this section, we'll explore each of these performance metrics in detail, their formulas, and their use cases, helping you understand when and why to use each metric in your model evaluation.

1. Accuracy

Accuracy is one of the most widely used performance metrics in classification problems. It measures the proportion of correct predictions made by the model out of all predictions. While it's easy to calculate, accuracy can be misleading, especially when dealing with imbalanced datasets.

$$\text{Accuracy} = \frac{\text{Number of Correct Predictions}}{\text{Total Number of Predictions}}$$

In terms of the confusion matrix, where:

- **True Positives** (TP) are correctly predicted positive instances.
- **True Negatives** (TN) are correctly predicted negative instances.
- **False Positives** (FP) are negative instances incorrectly classified as positive.
- **False Negatives** (FN) are positive instances incorrectly classified as negative.

The formula for accuracy is:

$$\text{Accuracy} = \frac{TP + TN}{TP + TN + FP + FN}$$

B. When to Use Accuracy

- **Balanced Datasets**: Accuracy is a good metric when the classes in the dataset are balanced (i.e., both classes have similar frequencies).
- **Simple Tasks**: For tasks where the costs of false positives and false negatives are equal, accuracy can provide a quick, easy measure of performance.

C. Limitations of Accuracy

- **Imbalanced Classes**: Accuracy can be misleading when the dataset has a large class imbalance. For example, if you are predicting whether an email is spam or not, and only 5% of emails are spam, a model that classifies all emails as "not spam" will have a high accuracy (95%) but will fail to detect any actual spam emails.

- **Doesn't Capture Class-Specific Performance**: Accuracy treats all types of errors equally, which may not be suitable in cases where one type of error is more costly than the other.

2. Precision

Precision is a performance metric that focuses on the quality of the positive predictions made by the model. It tells us how many of the predicted positive instances are actually positive. In other words, precision measures the proportion of true positives out of all instances that were predicted as positive.

A. Formula for Precision

$$\text{Precision} = \frac{TP}{TP + FP}$$

Where:

- **TP** is the number of true positives.
- **FP** is the number of false positives.

B. When to Use Precision

- **Minimizing False Positives**: Precision is particularly important when the cost of false positives is high. For example, in medical diagnostics, you may want to ensure that when the model predicts a patient has a disease, it is actually the case (e.g., predicting cancer). Misclassifying healthy patients as sick (false positives) can lead to unnecessary treatments or tests.
- **Imbalanced Datasets**: When working with imbalanced datasets, precision gives a more meaningful measure of the classifier's performance than accuracy, as it focuses on how well the model handles positive instances.

C. Limitations of Precision

- **Ignores False Negatives**: Precision does not account for false negatives, so a model with high precision could still be performing poorly if it fails to identify many positive instances (high FN).

3. Recall

Recall, also known as sensitivity or true positive rate, measures how well the model identifies positive instances. Specifically, recall calculates the proportion of true positives out of all the actual positive instances in the dataset. Recall is a critical metric when the goal is to minimize false negatives, i.e., missing positive instances.

A. Formula for Recall

$$\text{Recall} = \frac{TP}{TP + FN}$$

Where:

- **TP** is the number of true positives.
- **FN** is the number of false negatives.

B. When to Use Recall

- **Minimizing False Negatives**: Recall is particularly important when the cost of false negatives is high. For example, in fraud detection, missing a fraudulent transaction (false negative) could lead to financial losses.
- **Imbalanced Datasets**: In situations with imbalanced datasets where the positive class is underrepresented, recall helps measure the model's ability to detect all positive instances.

C. Limitations of Recall

- **Ignores False Positives**: While recall focuses on detecting all positives, it ignores false positives. A model with high recall could end up predicting a lot of false positives (which could be problematic depending on the application).

4. F1-Score

The F1-score is the harmonic mean of precision and recall. It is a balanced metric that takes both false positives and false negatives into account, making it especially useful when dealing with imbalanced datasets. The F1-score provides a more nuanced evaluation of a model's performance, especially when you need to balance the importance of both precision and recall.

A. Formula for F1-Score

$$\text{F1-Score} = 2 \times \frac{\text{Precision} \times \text{Recall}}{\text{Precision} + \text{Recall}}$$

Alternatively, using the confusion matrix:

$$\text{F1-Score} = 2 \times \frac{TP}{2TP + FP + FN}$$

B. When to Use F1-Score

- **Imbalanced Classes**: F1-score is a great metric to use when dealing with imbalanced classes, as it helps you consider both false positives and false negatives.
- **Balancing Precision and Recall**: If you need to strike a balance between precision and recall (i.e., when false positives and false negatives are equally important), F1-score is a more balanced evaluation metric than accuracy.

C. Limitations of F1-Score

- **Complexity**: While the F1-score balances precision and recall, it can be harder to interpret than accuracy, precision, or recall on their own.
- **Does Not Reflect Class-Specific Performance**: F1-score does not provide insight into the performance of each individual class. For instance, it does not allow you to see if the model is missing important instances of one particular class while performing well on the other.

5. Confusion Matrix

To better understand how these metrics work, it's essential to look at the confusion matrix, which summarizes the performance of a classification model by comparing the predicted class labels to the true labels. The confusion matrix provides the following values:

	Predicted Positive	Predicted Negative
Actual Positive	True Positive (TP)	False Negative (FN)
Actual Negative	False Positive (FP)	True Negative (TN)

From the confusion matrix, you can calculate accuracy, precision, recall, and F1-score, as they are derived from the four values: TP, TN, FP, and FN.

6. Choosing the Right Metric

- **Accuracy**: Use when the dataset is balanced and all errors are equally important.
- **Precision**: Use when the cost of false positives is high, and you want to be confident in your positive predictions.
- **Recall**: Use when the cost of false negatives is high, and you want to capture as many true positives as possible.
- **F1-Score**: Use when you need to balance precision and recall, especially with imbalanced classes.

In practice, you often have to choose the right metric based on the specific problem and the consequences of different types of errors. For example, in fraud detection, recall is critical, as missing a fraudulent transaction can be very costly. However, in spam email detection, precision is more important to avoid marking important emails as spam.

Understanding performance metrics like accuracy, precision, recall, and F1-score is essential for evaluating machine learning models. Each metric provides unique insights into different aspects of model performance. When developing and evaluating models, it's important to choose the right metric based on the problem at hand and the consequences of various types of errors. By understanding these metrics, you can make more informed decisions about model selection and optimization, ensuring that your machine learning system meets the desired goals.

7.3 Overfitting & Underfitting

In machine learning, one of the primary goals is to build models that generalize well to unseen data, rather than simply memorizing the training data. Two common issues that arise during model training are overfitting and underfitting. These terms refer to how well a model fits the training data and how well it can make predictions on new, unseen data.

In this section, we'll dive into what overfitting and underfitting mean, their causes, their impact on model performance, and strategies for mitigating them.

1. Overfitting

Overfitting occurs when a model learns not only the underlying patterns in the training data but also the noise and outliers. This means that the model is too complex and captures patterns that do not generalize well to new data. Essentially, the model is "overly fitted" to the training data, which can result in poor performance when it encounters new, unseen data.

A. How Overfitting Happens

Overfitting typically occurs when:

- The model is too complex for the data at hand, such as using a highly complex algorithm or a very deep neural network for a small dataset.
- The model has too many parameters relative to the amount of data, which allows it to "memorize" the data rather than learning generalizable patterns.
- Insufficient training data to allow the model to learn the true underlying patterns without memorizing specific details of the training set.

For instance, in a regression model, a very high-degree polynomial curve might fit the training data perfectly but fail to predict future data accurately because it has captured noise (random fluctuations) in the training set.

B. Consequences of Overfitting

- **Poor Generalization**: A model that overfits performs well on the training data but poorly on new, unseen data (test data). This is because it has essentially memorized the training data, making it less flexible and unable to adapt to variations in new data.
- **Increased Variance**: Overfitting leads to high variance in the model. This means that small changes in the training data can result in large changes in the model's predictions, making it unreliable and unstable.

C. Identifying Overfitting

To identify overfitting, you can compare the performance of the model on both the training set and the test set:

If the model has a significantly higher accuracy on the training data compared to the test data, it is likely overfitting.

Learning Curves: By plotting learning curves for training and validation (test) performance over time, you can often see signs of overfitting. If the model's training error continues to decrease while the validation error starts to increase, this is a clear sign of overfitting.

D. Mitigating Overfitting

There are several techniques to reduce or prevent overfitting:

- **Use Simpler Models**: Choose a model with fewer parameters or less complexity. For example, instead of a high-degree polynomial regression, consider a linear regression or a simpler model.
- **Regularization**: Regularization techniques like L1 (Lasso) and L2 (Ridge) regularization add a penalty to the model for having large weights or coefficients. This encourages the model to prefer simpler solutions and avoids overfitting to the noise in the data.
- **Cross-Validation**: Using cross-validation helps ensure that the model is not overfitting to a particular subset of the data. It provides a more robust measure of the model's performance.
- **More Data**: Increasing the amount of training data can help the model learn more generalizable patterns and reduce the risk of overfitting. Larger datasets provide more examples, making it less likely that the model will memorize noise.
- **Pruning (for Decision Trees):** In decision trees, overfitting can occur when the tree becomes too complex with too many splits. Pruning involves cutting back the tree to avoid overfitting.
- **Early Stopping (for Neural Networks):** When training deep learning models, early stopping can help prevent overfitting. This involves monitoring the model's performance on the validation data and stopping training when the validation performance stops improving.

2. Underfitting

Underfitting occurs when a model is too simple to capture the underlying patterns in the data. An underfit model does not learn enough from the training data and fails to generalize to both the training data and new, unseen data. This results in poor performance across both training and test datasets.

A. How Underfitting Happens

Underfitting typically occurs when:

- The model is too simple for the data at hand. For example, using a linear model for data that has complex, non-linear relationships can result in underfitting.
- The model doesn't have enough capacity to learn the important patterns in the data. This could be due to using a model with too few parameters or a model that is overly constrained.
- Insufficient training time or data: If the model has not been trained adequately or with enough data, it may fail to learn meaningful relationships.

For instance, in a regression problem, a simple linear model might underfit data that has a quadratic relationship because it cannot capture the non-linear trend.

B. Consequences of Underfitting

- **Low Accuracy**: An underfit model will generally have poor performance on both the training and test sets, as it is not able to capture the underlying patterns in the data.
- **High Bias**: Underfitting is often associated with high bias, meaning the model makes strong assumptions about the data and fails to learn important patterns. The model will consistently make errors that it cannot correct.

C. Identifying Underfitting

Signs of underfitting can be detected by:

Poor performance on both training and test data: If the model performs poorly on the training data and also poorly on the test data, it is likely underfitting.

Learning Curves: If both training and validation error are high and do not decrease significantly with additional training, the model may be underfitting.

D. Mitigating Underfitting

To prevent underfitting, consider the following strategies:

- **Use More Complex Models**: If your model is too simple (e.g., using linear regression for a non-linear problem), try using more complex models such as decision trees, support vector machines (SVM), or neural networks.
- **Increase Model Capacity**: Use a model with more parameters or a larger capacity (e.g., more hidden layers in a neural network) so that it can learn more complex patterns in the data.
- **Increase Training Time**: If your model is underfitting due to insufficient training, consider training it for a longer period, giving it more opportunity to learn the underlying patterns.
- **Remove Regularization**: If you have used regularization to prevent overfitting, it may have constrained the model too much. Reducing or removing the regularization term can allow the model to fit the data more effectively.

3. The Bias-Variance Tradeoff

Overfitting and underfitting are both consequences of the bias-variance tradeoff, a fundamental concept in machine learning:

Bias refers to the error introduced by the model's assumptions. A high-bias model makes strong assumptions about the data and often underfits.

Variance refers to the model's sensitivity to small changes in the training data. A high-variance model has overfitted the data and is overly sensitive to noise.

The goal is to find the right balance between bias and variance, where the model has enough flexibility to capture the underlying patterns in the data (low bias) but is not so complex that it overfits the data (low variance).

Underfitting corresponds to high bias and low variance (too simple a model that cannot capture the data's complexity).

Overfitting corresponds to low bias and high variance (a model that is too complex and fits the noise in the data).

Finding the optimal model involves balancing bias and variance to achieve the lowest total error.

Both overfitting and underfitting represent problems in building machine learning models that fail to generalize well to new data. Overfitting happens when the model is too complex and learns noise in the data, while underfitting occurs when the model is too simple and fails to capture the important patterns in the data. By understanding these issues and applying strategies to mitigate them—such as using simpler models, increasing data, regularization techniques, and cross-validation—you can build models that generalize well and perform effectively on unseen data. The key is to find a balance between complexity and simplicity to avoid both overfitting and underfitting.

7.4 Hyperparameter Tuning (Grid Search, Random Search, Bayesian Optimization)

One of the key steps in improving a machine learning model is hyperparameter tuning. Hyperparameters are parameters that are set before training a model and are not updated during training (unlike model parameters, which are learned from the data). Examples of hyperparameters include the learning rate in gradient descent, the number of trees in a random forest, or the depth of a decision tree. Choosing the right hyperparameters can significantly improve a model's performance.

In this section, we will explore three common methods of hyperparameter tuning: Grid Search, Random Search, and Bayesian Optimization. We'll cover how each technique works, their advantages, disadvantages, and use cases.

1. Grid Search

Grid Search is one of the simplest and most exhaustive methods of hyperparameter tuning. It involves specifying a set of hyperparameters to tune, and for each hyperparameter, you provide a list of possible values. The algorithm then trains the model with all possible combinations of hyperparameters and evaluates each combination's performance to determine the best one.

A. How Grid Search Works

- Define a grid of hyperparameters with different values.
- Train the model with every combination of hyperparameters in the grid.
- Evaluate each combination using a cross-validation approach (or a validation set).
- Select the combination that results in the best performance (based on a performance metric like accuracy, precision, recall, etc.).

B. Advantages of Grid Search

- Exhaustive: Grid Search evaluates all possible combinations of hyperparameters, ensuring that you don't miss any potentially good configurations.
- Easy to Understand and Implement: It is a straightforward approach and easy to implement in most machine learning frameworks, such as Scikit-learn.

C. Disadvantages of Grid Search

- **Computationally Expensive**: The number of possible combinations grows exponentially as the number of hyperparameters and their values increases. This can make Grid Search very slow, especially for models with many hyperparameters.
- **No Guarantee of Optimal Solution**: Grid search may not find the best solution, especially if the grid is not fine-grained enough or if the search space is very large.
- **Limited Flexibility**: It can be inefficient because it evaluates all combinations, even those that may not be promising, which results in wasted computations.

D. When to Use Grid Search

- **Small to Moderate Hyperparameter Spaces**: If you are tuning a small set of hyperparameters with relatively few choices, Grid Search can be a great option.
- **Exhaustive Search**: When you want to ensure that you explore every combination of hyperparameters and don't miss any important configurations.

2. Random Search

Random Search is another popular method for hyperparameter tuning, but instead of evaluating every combination of hyperparameters (like Grid Search), it randomly selects combinations of hyperparameters to evaluate. This randomness helps explore the hyperparameter space more efficiently than Grid Search, especially when the search space is large.

A. How Random Search Works

- Define a distribution or range for each hyperparameter.
- Randomly sample combinations from these ranges or distributions.
- Train the model with each randomly sampled combination and evaluate its performance.
- Select the combination that gives the best performance.

B. Advantages of Random Search

- **More Efficient than Grid Search**: By sampling randomly, it can explore a larger number of hyperparameter combinations in less time, especially when there are many hyperparameters to tune.
- **Better for High-Dimensional Spaces**: Random Search works better than Grid Search when the number of hyperparameters or the range of possible values is large. Since it samples randomly, it is more likely to find a good combination without having to evaluate every possibility.
- **Flexibility**: You can define continuous or discrete ranges for hyperparameters, which allows more flexibility in the search.

C. Disadvantages of Random Search

- **Not Exhaustive**: Because it randomly selects combinations, Random Search might miss the best combination of hyperparameters, especially if the number of evaluations is limited.
- **Possibly Suboptimal**: There is no guarantee that it will find the optimal hyperparameters, and it might stop early without fully exploring the search space.

D. When to Use Random Search

- **Large Hyperparameter Space**: If you have many hyperparameters or continuous variables that would make Grid Search computationally expensive, Random Search is often a more efficient alternative.
- **Exploratory Search**: When you want to quickly get an idea of which regions of the hyperparameter space may be promising, Random Search provides a good starting point.

3. Bayesian Optimization

Bayesian Optimization is a more sophisticated approach to hyperparameter tuning. It is based on building a probabilistic model of the objective function (usually performance metrics like accuracy or loss), and then using this model to guide the search for optimal hyperparameters. Unlike Grid Search and Random Search, Bayesian Optimization aims to find the best hyperparameters more efficiently by using the results of previous trials to inform future trials.

A. How Bayesian Optimization Works

- Define a probabilistic model (usually Gaussian Process) that models the function mapping hyperparameters to performance scores.
- Initialize the search with a few random samples from the hyperparameter space.
- Use the model to predict the performance of unexplored hyperparameters.
- Select the next set of hyperparameters to evaluate by maximizing an acquisition function, which balances exploring areas of the search space with the highest uncertainty and exploiting areas that are expected to yield high performance.
- Train the model with these new hyperparameters and update the probabilistic model.
- Repeat steps 3-5 iteratively until convergence or a set number of iterations is reached.

B. Advantages of Bayesian Optimization

- **Efficient Search**: Bayesian Optimization is more efficient than Grid Search and Random Search because it uses the results of previous evaluations to focus the search on areas of the hyperparameter space that are likely to yield good results. This reduces the number of evaluations required.
- **Handles Expensive Evaluations**: It is particularly useful when model training is time-consuming, as it minimizes the number of trials needed to find good hyperparameters.
- **Less Computationally Expensive**: By focusing on promising regions of the hyperparameter space, Bayesian Optimization typically requires fewer function evaluations than other methods.

C. Disadvantages of Bayesian Optimization

- **Complex to Implement**: Bayesian Optimization requires building and maintaining a probabilistic model and may involve more advanced techniques to implement and fine-tune.
- **Scalability**: It may struggle with very large hyperparameter spaces or models with a large number of hyperparameters.
- **Computational Overhead**: While Bayesian Optimization is more efficient than exhaustive methods, the optimization process itself (building and updating the model) can still introduce overhead.

D. When to Use Bayesian Optimization

- **Expensive Evaluations**: If training the model takes a long time (e.g., training deep learning models), Bayesian Optimization can help find optimal hyperparameters with fewer trials.
- **Complex Search Spaces**: When the relationship between hyperparameters and performance is complex, Bayesian Optimization can effectively explore the search space.
- **Efficiency is a Priority**: If you need to tune hyperparameters quickly without trying every possible combination, Bayesian Optimization is a great choice.

4. Comparison of Hyperparameter Tuning Methods

Method	Exploration	Computational Efficiency	Use Case	Key Advantages
Grid Search	Exhaustive (tries all combinations)	Computationally expensive for large search spaces	Small to moderate hyperparameter spaces, exhaustive search	Simple to implement, exhaustive, easy to understand
Random Search	Random (samples randomly)	More efficient than Grid Search, especially with large spaces	Large search spaces, exploratory search	Faster than Grid Search, works well with high-dimensional spaces
Bayesian Optimization	Probabilistic (builds model of performance)	Highly efficient, especially for expensive evaluations	Expensive or slow models, large, complex search spaces	More efficient than Grid and Random Search, fewer trials needed

Hyperparameter tuning is a critical step in optimizing machine learning models. The choice of tuning method depends on the complexity of the model, the size of the hyperparameter search space, and the computational resources available. Grid Search is exhaustive but computationally expensive, Random Search is more efficient for large search spaces, and Bayesian Optimization offers a sophisticated and efficient approach that can work particularly well for expensive or slow-to-train models.

By selecting the right hyperparameter tuning strategy, you can significantly improve your model's performance and avoid wasting computational resources on ineffective configurations.

8. Clustering Algorithms

Clustering helps discover hidden patterns in data. This chapter introduces K-Means, DBSCAN, and Hierarchical Clustering, showing how these algorithms group similar data points and their applications in market segmentation and customer analytics.

8.1 K-Means Clustering

K-Means Clustering is one of the most popular and widely used unsupervised learning algorithms for clustering tasks. Clustering is a type of unsupervised learning where the goal is to group similar data points together based on their features, without any predefined labels. K-Means is particularly useful when you have a dataset with no labeled categories, and your task is to uncover hidden patterns or groupings in the data.

In this section, we will explore what K-Means clustering is, how it works, its applications, and some common challenges associated with it.

1. What is K-Means Clustering?

K-Means clustering is an algorithm that partitions a dataset into K distinct, non-overlapping clusters based on similarity. The main idea is to group data points such that points within the same cluster are similar to each other, while points from different clusters are as dissimilar as possible.

A. Key Concepts

- **Centroids**: Each cluster is represented by a centroid, which is the average of all data points in that cluster. The centroid is the central point of the cluster, and the algorithm iteratively updates the centroid's position as it assigns data points to the nearest cluster.
- **K**: The number of clusters is a predefined hyperparameter, denoted as K. The challenge is to determine the optimal value of K, which dictates the number of groups the algorithm should create.

2. How Does K-Means Clustering Work?

K-Means clustering works through an iterative process to group data points into clusters. The basic steps are as follows:

A. Step 1: Initialize Centroids

The first step is to randomly select K data points from the dataset as initial cluster centroids. These centroids will represent the initial "centers" of the clusters.

B. Step 2: Assign Data Points to Nearest Centroid

Each data point is assigned to the nearest centroid based on a distance metric, typically Euclidean distance. The data points closest to a particular centroid are grouped into that cluster.

C. Step 3: Update Centroids

Once all the data points are assigned to a cluster, the centroids are updated by calculating the mean (average) of all the data points in each cluster. The centroid now represents the center of the newly formed cluster.

D. Step 4: Repeat

Steps 2 and 3 are repeated iteratively: the data points are reassigned to the new centroids, and the centroids are recalculated. This process continues until the centroids no longer change significantly between iterations or until a specified number of iterations is reached.

E. Termination

The algorithm terminates when the centroids stop changing, meaning that the clustering has converged, or when the algorithm reaches a predefined maximum number of iterations.

3. Choosing the Number of Clusters (K)

One of the key challenges with K-Means is selecting the right number of clusters (K). If K is too small, the algorithm may merge distinct clusters, leading to poor performance. If K is too large, the algorithm may overfit the data and create too many small, potentially meaningless clusters.

A. Elbow Method

The Elbow Method is a common technique to determine the optimal value of K. Here's how it works:

- Run K-Means clustering for different values of K (e.g., from 1 to 10).
- For each value of K, calculate the within-cluster sum of squares (WCSS), which measures the total variance within each cluster. The WCSS tends to decrease as K increases because the algorithm is able to form smaller and more precise clusters.
- Plot K versus WCSS and look for an "elbow" in the curve. The point at which the decrease in WCSS slows down significantly is often considered the optimal value for K.

B. Silhouette Score

The Silhouette Score measures how similar each point is to its own cluster compared to other clusters. The score ranges from -1 to 1, where a score closer to 1 indicates that points are well-matched to their cluster, and a score closer to -1 indicates that points are misclassified. By evaluating the Silhouette Score for different values of K, you can determine the number of clusters that maximizes the clustering quality.

4. Advantages of K-Means Clustering

- **Simplicity**: K-Means is easy to understand and implement, making it one of the most popular clustering algorithms.
- **Efficiency**: K-Means can handle large datasets relatively efficiently. Its time complexity is $O(K * N * T)$, where K is the number of clusters, N is the number of data points, and T is the number of iterations. This makes it much faster than other algorithms like hierarchical clustering for large datasets.
- **Scalability**: K-Means scales well to large datasets and is a suitable option for clustering high-dimensional data (although with some limitations).

5. Disadvantages of K-Means Clustering

- **Choosing K**: The number of clusters K must be predefined, which can be difficult when there is no clear indication of how many clusters should be formed.
- **Sensitivity to Initial Centroids**: The algorithm's performance can be significantly influenced by the initial selection of centroids. Poor initialization can lead to suboptimal clustering or convergence to a local minimum rather than the global minimum.

- **Non-Globally Optimal Solution**: K-Means only finds a local minimum in the loss function, and it might not always converge to the optimal solution, especially if the data has complex structures or if clusters are not spherical or of equal size.
- **Sensitivity to Outliers**: K-Means is sensitive to outliers, as they can significantly affect the position of centroids. Since K-Means uses the mean to update centroids, the presence of outliers can distort the cluster centers.

6. Applications of K-Means Clustering

K-Means clustering has many practical applications across various fields:

A. Customer Segmentation

In marketing and customer analytics, K-Means is used to segment customers into distinct groups based on purchasing behavior, demographics, or other features. This allows businesses to tailor their marketing strategies to different customer groups.

B. Image Compression

K-Means can be used to compress images by reducing the number of unique colors in the image. The algorithm groups similar colors into clusters and replaces the colors in each cluster with the centroid color, reducing the image's color palette while maintaining visual quality.

C. Document Clustering

K-Means can be applied to cluster documents based on their content. This is often used in information retrieval systems, such as news categorization, topic modeling, or organizing large collections of text documents.

D. Anomaly Detection

In situations where the data is mostly homogeneous, K-Means can be used for anomaly detection. Points that do not fit well into any cluster (i.e., have large distances from their assigned centroids) can be flagged as anomalies or outliers.

7. Improving K-Means Clustering

To improve the performance of K-Means clustering and overcome some of its limitations, there are a few variations and enhancements:

A. K-Means++ Initialization

K-Means++ is an initialization method that spreads out the initial centroids, making it less likely to converge to a poor solution. It helps reduce the sensitivity of K-Means to the random initialization of centroids.

B. Mini-Batch K-Means

For very large datasets, Mini-Batch K-Means is a variation of the standard K-Means algorithm that uses small random batches of data instead of the entire dataset to update centroids. This can speed up the training process without significantly sacrificing the quality of the results.

C. Alternative Clustering Algorithms

In cases where K-Means is not suitable (e.g., non-spherical clusters, presence of outliers), you might consider alternative clustering algorithms such as DBSCAN (Density-Based Spatial Clustering of Applications with Noise), which can find clusters of arbitrary shapes, or Agglomerative Hierarchical Clustering, which does not require specifying the number of clusters in advance.

K-Means clustering is a powerful, efficient, and widely used algorithm for unsupervised learning tasks, especially when dealing with large datasets and the need to uncover patterns or groupings within the data. Although it has its limitations, including sensitivity to the choice of K and initial centroids, it remains a go-to algorithm due to its simplicity, speed, and effectiveness. Understanding how to properly tune the parameters and handle challenges like outliers and cluster initialization can significantly enhance its performance and applicability in real-world problems.

8.2 Hierarchical Clustering

Hierarchical Clustering is another powerful unsupervised learning algorithm used to group data points into clusters based on their similarity. Unlike K-Means, which partitions data into a pre-specified number of clusters, hierarchical clustering creates a tree-like structure (called a dendrogram) that illustrates the relationships between the data points. This approach doesn't require you to define the number of clusters upfront, making it particularly useful when you're unsure about the number of clusters needed in the data.

In this section, we will explore the concept of hierarchical clustering, its types, how it works, and its applications and limitations.

1. What is Hierarchical Clustering?

Hierarchical clustering is a method of cluster analysis that builds a hierarchy of clusters, represented as a dendrogram. The hierarchy can be constructed either in a bottom-up manner (agglomerative) or a top-down manner (divisive). The key idea is to repeatedly merge or split clusters based on a distance metric that quantifies the similarity between data points.

The resulting tree structure enables you to visually inspect the relationships between different data points and choose an appropriate level of granularity for the clustering.

2. Types of Hierarchical Clustering

There are two primary approaches to hierarchical clustering:

A. Agglomerative (Bottom-Up) Clustering

- Agglomerative hierarchical clustering is the most common approach. It starts with each data point as its own cluster and then iteratively merges the closest clusters.
- At the beginning, each data point is considered a separate cluster (or "leaf"), and the algorithm successively merges pairs of clusters based on a similarity metric.
- This process continues until all the data points are merged into a single cluster.

B. Divisive (Top-Down) Clustering

- Divisive hierarchical clustering starts with the entire dataset as one single cluster and then repeatedly splits the data into smaller clusters. The process continues until each data point is its own cluster (a leaf).
- Divisive clustering is less commonly used due to its higher computational cost compared to agglomerative clustering.
- In practice, agglomerative hierarchical clustering is more commonly applied because it's more computationally efficient and simpler to implement.

3. How Does Agglomerative Hierarchical Clustering Work?

Agglomerative hierarchical clustering follows a series of steps to merge the closest clusters at each iteration:

A. Step 1: Initialize Clusters

Start by treating each data point as its own cluster. Initially, there are as many clusters as data points.

B. Step 2: Compute Similarities

Calculate the distance or dissimilarity between every pair of clusters. This can be done using various distance metrics, such as Euclidean distance, Manhattan distance, or Cosine similarity. The choice of distance metric depends on the nature of the data and the problem.

C. Step 3: Merge the Closest Clusters

Identify the two clusters that are closest (i.e., have the smallest distance between them) and merge them into a single cluster.

D. Step 4: Update the Distance Matrix

After merging the two clusters, update the distance matrix, which now includes the newly formed cluster. This step is repeated at each iteration.

E. Step 5: Repeat the Process

Continue merging the closest clusters, recalculating distances after each merge, until all data points belong to a single cluster. The algorithm terminates when all points are in one cluster.

F. Step 6: Create the Dendrogram

As the algorithm progresses, it produces a dendrogram, a tree-like diagram that visually represents the sequence of merges. The dendrogram illustrates how data points or clusters are hierarchically grouped together, showing the distance at which each merge occurred.

4. Linkage Criteria in Hierarchical Clustering

To determine how clusters are merged, the algorithm relies on a linkage criterion, which defines how to measure the distance between two clusters. There are several popular linkage methods:

A. Single Linkage (Nearest Point Linkage)

In single linkage, the distance between two clusters is defined as the shortest distance between any two points, one from each cluster. This method tends to produce long, chain-like clusters.

B. Complete Linkage (Farthest Point Linkage)

Complete linkage calculates the distance between two clusters as the greatest distance between any two points, one from each cluster. This method tends to produce compact, spherical clusters.

C. Average Linkage

Average linkage computes the distance between two clusters as the average distance between all pairs of points, one from each cluster. This is a compromise between single and complete linkage.

D. Ward's Linkage

Ward's linkage minimizes the total within-cluster variance. The distance between two clusters is calculated based on the increase in the sum of squared differences (variance) after merging them. Ward's method often leads to more balanced clusters.

Each of these linkage methods affects the shape and structure of the resulting clusters, and the choice of linkage criterion depends on the data and the desired clustering properties.

5. Distance Metrics in Hierarchical Clustering

The choice of distance metric is critical in hierarchical clustering, as it defines how the similarity (or dissimilarity) between data points is measured. Common distance metrics include:

Euclidean Distance: The straight-line distance between two points in multi-dimensional space. It's the most common distance measure for continuous data.

Manhattan Distance: The sum of the absolute differences between the coordinates of two points, often used for grid-like data (e.g., city blocks).

Cosine Similarity: Measures the cosine of the angle between two vectors. It is particularly useful for high-dimensional data like text or documents.

Correlation-Based Distance: Measures how strongly the variables are correlated. This can be useful for time-series data or data with relationships that may not be captured by geometric distances.

6. Advantages of Hierarchical Clustering

No Need to Predefine the Number of Clusters: Unlike K-Means, you don't need to specify the number of clusters ahead of time. The dendrogram provides a visual representation that allows you to decide the number of clusters based on the level of granularity you want.

Hierarchical Structure: The dendrogram provides a visual and intuitive representation of the hierarchical relationships between data points, making it easy to understand the structure of the data.

Works Well with Complex Data: Hierarchical clustering is more flexible than K-Means, and it can handle data with complex cluster structures, such as irregular shapes or varying densities.

No Need for Preprocessing: Unlike K-Means, which may require scaling or normalization of the data, hierarchical clustering doesn't have these prerequisites. However, choosing an appropriate distance metric and linkage method is important.

7. Disadvantages of Hierarchical Clustering

Computational Complexity: Hierarchical clustering has a high time complexity of $O(N^2 \log N)$ (where N is the number of data points), making it less efficient for very large datasets.

Memory Usage: Storing the distance matrix and updating it at each iteration can require a significant amount of memory, especially for large datasets.

Sensitive to Noise and Outliers: Hierarchical clustering can be sensitive to noisy data and outliers, especially in the early stages of the merging process. This can result in poor clustering quality if the data is not preprocessed carefully.

Difficulty with Non-Globular Clusters: While hierarchical clustering is flexible, it can still struggle with clusters of different shapes or densities, especially if the wrong linkage method is used.

8. Applications of Hierarchical Clustering

Hierarchical clustering has several real-world applications across different fields:

Gene Expression Data: In bioinformatics, hierarchical clustering is often used to group genes with similar expression patterns, helping to identify genes that behave similarly under certain conditions.

Document Clustering: Hierarchical clustering is used in natural language processing (NLP) to group similar documents or text based on content or topic.

Market Segmentation: In marketing, hierarchical clustering can be used to segment customers into groups based on purchasing behavior or demographics.

Image Analysis: It is used for grouping similar images or features in computer vision, especially when dealing with complex or multi-dimensional data.

Hierarchical clustering is a flexible and powerful unsupervised learning technique that creates a tree-like structure of data points based on similarity. It's particularly useful when the number of clusters is not known in advance or when the hierarchical relationships between clusters need to be visualized. Although it has some drawbacks, such as computational inefficiency for large datasets and sensitivity to noise, it remains an essential tool for clustering tasks in fields like bioinformatics, text analysis, and customer segmentation. Understanding the different linkage criteria, distance metrics, and how to interpret dendrograms can help you leverage hierarchical clustering effectively.

8.3 DBSCAN (Density-Based Clustering)

DBSCAN (Density-Based Spatial Clustering of Applications with Noise) is a powerful unsupervised learning algorithm that finds clusters based on the density of data points in a dataset. Unlike K-Means and hierarchical clustering, which divide the data into a predefined number of clusters, DBSCAN identifies clusters of varying shapes and sizes by considering the local density of data points. It's particularly effective at discovering clusters that are not necessarily spherical and can handle noise (outliers) in the dataset.

In this section, we will explore what DBSCAN is, how it works, its advantages and disadvantages, and real-world applications.

1. What is DBSCAN?

DBSCAN is a density-based clustering algorithm, which means it groups data points that are close together based on the density of points in the surrounding area. The basic idea is that clusters are regions of high point density, separated by regions of low point density.

DBSCAN works by identifying core points, border points, and noise points:

Core Points: A data point is a core point if there are at least a minimum number of points (including itself) within a specified distance (called epsilon, or ε) of the point.

Border Points: A border point is a point that has fewer than the minimum number of points within its ε radius, but is within the ε radius of a core point.

Noise Points: Points that are neither core points nor border points are considered noise (outliers).

DBSCAN is different from other clustering algorithms because it does not require you to specify the number of clusters in advance. It automatically detects the number of clusters based on the data's density and the parameters ε and MinPts (the minimum number of points required to form a dense region).

2. How Does DBSCAN Work?

DBSCAN works by iteratively expanding clusters from core points and categorizing all points into one of three groups: core points, border points, or noise points. Here's how the algorithm proceeds:

A. Step 1: Initialization

The algorithm begins by choosing an arbitrary point in the dataset and checking if it is a core point by looking at how many points are within its ε neighborhood (within a specified radius).

B. Step 2: Core Point Identification

If the point has enough neighbors (at least MinPts), it is marked as a core point, and a new cluster is formed. All points within the ε radius of this core point are added to the cluster.

C. Step 3: Expand the Cluster

Once a core point has been found, DBSCAN tries to expand the cluster by checking the neighboring points. If a neighboring point is also a core point, DBSCAN continues expanding the cluster by adding the neighbors of the new core point.

D. Step 4: Border and Noise Points

- If a point is not a core point, but is within the ε radius of a core point, it is classified as a border point and added to the cluster.
- If a point is neither a core point nor a border point, it is considered noise and is not assigned to any cluster.

E. Step 5: Repeat for All Data Points

The process continues until all points in the dataset have been processed and classified as either core points, border points, or noise points.

3. Key Parameters of DBSCAN

DBSCAN has two key parameters that need to be defined:

A. Epsilon (ε)

Epsilon (ε) is the maximum distance between two points for them to be considered as neighbors. In other words, it determines the radius of the neighborhood around a point. Choosing an appropriate value for ε is crucial as it affects how clusters are formed.

B. MinPts

MinPts refers to the minimum number of points required to form a dense region (i.e., a cluster). Typically, MinPts is set to a value greater than or equal to the dimensionality of the data plus one (e.g., 4 for 2D data, 5 for 3D data).

Both parameters affect the final clustering result. The value of ε should be chosen such that it reflects the density of the clusters you want to find. MinPts controls the minimum size of a cluster.

4. Advantages of DBSCAN

DBSCAN has several advantages that make it a popular clustering algorithm:

A. No Need to Specify the Number of Clusters

Unlike K-Means, where you need to specify the number of clusters beforehand, DBSCAN does not require you to set the number of clusters. The algorithm automatically identifies clusters based on the density of points in the dataset.

B. Can Find Clusters of Arbitrary Shape

DBSCAN is capable of finding clusters of any shape, as opposed to K-Means, which assumes that clusters are spherical. This makes DBSCAN particularly useful when working with data that has irregular or non-convex clusters.

C. Handles Noise and Outliers

DBSCAN automatically labels points that do not belong to any cluster as noise. This is particularly useful in datasets where there are a significant number of outliers or irrelevant data points that do not fit into any cluster.

D. Works Well with High-Dimensional Data

DBSCAN can perform well on high-dimensional datasets, as long as you can effectively define the distance measure (e.g., Euclidean distance, cosine similarity). This makes it suitable for applications like document clustering or anomaly detection in large datasets.

5. Disadvantages of DBSCAN

Despite its many advantages, DBSCAN has some limitations:

A. Sensitive to ε and MinPts

Choosing appropriate values for ε and MinPts can be challenging. If ε is too large, the algorithm may merge distinct clusters into a single cluster. If ε is too small, the algorithm may classify most points as noise, leading to poor clustering results. A similar issue arises with MinPts, where too small a value might lead to too many small clusters or noise, and too large a value might merge dissimilar clusters.

B. Not Suitable for Varying Densities

DBSCAN works best when clusters have similar densities. If the dataset has clusters with very different densities, DBSCAN may fail to properly identify them. This is because the same value of ε and MinPts may not work well for clusters with different densities.

C. Computational Complexity

While DBSCAN is generally more efficient than hierarchical clustering, its time complexity can still be high, especially when using a brute-force distance calculation. The time complexity for DBSCAN is generally $O(N \log N)$ with spatial indexing (e.g., using KD-trees or ball trees), but without such optimizations, it can be $O(N^2)$.

6. Applications of DBSCAN

DBSCAN is widely used in many fields due to its ability to handle noisy data and identify clusters of arbitrary shapes. Some common applications include:

A. Geospatial Data Analysis

DBSCAN is commonly used in geospatial clustering, such as grouping geographical locations based on proximity. For example, it can be used in identifying hot spots for criminal activity, clustering locations of events, or finding clusters of stores in retail analytics.

B. Anomaly Detection

Since DBSCAN labels points that do not fit well into any cluster as noise, it can be used effectively for anomaly detection. Outliers in the data can be automatically flagged as noise, which is particularly useful in fraud detection, network security, and quality control.

C. Image Segmentation

In image processing, DBSCAN can be used to identify regions of interest in an image by clustering pixels that share similar properties. It's particularly useful when segments are irregularly shaped or contain noise, making it more flexible than traditional methods like K-Means.

D. Biological Data Analysis

In bioinformatics, DBSCAN has been used to cluster biological data such as gene expression patterns, protein structures, and microarray data. The algorithm can identify groups of genes with similar expression profiles or groups of proteins with similar functions.

E. Social Network Analysis

DBSCAN can be applied to social network analysis to identify communities of users who interact frequently. The algorithm can help in clustering social media users or finding groups of users with similar behaviors.

7. Improving DBSCAN Clustering

Here are a few techniques to improve DBSCAN clustering:

A. Selecting Appropriate Parameters

Use k-distance plots to visualize the distance to the k-th nearest neighbor for each point. The plot can help you select a good value for ε by looking for an "elbow" in the graph, which represents a transition from low to high density.

B. Use of Spatial Indexing

Using spatial indexing techniques like KD-Trees or Ball Trees can significantly speed up the computation of nearest neighbor distances and improve DBSCAN's efficiency.

C. Using Variants of DBSCAN

OPTICS (Ordering Points to Identify the Clustering Structure) is a variant of DBSCAN that addresses some of its limitations, such as sensitivity to the ε parameter and varying cluster densities. It can generate a more flexible clustering structure, useful for complex datasets.

DBSCAN is a versatile and powerful clustering algorithm that is well-suited for data with arbitrary-shaped clusters, noise, and outliers. By automatically determining the number of clusters and identifying noise points, DBSCAN offers a major advantage over other clustering algorithms like K-Means, which require the user to specify the number of clusters upfront. However, choosing the right ε and MinPts parameters remains a challenge, and DBSCAN is less effective when clusters have varying densities. Despite these limitations, DBSCAN is widely used in fields such as geospatial data analysis, image segmentation, and anomaly detection, and remains a go-to algorithm for many clustering tasks.

8.4 Choosing the Right Clustering Method

Clustering is one of the fundamental tasks in unsupervised machine learning, and the success of a clustering algorithm depends on the nature of the data, the underlying problem, and the objectives of the analysis. Choosing the right clustering method is crucial, as different algorithms excel under different conditions and come with their own strengths and weaknesses.

In this section, we will explore factors to consider when choosing a clustering algorithm, compare some of the most popular clustering methods, and discuss how to select the best method based on the specific characteristics of your data.

1. Factors to Consider When Choosing a Clustering Method

There are several factors to consider when choosing a clustering algorithm. These factors will guide you toward selecting the most suitable method for your particular use case:

A. Shape and Size of Clusters

- Some clustering algorithms, such as K-Means, assume that clusters are spherical and have approximately the same size. If your data consists of clusters that have complex shapes or different sizes, these algorithms might perform poorly.
- DBSCAN, on the other hand, can detect clusters of arbitrary shapes and sizes, which makes it more appropriate for data with clusters that are not well-separated or have irregular boundaries.
- Hierarchical clustering can also capture non-globular shapes and create a hierarchy of clusters based on distance.

B. Data Density

- The density of clusters plays a key role in algorithm selection. DBSCAN is particularly effective for datasets with varying densities because it forms clusters based on local density and can handle noise.
- K-Means assumes roughly equal density for all clusters, and can struggle if the clusters vary in density, with sparse regions potentially being ignored or misclassified.
- Gaussian Mixture Models (GMM) can also handle clusters with different densities, as it assumes that each cluster is represented by a Gaussian distribution, which can model different shapes and densities.

C. Number of Clusters

- Some algorithms, like K-Means, require you to specify the number of clusters (K) beforehand. This can be a limitation if you don't know the exact number of clusters in your data.
- DBSCAN and hierarchical clustering, however, do not require you to specify the number of clusters. Instead, they form clusters based on density or distance criteria. This can be an advantage if the number of clusters is not known in advance.

D. Scalability

- The size of your dataset significantly affects the choice of clustering method. K-Means is relatively fast and scales well with large datasets, making it a good choice when you need to cluster large volumes of data quickly.
- DBSCAN can be slower for large datasets, especially if it requires exhaustive distance calculations between all pairs of points. However, spatial indexing techniques can speed up DBSCAN's performance.
- Hierarchical clustering tends to have higher time complexity ($O(N^2 \log N)$), making it less efficient for large datasets.

E. Handling Outliers

- Outliers or noise points in the data can affect the clustering process. DBSCAN has a built-in mechanism for identifying and handling noise points, marking them as outliers.
- K-Means and Gaussian Mixture Models may assign outliers to a cluster, potentially distorting the results, since they treat all data points equally without distinguishing noise.

- Hierarchical clustering can also be affected by outliers, though the effect may be less significant if the outliers do not belong to the densest regions.

F. Dimensionality

- High-dimensional data can present challenges for many clustering algorithms due to the curse of dimensionality. K-Means can work well on moderately high-dimensional data but may struggle as the dimensionality increases.
- DBSCAN and hierarchical clustering can also face issues with high-dimensional data, as the concept of distance becomes less meaningful in high-dimensional spaces, and computational complexity increases.
- Gaussian Mixture Models can perform better in high-dimensional spaces, as long as the number of dimensions is manageable.

G. Interpretability

- The interpretability of clustering results is another important factor. K-Means and hierarchical clustering are relatively simple to understand, as they provide clear cluster assignments and easy-to-interpret cluster centroids or hierarchical trees.
- DBSCAN and Gaussian Mixture Models may be harder to interpret, especially when clusters are formed based on density or probabilistic models. However, the results can still be useful for exploratory data analysis, even if they are not as straightforward to interpret.

2. Comparing Clustering Algorithms

Let's now compare some of the most common clustering algorithms based on the factors mentioned above:

A. K-Means

- **Best for**: Large datasets, spherical clusters of similar size and density.
- **Strengths**: Fast and scalable, works well for large datasets with a predefined number of clusters.
- **Weaknesses**: Assumes clusters are spherical, struggles with non-globular clusters, sensitive to outliers, requires specifying the number of clusters.
- **Use cases**: Customer segmentation, document clustering, image compression.

B. DBSCAN

- **Best for**: Data with arbitrary-shaped clusters, datasets with noise and outliers.
- **Strengths**: Does not require specifying the number of clusters, can detect clusters of any shape, handles outliers.
- **Weaknesses**: Sensitive to the choice of ε and MinPts, can struggle with clusters of varying density.
- **Use cases**: Geospatial data, anomaly detection, image segmentation, noise filtering.

C. Hierarchical Clustering

- **Best for**: Small to medium datasets, when you want to visualize the hierarchy of clusters.
- **Strengths**: Does not require the number of clusters to be specified, produces a dendrogram that provides insight into data relationships.
- **Weaknesses**: Computationally expensive ($O(N^2 \log N)$), sensitive to noise, can struggle with large datasets.
- **Use cases**: Gene expression analysis, document clustering, biological data clustering.

D. Gaussian Mixture Models (GMM)

- **Best for**: Data with clusters that follow Gaussian (normal) distributions, varying densities.
- **Strengths**: Can model clusters of different shapes and densities, provides probabilistic cluster assignments.
- **Weaknesses**: Requires the number of clusters to be specified, assumes data points come from a mixture of Gaussian distributions.
- **Use cases**: Anomaly detection, speech recognition, image segmentation, density estimation.

E. Mean Shift

- **Best for**: Data with arbitrary shapes and varying densities.
- **Strengths**: Can detect clusters without needing to specify the number of clusters, does not assume any prior distribution.
- **Weaknesses**: Computationally expensive, sensitive to bandwidth parameter.
- **Use cases**: Image segmentation, object tracking, computer vision tasks.

3. How to Choose the Right Clustering Method

Given the various clustering algorithms and their strengths and weaknesses, the right choice largely depends on your specific use case and the nature of your data. Here are some practical steps to help you choose the right clustering method:

A. Examine the Nature of Your Data

- **Cluster shapes**: If you know that your clusters are non-globular or have varying densities, DBSCAN or GMM might be better options than K-Means.
- **Noise and outliers**: If your data has a lot of noise or outliers, DBSCAN is a great choice, as it can identify and separate outliers effectively.

B. Consider the Number of Clusters

- If you don't know the number of clusters beforehand, DBSCAN and hierarchical clustering are good options, as they don't require specifying the number of clusters.
- If you do know the number of clusters or have a good estimate, K-Means or Gaussian Mixture Models can be suitable choices.

C. Scalability and Efficiency

- For large datasets, K-Means is the fastest and most scalable option. If you are dealing with very high-dimensional data, GMM may offer better performance than DBSCAN or hierarchical clustering.
- If computational efficiency is a concern and the dataset is not too large, hierarchical clustering may provide valuable insight despite its higher computational cost.

D. Visualize the Data

- If possible, visualize your data to get an idea of the clustering structure. In some cases, you may observe clear separation between clusters or complex, irregular shapes. For simple spherical clusters, K-Means will likely suffice. For more complicated shapes, DBSCAN or hierarchical clustering might be a better choice.

Choosing the right clustering algorithm is essential to obtaining meaningful insights from your data. There is no one-size-fits-all answer; the best algorithm depends on the characteristics of the data, the number of clusters, the presence of noise, and the computational resources available. By carefully considering these factors, you can select the most appropriate clustering method that will give you accurate and interpretable results.

9. Dimensionality Reduction

High-dimensional data can be complex and inefficient. This chapter introduces Principal Component Analysis (PCA), t-SNE, and Autoencoders—techniques that simplify data while preserving its essential features, making ML models faster and more efficient.

9.1 Why Dimensionality Reduction?

Dimensionality reduction is a crucial concept and technique in machine learning and data science. In simple terms, it involves reducing the number of input features or variables in a dataset while retaining as much of the important information as possible. It is often used in high-dimensional datasets where the number of features or variables is large.

In this section, we will explore why dimensionality reduction is important, the challenges it addresses, and how it benefits machine learning models. We will also examine the key reasons for applying dimensionality reduction and how it contributes to data analysis and model performance.

1. The Curse of Dimensionality

One of the main reasons for using dimensionality reduction is to address the curse of dimensionality. The curse of dimensionality refers to the phenomenon where the feature space becomes increasingly sparse as the number of dimensions (features) grows. This has several negative consequences, including:

A. Data Sparsity

As the number of dimensions increases, the amount of data required to maintain a meaningful representation of the dataset grows exponentially. In high-dimensional spaces, data points become sparse, and distances between data points increase, making it harder to find meaningful patterns.

B. Increased Computational Complexity

High-dimensional data often results in longer training times, higher computational costs, and increased memory requirements. With more features to process, machine learning algorithms have to handle a larger feature space, leading to more complex models that are computationally expensive to train and evaluate.

C. Model Overfitting

With high-dimensional data, models may become too complex and overfit to the training data. Overfitting happens when the model captures noise or random fluctuations in the data rather than general patterns, leading to poor performance on unseen data (test data). By reducing the number of dimensions, we can simplify the model, making it less likely to overfit.

2. Improving Model Performance

Dimensionality reduction can enhance the performance of machine learning models in several ways:

A. Faster Training and Prediction

Reducing the number of features in the dataset makes the learning process faster. This results in faster training times and, in many cases, more efficient predictions once the model is deployed. For instance, in models like K-Nearest Neighbors (K-NN) or Support Vector Machines (SVM), the computational cost increases with the number of features, so reducing the dimensionality can help improve efficiency.

B. Mitigating Overfitting

With fewer features, the risk of overfitting decreases. High-dimensional data can introduce noise that may cause the model to fit to irrelevant patterns in the data. By reducing the number of features and retaining only the most important ones, dimensionality reduction helps in creating simpler models that generalize better to new, unseen data.

C. Noise Reduction

In many high-dimensional datasets, some features may not contribute significantly to the underlying patterns. These features could introduce noise, making it harder for the model to identify the true relationships in the data. Dimensionality reduction techniques help eliminate these irrelevant or redundant features, improving model accuracy and robustness.

3. Visualization and Interpretation

Dimensionality reduction is essential for the interpretation and visualization of high-dimensional data. Data with hundreds or thousands of features can be hard to visualize and understand. By reducing the number of dimensions, it becomes easier to visualize the relationships between the data points and gain insights.

A. Visualization

For example, if you have data with 100 features, it's impossible to plot the data in a 2D or 3D space. By reducing the dimensions, you can project the data into two or three dimensions, allowing you to visualize it and better understand the structure. This is especially useful in exploratory data analysis, where you want to get an initial sense of the data distribution and possible clusters.

Popular dimensionality reduction techniques, such as Principal Component Analysis (PCA), project high-dimensional data onto lower-dimensional subspaces while preserving the variance in the data, allowing you to plot and interpret complex datasets visually.

B. Better Feature Understanding

Reducing dimensions can also help identify the most important features that contribute to the data's underlying patterns. By focusing on the most significant components or features, dimensionality reduction can highlight the factors that have the most influence on the predictions, leading to better interpretability and understanding of the model.

4. Dealing with Multicollinearity

In some datasets, certain features may be highly correlated with one another. For example, in financial data, metrics like total revenue and net income may be strongly related. This can cause multicollinearity, where the redundancy between features can distort model coefficients, leading to instability in the model's predictions.

Dimensionality reduction can help mitigate multicollinearity by transforming correlated features into a smaller number of independent components, ensuring that the machine learning model is not unduly influenced by correlated variables. Techniques such as PCA project the data onto orthogonal components, removing redundancy and improving the stability and performance of linear models.

5. Feature Selection vs. Dimensionality Reduction

It's important to differentiate between feature selection and dimensionality reduction, as both aim to reduce the number of features in a dataset but in different ways:

A. Feature Selection

Feature selection involves selecting a subset of the original features based on certain criteria (e.g., statistical tests, importance scores, etc.). In feature selection, the original features are preserved, and irrelevant or redundant features are removed.

B. Dimensionality Reduction

Dimensionality reduction, on the other hand, creates new features by transforming the original features into a lower-dimensional space. These new features (e.g., the principal components in PCA) are linear combinations of the original features, and they capture the most important variance in the data.

Both approaches can be useful depending on the problem, but dimensionality reduction is typically employed when you want to preserve the data's underlying structure in a reduced form, while feature selection is preferred when you want to maintain the original features but remove irrelevant ones.

6. Popular Dimensionality Reduction Techniques

Several dimensionality reduction techniques are commonly used, each with its strengths and applications. Here are some popular methods:

A. Principal Component Analysis (PCA)

PCA is one of the most widely used dimensionality reduction techniques. It works by finding the directions (principal components) in the feature space that capture the most variance in the data. PCA projects the data onto these directions, reducing the dimensionality while retaining as much variance as possible. PCA is often used in exploratory data analysis and preprocessing for machine learning.

B. t-Distributed Stochastic Neighbor Embedding (t-SNE)

t-SNE is a nonlinear dimensionality reduction technique that is particularly useful for visualizing high-dimensional data in 2D or 3D. t-SNE focuses on preserving the pairwise distances between data points in high-dimensional space, making it effective for visualizing clusters or complex patterns.

C. Linear Discriminant Analysis (LDA)

LDA is a supervised dimensionality reduction technique often used for classification tasks. It works by maximizing the separability between different classes in the data, making it particularly useful when you want to reduce dimensions for a classification problem while preserving the class structure.

D. Autoencoders

Autoencoders are a type of neural network used for dimensionality reduction. The encoder part of the network compresses the data into a lower-dimensional representation, while the decoder attempts to reconstruct the original data. Autoencoders are particularly useful for complex datasets with nonlinear relationships between features.

Dimensionality reduction is a powerful tool in machine learning that helps mitigate the curse of dimensionality, improve model performance, reduce noise, and enhance the interpretability of data. By reducing the number of features in a dataset, dimensionality reduction allows for faster computation, better generalization, and easier visualization of high-dimensional data.

Whether you're dealing with large datasets, high-dimensional feature spaces, or seeking to improve model efficiency and interpretability, dimensionality reduction techniques provide a valuable way to extract the most meaningful information while simplifying the data. Understanding when and why to apply dimensionality reduction is an essential skill for data scientists and machine learning practitioners, as it enables them to tackle complex problems with more manageable datasets.

9.2 Principal Component Analysis (PCA)

Principal Component Analysis (PCA) is one of the most widely used techniques in machine learning and data science for dimensionality reduction. It is a linear transformation technique that reduces the number of features in a dataset while preserving as much variance (or information) as possible. PCA is particularly useful when dealing with high-dimensional data, and it helps in visualizing, understanding, and simplifying complex datasets.

In this section, we will explore how PCA works, its steps, and its applications in machine learning. We will also examine the mathematical foundations of PCA, its advantages, limitations, and real-world use cases.

1. What is Principal Component Analysis (PCA)?

PCA is a statistical technique used to transform a dataset of potentially correlated features into a set of linearly uncorrelated features called principal components. These principal components are ordered by the amount of variance they capture from the original data. The first principal component accounts for the most variance, the second component accounts for the second most, and so on.

The primary goal of PCA is to reduce the dimensionality of a dataset, making it easier to work with, while preserving as much information as possible. By focusing on the directions that capture the most variance, PCA reduces redundancy in the data, leading to simpler models and more efficient computations.

2. How Does PCA Work?

PCA involves several key steps, which we'll outline in detail:

A. Step 1: Standardize the Data

PCA is sensitive to the scale of the features, so it is important to standardize the dataset before applying PCA. This involves transforming the data so that each feature has a mean of 0 and a standard deviation of 1.

Mathematically, standardization is done by subtracting the mean of each feature from the data and dividing by the standard deviation:

$$X' = \frac{X - \mu}{\sigma}$$

where X is the original data, μ is the mean, and σ is the standard deviation of each feature.

B. Step 2: Compute the Covariance Matrix

After standardizing the data, PCA proceeds by calculating the covariance matrix, which captures the relationships between the features. The covariance matrix is a square matrix that shows how pairs of features vary with respect to each other.

The covariance matrix C for a dataset X' with n samples and m features is calculated as:

$$C = \frac{1}{n}X'^{T}X'$$

where X'^{T} is the transpose of the standardized data matrix.

A key point to note is that if features are highly correlated, the covariance between them will be high, indicating redundancy in the data.

C. Step 3: Compute the Eigenvalues and Eigenvectors

The next step in PCA is to compute the eigenvalues and eigenvectors of the covariance matrix. Eigenvectors represent the directions of maximum variance in the data, and eigenvalues represent the magnitude of the variance along each eigenvector.

Mathematically, an eigenvalue λ and eigenvector v satisfy the equation:

$$Cv = \lambda v$$

where C is the covariance matrix, v is the eigenvector, and λ is the eigenvalue.

The eigenvectors define the directions (or axes) of the new feature space, and the eigenvalues tell us how much variance is captured along each axis. The eigenvector with the largest eigenvalue corresponds to the direction of maximum variance in the data.

D. Step 4: Sort Eigenvalues and Eigenvectors

After calculating the eigenvalues and eigenvectors, the next step is to sort the eigenvalues in descending order. This allows us to prioritize the components (eigenvectors) that capture the most variance in the data.

By sorting the eigenvalues, we can then rank the eigenvectors and select the top ones that capture the most significant variance in the data.

E. Step 5: Project the Data onto the Principal Components

The final step is to **project** the original data onto the top k principal components. To do this, we take the eigenvectors corresponding to the k largest eigenvalues and form a new matrix. The original data is then multiplied by this matrix to obtain the transformed dataset in the new lower-dimensional space.

If we have k components, the transformation is:

$$X_{\text{new}} = X' \cdot W$$

where W is the matrix of eigenvectors corresponding to the top k eigenvalues, and X_{new} is the transformed dataset.

This transformed data is now in a lower-dimensional space, with the most important information retained.

3. Mathematical Intuition Behind PCA

At the heart of PCA is the concept of variance. PCA aims to find directions (principal components) in which the data exhibits the most variance. These directions are determined by the eigenvectors of the covariance matrix, and the magnitude of variance along these directions is given by the corresponding eigenvalues.

The intuition behind PCA can be understood as follows:

- The data points in the original feature space are spread out in multiple directions. Some of these directions may have little or no variation (i.e., the data points are closely packed together along these axes).
- PCA identifies the directions where the data varies the most and projects the data along these new axes, effectively reducing the dimensionality while maintaining the most important variations in the data.

4. Benefits of PCA

PCA has several key benefits, especially when working with high-dimensional data:

A. Dimensionality Reduction

PCA is primarily used to reduce the number of features or dimensions in a dataset while retaining as much of the original variance as possible. This makes the dataset easier to visualize and process, and it helps speed up machine learning algorithms.

B. Noise Reduction

By focusing on the principal components that capture the most variance, PCA reduces the impact of noise or small fluctuations in the data that may not be important. It can thus lead to more stable and generalizable models.

C. Improved Interpretability

PCA can make it easier to interpret complex datasets by reducing the number of features. In some cases, the principal components may provide insight into the underlying structure of the data that was not apparent in the high-dimensional space.

D. Avoiding Overfitting

Reducing the number of features in the data can help prevent overfitting, especially when the number of samples is small relative to the number of features. PCA removes less important features that might lead to overfitting and improves the generalization ability of models.

5. Applications of PCA

PCA is widely used in various fields, from machine learning to signal processing. Some common applications include:

A. Data Preprocessing for Machine Learning

PCA is often used as a preprocessing step to reduce the dimensionality of the data before feeding it into machine learning models. It is especially useful when dealing with datasets with many features, as it can help speed up training and improve model performance.

B. Image Compression

In image processing, PCA can be used to compress images by reducing the number of pixels while retaining the most important features. This is done by applying PCA to the pixel values and keeping only the most significant components.

C. Visualization

PCA is used for visualizing high-dimensional data by reducing it to two or three dimensions. This makes it easier to visualize the structure of the data, such as clusters or patterns, in a 2D or 3D plot.

D. Gene Expression Analysis

In bioinformatics, PCA is often used to analyze gene expression data, where the number of genes (features) can be very large. By reducing the dimensions, PCA helps identify patterns or groupings in the gene expression profiles.

E. Speech and Audio Signal Processing

PCA is used in speech recognition and audio signal processing to reduce the complexity of audio data and extract key features for analysis.

6. Limitations of PCA

While PCA is a powerful tool, it does have some limitations:

A. Linear Assumption

PCA assumes that the relationships between features are linear. It may not perform well if the underlying relationships in the data are non-linear, as it will not capture complex patterns that require non-linear transformations.

B. Interpretability of Principal Components

The principal components generated by PCA are linear combinations of the original features, which can sometimes make it difficult to interpret the meaning of these components in the context of the original data.

C. Sensitivity to Scaling

PCA is sensitive to the scaling of features. If the features are not standardized (i.e., having different units or ranges), the results of PCA may be biased toward the features with larger ranges.

Principal Component Analysis (PCA) is a powerful technique for dimensionality reduction, which helps in simplifying complex datasets while retaining most of their important information. By transforming the data into a new coordinate system where the axes (principal components) capture the most variance, PCA reduces the number of features, improves computational efficiency, and mitigates issues such as multicollinearity and overfitting.

PCA is widely used in various fields, including machine learning, image processing, bioinformatics, and signal processing. Despite its limitations, such as the linearity assumption and sensitivity to scaling, PCA remains one of the most effective and widely used techniques for reducing dimensionality in high-dimensional datasets.

9.3 t-SNE for Visualization

t-SNE (t-Distributed Stochastic Neighbor Embedding) is a popular dimensionality reduction technique specifically designed for the visualization of high-dimensional data. Unlike traditional methods like Principal Component Analysis (PCA), which focus on retaining variance, t-SNE emphasizes preserving the local structure of the data. This makes t-SNE particularly well-suited for visualizing complex datasets, such as clusters, while reducing the number of dimensions for easier interpretation.

In this section, we'll explore how t-SNE works, its key advantages, its limitations, and its practical applications, especially in the context of data visualization.

1. What is t-SNE?

t-SNE is a non-linear dimensionality reduction technique that converts high-dimensional data into two or three dimensions for visualization purposes. It is often used to project data points from a high-dimensional space into a lower-dimensional space while preserving the relationships between data points. Unlike PCA, which uses linear projections, t-SNE focuses on preserving the local structure of the data, such as clusters or neighborhoods, in the lower-dimensional representation.

The primary objective of t-SNE is to minimize the difference between the pairwise similarities of points in the original high-dimensional space and their corresponding points in the lower-dimensional space. The resulting lower-dimensional space can then be plotted, making it easier to visualize the structure of complex data.

2. How Does t-SNE Work?

The working of t-SNE can be broken down into several steps:

A. Pairwise Similarities in High-Dimensional Space

t-SNE starts by calculating the pairwise similarities between data points in the high-dimensional space. The similarity between two points is defined using a probability distribution, where nearby points have higher probabilities of being similar.

The similarity between two points x_i and x_j is calculated using a Gaussian distribution, where the variance depends on the distance between the points:

$$p_{ij} = \frac{\exp(-\|x_i - x_j\|^2/2\sigma^2)}{\sum_{k \neq i} \exp(-\|x_i - x_k\|^2/2\sigma^2)}$$

where $\|x_i - x_j\|$ is the Euclidean distance between points x_i and x_j, and σ is a parameter that controls the scale of the similarities.

B. Probabilities in Lower-Dimensional Space

Next, t-SNE constructs a similar probability distribution in the lower-dimensional space. The challenge is to preserve the pairwise relationships between points as much as possible when projecting them into lower dimensions.

In the low-dimensional space, the similarities between points are represented by another probability distribution, which is typically a Student's t-distribution with one degree of freedom (also known as the Cauchy distribution). The heavy tails of this distribution allow t-SNE to focus on maintaining local pairwise distances and avoid crowding points that are far apart.

C. Minimizing the Kullback-Leibler Divergence

The goal of t-SNE is to minimize the difference between the probability distributions in the high-dimensional and low-dimensional spaces. This is done by minimizing the Kullback-Leibler (KL) divergence, a measure of how one probability distribution diverges from a second, expected probability distribution. The objective is to make the pairwise similarities between data points in both spaces as similar as possible.

The KL divergence for t-SNE is defined as:

$$KL(P\|Q) = \sum_i \sum_j p_{ij} \log \frac{p_{ij}}{q_{ij}}$$

where p_{ij} and q_{ij} are the probabilities in the high-dimensional and low-dimensional spaces, respectively. The optimization process adjusts the points in the lower-dimensional space to minimize this divergence.

D. Gradient Descent Optimization

t-SNE uses gradient descent to minimize the KL divergence. Starting with a random initialization of points in the lower-dimensional space, t-SNE iteratively updates the positions of the points to minimize the divergence. This process can be computationally expensive, especially with large datasets, as it involves calculating pairwise distances and optimizing the positions of all points.

3. Advantages of t-SNE

t-SNE offers several advantages, especially for visualizing complex, high-dimensional data:

A. Preservation of Local Structure

One of the key strengths of t-SNE is its ability to preserve the local structure of the data. This means that points that are similar or close together in the high-dimensional space will also be close together in the lower-dimensional representation. t-SNE excels at revealing clusters or patterns that might be hard to identify in high-dimensional data.

B. Non-Linear Dimensionality Reduction

Unlike PCA, which uses linear projections, t-SNE is a non-linear technique. This makes it well-suited for data with non-linear relationships. t-SNE can capture more complex relationships and reveal underlying structures that PCA might miss.

C. Intuitive Visualizations

t-SNE is particularly useful for visualizing high-dimensional data in 2D or 3D. The resulting plots often show clear clusters or groupings of data points, making it easier to interpret and understand the data. For example, t-SNE is frequently used in clustering tasks to visualize the formation of groups or categories in the data.

D. Works Well with Sparse Data

t-SNE can handle sparse data well, where many of the features are zero. It can capture underlying patterns even when the data is sparse, which is useful in applications like text analysis and natural language processing (NLP).

4. Limitations of t-SNE

While t-SNE is powerful, it also has several limitations:

A. Computational Complexity

t-SNE can be computationally expensive, especially when working with large datasets. The optimization process requires calculating pairwise distances between all data points, which can be slow as the number of points increases. For very large datasets, the algorithm may become impractical without optimizations or approximations.

B. Loss of Global Structure

While t-SNE does a great job of preserving the local structure, it does not necessarily preserve the global structure of the data. This means that while clusters or groups in the data will be maintained in the lower-dimensional space, the relative distances between clusters may not be accurate.

C. Parameter Sensitivity

The results of t-SNE can be sensitive to its hyperparameters, such as the learning rate and the number of iterations. Different choices for these parameters can lead to different visualizations, which can sometimes be misleading if the parameters are not tuned correctly.

D. Non-deterministic Results

t-SNE is not a deterministic algorithm, meaning that different runs can produce slightly different results. This is due to the random initialization of the points in the lower-dimensional space. To obtain more stable results, it is common practice to run t-SNE multiple times and examine the consistency of the visualizations.

5. Applications of t-SNE

t-SNE is widely used in data exploration and visualization, particularly in the following areas:

A. Clustering and Pattern Recognition

t-SNE is often used in unsupervised learning to visualize the structure of clusters or patterns in the data. By reducing the data to two or three dimensions, it becomes easier to identify clusters that might not be apparent in the high-dimensional space.

B. Image Analysis

In computer vision, t-SNE is commonly used to visualize the features learned by deep neural networks. After training a model, t-SNE can be applied to the activations of intermediate layers to understand how the model is organizing features and capturing patterns in images.

C. Natural Language Processing (NLP)

t-SNE is also popular in NLP for visualizing word embeddings (e.g., Word2Vec or GloVe). These embeddings represent words in high-dimensional vector spaces, and t-SNE can be used to project them into 2D or 3D space for visual inspection. This can help reveal relationships between words, such as semantic similarity or clustering of words with similar meanings.

D. Gene Expression Analysis

t-SNE is frequently applied to gene expression data to visualize how genes cluster based on their expression levels. This can help identify patterns in genetic data, such as groupings of genes that have similar functions or behaviors.

t-SNE is a powerful technique for visualizing high-dimensional data. Its ability to preserve the local structure of the data makes it particularly useful for identifying clusters and patterns in complex datasets. While it excels at revealing relationships in data that are difficult to see in higher dimensions, it does have some limitations, such as computational complexity and sensitivity to hyperparameters.

Despite these limitations, t-SNE remains a valuable tool in the data scientist's toolkit, especially for exploratory data analysis, clustering, and visualization tasks. By using t-

SNE, practitioners can gain a deeper understanding of their data and uncover hidden patterns that might otherwise go unnoticed.

9.4 Autoencoders for Dimensionality Reduction

Autoencoders are a type of neural network that are designed to learn an efficient representation of data, typically for the purpose of dimensionality reduction, noise reduction, or feature extraction. Unlike traditional linear methods like Principal Component Analysis (PCA), autoencoders are non-linear models that can capture more complex patterns and relationships in the data. They are a powerful tool in the deep learning toolbox, and they have applications across various fields, including image processing, anomaly detection, and data compression.

In this section, we will explore the workings of autoencoders, how they can be used for dimensionality reduction, their advantages and limitations, and their practical applications.

1. What is an Autoencoder?

An autoencoder is a type of artificial neural network designed to learn a compressed, low-dimensional representation (encoding) of the input data. The network consists of two main parts:

Encoder: This part of the autoencoder compresses the input data into a lower-dimensional space. The encoder learns to map the high-dimensional input to a smaller representation by using a series of layers (usually fully connected layers).

Decoder: This part reconstructs the input data from the compressed representation created by the encoder. The goal of the decoder is to recreate the input as accurately as possible from its lower-dimensional encoding.

The network is trained in such a way that the reconstruction error (typically measured as mean squared error or binary cross-entropy) between the input and the output is minimized. Essentially, the autoencoder learns to represent the data in a compressed form that retains the most significant features of the original data.

2. How Does an Autoencoder Work for Dimensionality Reduction?

Autoencoders are commonly used for dimensionality reduction because they can learn a compact representation of data that captures its most important features. Here's how they work for this purpose:

A. Encoder Phase:

The encoder takes the high-dimensional input data and compresses it into a smaller set of variables, typically by passing the data through one or more layers of the neural network.

The encoder's goal is to capture the most important features of the input data in the compressed representation. The layer in the middle of the network, often referred to as the bottleneck layer, contains this low-dimensional representation, which is a compressed version of the input data.

Mathematically, the encoder function is:

$$h = f_{encoder}(x)$$

B. Decoder Phase:

The decoder takes this low-dimensional representation and tries to reconstruct the original high-dimensional data as closely as possible.

The decoder is trained to minimize the reconstruction error, which measures how close the output of the decoder is to the input data. This error is used to adjust the parameters of both the encoder and decoder during training.

Mathematically, the decoder function is:

$$\hat{x} = f_{decoder}(h)$$

C. Training the Autoencoder:

During training, the goal is to minimize the difference between the original input data x and the reconstructed output $\hat{x}$. This is typically done using a loss function, such as mean squared error (MSE):

$$L(x, \hat{x}) = \|x - \hat{x}\|^2$$

The network is trained using backpropagation and gradient descent, adjusting the weights of the encoder and decoder to minimize the reconstruction error.

Once the autoencoder is trained, the encoder part of the network can be used independently to map new input data into its compressed, lower-dimensional representation.

3. Types of Autoencoders

There are several variations of autoencoders, each designed for specific use cases or to overcome certain limitations of the basic model. Some common types include:

A. Vanilla Autoencoder

The standard autoencoder architecture, consisting of a symmetric encoder and decoder. It is suitable for simple applications where the data is relatively straightforward and there is no need for advanced features such as noise handling or regularization.

B. Denoising Autoencoder (DAE)

A denoising autoencoder is trained to reconstruct the original, noise-free input from a corrupted version of the input. This makes it particularly useful for noise reduction, where the goal is to remove noise from the data while preserving the important features.

In this case, the encoder takes the noisy data as input, and the decoder learns to output the clean version of the data. This approach can be used for image denoising or recovering missing values in data.

C. Sparse Autoencoder

A sparse autoencoder includes a sparsity constraint on the encoding. This forces the network to learn representations where only a small number of neurons in the bottleneck layer are active at any given time. This can help the model focus on the most important features of the data and is often used for feature extraction in high-dimensional data.

D. Variational Autoencoder (VAE)

A variational autoencoder is a generative model that learns a probabilistic mapping between the input data and the compressed representation. Unlike the standard autoencoder, which maps data to a single point in the latent space, VAEs map data to a distribution. This makes VAEs particularly useful for tasks like image generation or data augmentation.

4. Advantages of Autoencoders for Dimensionality Reduction

Autoencoders offer several advantages for dimensionality reduction over traditional methods like PCA:

A. Non-Linear Dimensionality Reduction

Unlike PCA, which is a linear technique, autoencoders can capture non-linear relationships in the data. This makes them more powerful for data that is highly complex or non-linear, such as images, audio, or text data.

B. Learned Features

Autoencoders learn to extract important features from the data automatically. This is particularly useful when the data is high-dimensional and manually selecting features may not be feasible.

C. Adaptable Architecture

The architecture of autoencoders can be easily adjusted to suit different types of data. For instance, convolutional autoencoders are often used for image data, while recurrent autoencoders are used for sequential data like time series or text.

D. Effective for Unsupervised Learning

Autoencoders are unsupervised models, meaning they do not require labeled data to train. This makes them ideal for situations where labeled data is scarce or expensive to obtain, but large amounts of unlabeled data are available.

5. Applications of Autoencoders

Autoencoders have a wide range of applications across different domains:

A. Data Compression

Autoencoders are often used for data compression, where the encoder reduces the dimensionality of the data and the decoder reconstructs the data. This can be useful for storing or transmitting large amounts of data more efficiently, such as compressing images or video files.

B. Anomaly Detection

Autoencoders can be trained to learn the normal distribution of the data. Once trained, the reconstruction error can be used to detect anomalies. If the model is unable to reconstruct a new data point accurately (i.e., if the reconstruction error is large), the data point is considered an anomaly. This technique is used in fraud detection, equipment monitoring, and cybersecurity.

C. Denoising and Image Restoration

Denoising autoencoders can be used to remove noise from images or other types of data. They are particularly useful in tasks like image enhancement, where the goal is to recover a clean image from a noisy version.

D. Feature Learning and Preprocessing

Autoencoders can be used to learn compressed representations of data, which can be used as features for downstream machine learning tasks. This is particularly useful when the original features are high-dimensional or not well-suited for use in traditional machine learning models.

E. Generative Modeling

Variational Autoencoders (VAEs) are widely used in generative tasks such as image generation, data augmentation, and unsupervised learning. They can generate new data samples by sampling from the learned latent space.

6. Limitations of Autoencoders

While autoencoders are powerful, they do have some limitations:

A. Training Complexity

Training autoencoders can be computationally intensive and time-consuming, especially for large datasets. Proper tuning of the network architecture, regularization techniques, and hyperparameters is required for good performance.

B. Overfitting

Autoencoders are prone to overfitting, especially when the network is too complex or when there is not enough training data. Regularization techniques such as dropout or early stopping can help mitigate this risk.

C. Interpretability

The features learned by an autoencoder in the bottleneck layer may be difficult to interpret. While the encoder learns to compress the data, the resulting low-dimensional representation may not always correspond to easily interpretable features.

Autoencoders are a versatile and powerful tool for dimensionality reduction, offering significant advantages over traditional linear methods like PCA, especially when dealing with non-linear data. They can learn efficient representations of high-dimensional data, handle complex relationships, and are widely used in fields such as image processing, anomaly detection, and feature extraction.

Despite their strengths, autoencoders have limitations, such as training complexity and susceptibility to overfitting, but these can often be mitigated through careful design and regularization techniques. When used appropriately, autoencoders can provide a robust solution for many machine learning tasks requiring dimensionality reduction and feature learning.

10. Anomaly Detection & Association Rules

Detecting fraud, network intrusions, and unusual patterns requires anomaly detection techniques. This chapter explores Isolation Forest, One-Class SVM, and Association Rule Learning (Apriori, FP-Growth), showing how they uncover valuable insights from data.

10.1 Identifying Outliers in Data

Outliers are data points that differ significantly from the majority of the data in a dataset. These anomalies or outliers may represent rare events, errors in data collection, or points that do not conform to expected patterns. Identifying outliers is crucial in data preprocessing, as they can have a significant impact on the performance of machine learning models, skew statistical analyses, or indicate important insights.

In this section, we will explore the concept of outliers, why identifying them is important, and the various methods used to detect outliers in data.

1. What Are Outliers?

An outlier is an observation that lies an abnormal distance from other values in a dataset. Outliers are values that appear to deviate significantly from the pattern of the rest of the data. They can either be:

Univariate Outliers: Outliers that occur when considering only one variable or feature. For example, a person's age being recorded as 200 years old in a dataset of typical human ages.

Multivariate Outliers: Outliers that occur when considering multiple variables or features. These points may not appear to be outliers when examined individually but may stand out when considering the relationships between multiple features.

Outliers may arise for several reasons, including errors during data collection, input mistakes, or the presence of rare but important phenomena that the model should learn from.

2. Why is Identifying Outliers Important?

Identifying outliers is a key step in data preprocessing because outliers can affect the results of statistical analyses and machine learning models in the following ways:

A. Impact on Model Performance

Many machine learning algorithms, such as linear regression and k-nearest neighbors (k-NN), are sensitive to outliers. For example, an outlier can disproportionately influence the slope of a regression line in linear regression, leading to biased predictions. Similarly, outliers can affect distance-based algorithms like k-NN, making them less accurate.

B. Statistical Distortion

In statistical modeling, outliers can distort results, leading to incorrect conclusions. For example, the mean can be heavily influenced by extreme values, whereas the median provides a more robust measure of central tendency when outliers are present.

C. Signal for Important Insights

Not all outliers are detrimental. In some cases, outliers represent valuable insights into rare events, fraud detection, or system malfunctions. For example, outliers in financial transactions might indicate fraudulent activity.

D. Quality Control

In data cleaning processes, identifying outliers helps in removing erroneous data points that may have resulted from faulty sensors, incorrect data entry, or technical issues, leading to more accurate analyses.

3. Types of Outliers

There are various types of outliers, each requiring different detection methods:

A. Global Outliers (Point Outliers)

These are data points that stand far away from the rest of the data. They typically represent rare events or errors in the data. For example, a data point with an extremely high or low value that is far removed from the typical range of the dataset.

B. Contextual Outliers (Conditional Outliers)

Contextual outliers occur when a data point is considered an outlier within a specific context or under certain conditions. For example, a temperature of 40°C might be normal in the summer but an outlier in the winter.

C. Collective Outliers

Collective outliers refer to a group of data points that are anomalous when considered together, but individually might not appear to be outliers. For instance, in time series data, a sudden spike or dip in a series of points can be a collective outlier, even if each individual point is not an outlier.

4. Methods for Identifying Outliers

Several techniques are used to detect outliers in datasets. The appropriate method depends on the type of data (univariate or multivariate) and the nature of the dataset (continuous or categorical).

A. Visual Methods

Visual methods are often the first step in identifying outliers, especially when working with small datasets. Common techniques include:

Boxplots: A boxplot is a graphical representation of the distribution of a dataset. Outliers are typically represented as points outside of the "whiskers" of the boxplot, which indicate the range within 1.5 times the interquartile range (IQR) of the data.

IQR (Interquartile Range): The IQR is the range between the 25th (Q1) and 75th (Q3) percentiles of the data. Outliers are defined as points that fall below $Q1 - 1.5 \times IQR$ or above $Q3 + 1.5 \times IQR$.

Scatter Plots: A scatter plot is useful for visualizing relationships between two variables. Outliers appear as points that lie far from the general distribution of points.

B. Statistical Methods

Statistical methods involve calculating specific thresholds to determine if a data point is an outlier.

Z-Score: The Z-score measures how many standard deviations a data point is from the mean of the data. A Z-score greater than 3 or less than -3 typically indicates an outlier in a normally distributed dataset. Mathematically:

$$Z = \frac{x - \mu}{\sigma}$$

Modified Z-Score: For datasets that are not normally distributed, the modified Z-score can be used, which is based on the median absolute deviation (MAD). This method is more robust to outliers in non-Gaussian data.

IQR Method: As mentioned earlier, the IQR method is another statistical technique. Data points outside the range defined by $Q1 - 1.5 \times IQR$ and $Q3 + 1.5 \times IQR$ are considered outliers.

C. Machine Learning Methods

Machine learning algorithms can also be used to detect outliers, particularly when dealing with high-dimensional or complex datasets. These methods include:

Isolation Forest: Isolation Forest is an unsupervised learning algorithm designed to detect outliers in high-dimensional datasets. The algorithm works by isolating data points through random partitioning. Outliers are identified as points that require fewer partitions to be isolated.

One-Class SVM: One-Class Support Vector Machine is another unsupervised learning method that is used for outlier detection. It tries to find a boundary that best separates the normal data points from the outliers in a high-dimensional space.

K-Means Clustering: K-means clustering can be used for outlier detection by clustering data points into groups and considering points that are far from any cluster centroid as outliers.

D. Distance-Based Methods

These methods measure the distance between a data point and its neighbors to identify outliers.

k-Nearest Neighbors (k-NN): The distance to the k-nearest neighbors can be used to identify outliers. Points that are far from their nearest neighbors are considered outliers. The outlier score can be defined based on the distance from the nearest neighbor or the density of points in the neighborhood.

DBSCAN (Density-Based Spatial Clustering of Applications with Noise): DBSCAN is a density-based clustering algorithm that can be used for outlier detection. It defines outliers as points that do not belong to any cluster (i.e., points with low density in their neighborhood).

5. Dealing with Outliers

Once outliers are identified, the next step is to decide how to handle them. The way outliers are treated depends on the specific problem, the type of outliers, and the impact they have on the analysis or model.

A. Removing Outliers

In some cases, it may be appropriate to remove outliers from the dataset if they are considered errors or noise. This is common when the outliers are due to incorrect data collection or data entry.

B. Transforming the Data

Instead of removing outliers, one could apply data transformations such as log or square root transformations to reduce the impact of extreme values. This can help stabilize variance and make the data more suitable for analysis.

C. Imputing Outliers

If the outliers represent missing or incomplete data, they can be imputed using techniques such as mean, median, or interpolation. However, this method should be used cautiously, as imputing extreme values may introduce bias into the dataset.

D. Modeling Robustly to Outliers

Some machine learning models, such as decision trees or robust regression models, are less sensitive to outliers. Choosing a robust model can help mitigate the impact of outliers while preserving the integrity of the data.

Identifying outliers in data is an essential step in data analysis and preprocessing. Outliers can significantly affect the performance of machine learning models and statistical analyses, so detecting and addressing them appropriately is crucial for obtaining accurate results. By using visual, statistical, machine learning, or distance-based methods, outliers can be identified and handled in a way that minimizes their negative impact on model accuracy and ensures better data quality.

In some cases, outliers may provide valuable insights, such as fraud detection or rare event identification, and should be investigated further. Understanding when to remove, transform, or leave outliers in the dataset depends on the context of the problem at hand.

10.2 Anomaly Detection Techniques

Anomaly detection is the process of identifying rare or unusual events, behaviors, or patterns in data that deviate significantly from the norm. These anomalies, also known as outliers or exceptions, can have significant implications depending on the context. For instance, in financial systems, detecting fraudulent transactions is critical, while in industrial settings, identifying sensor malfunctions or irregular equipment behavior can prevent costly downtime.

In this section, we will explore several techniques for anomaly detection, discussing their methods, use cases, advantages, and limitations. These techniques can be broadly classified into statistical, machine learning-based, distance-based, and clustering-based methods.

1. Why is Anomaly Detection Important?

Anomaly detection is essential for several reasons:

- **Fraud Detection**: Identifying fraudulent activities such as credit card fraud, insurance fraud, or cyber-attacks.
- **Network Security**: Detecting unusual patterns of behavior in network traffic to identify potential intrusions or cyber-attacks.
- **Medical Diagnosis**: Identifying rare diseases or anomalies in medical data that may require urgent attention.
- **Quality Control**: Detecting faulty products in manufacturing processes.
- **Intrusion Detection**: Identifying unusual access patterns in computer systems or networks that could indicate unauthorized access.

2. Types of Anomalies

Anomalies can manifest in different forms depending on the nature of the data:

- **Point Anomalies**: A single data point that deviates significantly from the rest of the data.
- **Example**: A sudden spike in a person's credit card expenditure.

- **Contextual Anomalies**: Data points that are considered anomalies based on the context or environment they occur in.
- **Example**: A high temperature reading of 40°C may be normal in the summer but anomalous during winter.

- **Collective Anomalies**: A collection of related data points that collectively deviate from the norm.
- **Example**: A sudden drop in network traffic followed by a burst of unusual traffic could indicate a security breach or network attack.

3. Anomaly Detection Techniques

There are various techniques used to detect anomalies in data. These techniques can be broadly classified into the following categories:

A. Statistical Methods

Statistical methods for anomaly detection assume that the majority of data points follow a known distribution (e.g., normal distribution) and that anomalies are rare and deviate significantly from this distribution.

Z-Score (Standard Score) Method:

This method involves calculating the Z-score for each data point, which measures how many standard deviations a data point is away from the mean. Points with a Z-score above a certain threshold (usually 3 or -3) are considered anomalies.

Formula:

$$Z = \frac{x - \mu}{\sigma}$$

Use Case: Suitable for data that follows a normal distribution. For example, detecting unusually high or low temperatures.

Grubbs' Test:

This statistical test identifies outliers in a univariate dataset that follows a normal distribution. The test works by iteratively removing the data point with the highest deviation from the mean until no further outliers can be found.

Use Case: Useful when the data follows a Gaussian distribution, often applied in quality control and scientific experiments.

Boxplot and IQR Method:

A boxplot visualizes the distribution of data, with outliers typically defined as points beyond 1.5 times the interquartile range (IQR). The IQR is the difference between the first (Q1) and third (Q3) quartiles of the data.

Use Case: Often used in exploratory data analysis (EDA) to detect univariate outliers.

B. Distance-Based Methods

Distance-based anomaly detection methods identify anomalies based on how far a data point is from others in the feature space. These methods are particularly useful for high-dimensional or continuous data.

k-Nearest Neighbors (k-NN):

This method identifies anomalies based on the distance to the k-nearest neighbors. Data points that are far away from their nearest neighbors are considered anomalies. An anomaly score is calculated as the average distance to the k nearest neighbors.

Use Case: Works well for low-dimensional and high-dimensional datasets, and is often used in detecting fraud or rare events.

Local Outlier Factor (LOF):

LOF is an extension of the k-NN approach that evaluates the density of data points in the neighborhood. It computes the local density deviation of a data point with respect to its neighbors. Points with significantly lower density than their neighbors are flagged as anomalies.

Use Case: Effective for detecting anomalies in datasets with varying densities, such as detecting fraudulent transactions in financial data.

DBSCAN (Density-Based Spatial Clustering of Applications with Noise):

DBSCAN is a clustering algorithm that groups together data points that are close to each other based on a distance metric. Points that do not belong to any cluster (low-density areas) are considered outliers.

Use Case: Suitable for detecting anomalies in spatial data or datasets with non-linear structures, like geographic data or time series data.

C. Machine Learning-Based Methods

Machine learning-based methods use algorithms to learn the structure of normal data and identify data points that deviate from this learned distribution. These methods are often unsupervised, meaning they do not require labeled data.

Isolation Forest:

Isolation Forest is an unsupervised anomaly detection algorithm that works by randomly partitioning the data and isolating the anomalies. It isolates anomalies by partitioning the feature space, making them easier to identify because they require fewer partitions to isolate.

Use Case: Efficient in high-dimensional datasets and for large datasets where speed is critical. Commonly used in fraud detection and network security.

One-Class Support Vector Machine (One-Class SVM):

One-Class SVM is a machine learning algorithm that learns a decision boundary around the normal data points. It works by mapping the data into a higher-dimensional space and finding a hyperplane that separates the normal data points from anomalies.

Use Case: Works well for high-dimensional data, particularly in fraud detection, outlier detection in images, and sensor data.

Autoencoders:

Autoencoders are a type of neural network that learns to compress the input data into a lower-dimensional representation and reconstruct it back. Anomalies are identified based on reconstruction error—data points that have high reconstruction error are considered anomalies.

Use Case: Effective for high-dimensional data, especially in image or time-series anomaly detection.

D. Clustering-Based Methods

Clustering methods assume that normal data points are grouped together in clusters, and anomalies are data points that do not belong to any cluster.

k-Means Clustering:

k-Means clustering can be used for anomaly detection by clustering data points into k groups. Data points that are far from any cluster center are considered anomalies. The distance between a data point and its closest cluster center is used as the anomaly score.

Use Case: Suitable for datasets with clear clusters. Used in customer segmentation and anomaly detection in sensor data.

Gaussian Mixture Models (GMM):

GMM is a probabilistic model that assumes the data is generated from a mixture of several Gaussian distributions. Anomalies are identified by calculating the likelihood of a data point belonging to any of the Gaussian distributions. Points with low likelihood are considered anomalies.

Use Case: Used when data follows a mixture of Gaussian distributions, such as in detecting fraudulent activity in financial data or identifying rare events in time series data.

4. Evaluating Anomaly Detection Models

Evaluating the performance of anomaly detection techniques can be challenging due to the lack of labeled data in many real-world applications. Some common evaluation metrics include:

Precision and Recall: Precision measures the percentage of true anomalies among all identified anomalies, while recall measures the percentage of actual anomalies that were correctly identified.

F1-Score: The F1-score is the harmonic mean of precision and recall, providing a balanced evaluation metric.

ROC-AUC: The area under the Receiver Operating Characteristic (ROC) curve measures the trade-off between true positives and false positives.

Confusion Matrix: A confusion matrix can help evaluate how well the anomaly detection model performs by comparing the predicted labels to the actual labels.

Anomaly detection is a critical process in identifying rare events, outliers, or unusual patterns in data. There are various techniques available, ranging from statistical methods like Z-scores and IQR, to machine learning methods like Isolation Forest, One-Class SVM, and Autoencoders. Each method has its strengths and weaknesses, and the choice of technique depends on the specific application, the type of data, and the desired accuracy.

By selecting the appropriate anomaly detection technique and carefully evaluating its performance, organizations can better identify fraud, network intrusions, sensor malfunctions, or other types of anomalies, ensuring better decision-making, improved security, and enhanced operational efficiency.

10.3 Market Basket Analysis and Association Rule Mining

Market Basket Analysis (MBA) is a technique used to understand patterns in customer behavior by analyzing transactions in a retail or transactional dataset. It helps businesses gain insights into which products are frequently purchased together, allowing for strategies like product bundling, promotions, and store layouts. The most widely used method for MBA is Association Rule Mining, which uncovers relationships between different items within a dataset.

In this section, we will explore the concept of Market Basket Analysis, the fundamentals of Association Rule Mining, key metrics used in evaluating association rules, and practical applications in business.

1. What is Market Basket Analysis?

Market Basket Analysis is a data mining technique that helps businesses analyze the purchasing behavior of customers by identifying patterns in their transaction data. The idea is to find associations between different items purchased together in a basket, or transaction, which could help retailers improve sales and product placement.

For example, when customers buy bread, they may also buy butter. Recognizing such patterns allows businesses to optimize product placement in stores, run effective promotions, and make data-driven decisions about inventory and pricing.

2. Association Rule Mining: An Overview

Association Rule Mining is a key technique used in Market Basket Analysis to discover interesting relationships (or associations) between different items in large datasets. It involves finding frequent itemsets—combinations of items that occur together in a transaction—and then generating association rules based on these itemsets.

Association rules are typically written as:

$$A \Rightarrow B$$

This means, "If item A is bought, then item B is likely to be bought as well."

Example:

- **Rule**: {bread} → {butter}
- **Interpretation**: If a customer buys bread, they are likely to also buy butter.

The goal of association rule mining is to discover relationships that can be used to influence marketing strategies, inventory management, and sales forecasting.

3. Key Concepts in Association Rule Mining

Association Rule Mining has several key concepts that are essential for understanding and implementing the technique effectively:

A. Itemset

An itemset is simply a collection of one or more items that appear in a transaction. For example, in the context of a supermarket, an itemset could be {bread, butter, jam}, which represents a transaction where the customer bought bread, butter, and jam together.

B. Frequent Itemsets

Frequent itemsets are combinations of items that appear together in transactions with a frequency higher than a specified threshold, known as the support threshold. Finding these frequent itemsets is the first step in association rule mining.

C. Association Rule

An association rule is a statement of the form:

$$A \Rightarrow B$$

where A and B are itemsets. The rule implies that the purchase of A leads to the purchase of B. Association rules are derived from frequent itemsets and represent the relationships between items that occur together in transactions.

D. Support

Support is a measure of how frequently an itemset appears in the dataset. It is calculated as:

$$\text{Support}(A) = \frac{\text{Number of transactions containing itemset A}}{\text{Total number of transactions}}$$

Support tells you the frequency of occurrence of the itemset, which helps to identify popular item combinations.

E. Confidence

Confidence is a measure of how often items in B are purchased when A is purchased. It is calculated as:

$$\text{Confidence}(A \Rightarrow B) = \frac{\text{Support}(A \cup B)}{\text{Support}(A)}$$

Confidence tells you the strength of the rule—how likely B is to be bought when A is bought. For example, a high confidence value for the rule {bread} → {butter} means that when bread is bought, butter is very likely to be bought too.

F. Lift

Lift is a measure of the strength of an association rule over random chance. It compares the observed support of the rule to the expected support if the items were independent of each other. It is calculated as:

$$\text{Lift}(A \Rightarrow B) = \frac{\text{Confidence}(A \Rightarrow B)}{\text{Support}(B)}$$

A lift greater than 1 indicates that A and B are more likely to be purchased together than would be expected by chance, while a lift of less than 1 indicates the opposite.

4. The Process of Association Rule Mining

Association Rule Mining typically follows a two-step process:

A. Step 1: Find Frequent Itemsets

The first step is to identify all the frequent itemsets in the dataset. This can be done using various algorithms, the most famous of which is the Apriori algorithm.

Apriori Algorithm: The Apriori algorithm uses a breadth-first search strategy to find frequent itemsets. It starts by identifying single items (1-itemsets) that meet the minimum support threshold. Then, it iteratively combines frequent itemsets to generate larger itemsets (2-itemsets, 3-itemsets, etc.) until no more frequent itemsets can be generated.

FP-Growth Algorithm: Another popular algorithm for mining frequent itemsets is the FP-Growth (Frequent Pattern Growth) algorithm. Unlike Apriori, which generates candidate itemsets, FP-Growth constructs a compact data structure called the FP-tree, which allows for efficient mining of frequent itemsets.

B. Step 2: Generate Association Rules

Once the frequent itemsets are identified, the next step is to generate association rules. For each frequent itemset, the algorithm computes the confidence and lift for potential rules and keeps only those that meet the specified thresholds for both support and confidence.

The rule generation step often involves filtering out weak rules (those with low confidence or lift) to focus on strong, actionable patterns.

5. Example: Market Basket Analysis in Retail

Let's look at an example of how Market Basket Analysis can be applied in a retail scenario:

Dataset:

Suppose we have the following transactions in a grocery store:

Transaction ID	Items Purchased
1	{bread, butter}
2	{bread, jam}
3	{bread, butter, jam}
4	{butter, jam}
5	{bread, butter}

Frequent Itemsets:

Using the Apriori algorithm, we can find the following frequent itemsets with a minimum support threshold of 40% (i.e., items that appear in at least 2 transactions):

- **{bread}**: 4 transactions (80% support)
- **{butter}**: 4 transactions (80% support)
- **{bread, butter}**: 3 transactions (60% support)
- **{bread, jam}**: 2 transactions (40% support)

- **{butter, jam}**: 2 transactions (40% support)

Association Rules:

From the frequent itemsets, we can now generate association rules. Let's focus on the rule {bread} → {butter}:

- Support: $\frac{3}{5} = 60\%$
- Confidence: $\frac{3}{4} = 75\%$
- Lift: $\frac{0.60}{0.80} = 0.75$

Interpretation:

- The rule {bread} → {butter} means that 75% of the transactions that include bread also include butter, which suggests a strong relationship between bread and butter in the store.
- The lift value of 0.75 is less than 1, suggesting that the items bread and butter are likely purchased together, but not as strongly as independent items.

Actionable Insights:

Based on this analysis, the store may consider bundling bread and butter together in promotions, optimizing shelf placement, or recommending butter when a customer purchases bread.

6. Applications of Market Basket Analysis and Association Rule Mining

Market Basket Analysis and Association Rule Mining have several real-world applications, especially in the retail industry. Some common use cases include:

Product Recommendations: By analyzing which items are commonly bought together, retailers can recommend complementary products to customers, both in physical stores and online (e.g., Amazon's "Customers who bought this item also bought...").

Cross-Selling and Up-Selling: Businesses can use association rules to create cross-selling opportunities. For instance, if a customer buys a laptop, the retailer might suggest accessories such as a mouse, keyboard, or laptop bag.

Inventory Management: Retailers can use the results of market basket analysis to optimize stock levels and ensure that related products are available together, reducing the chance of stockouts for high-demand item pairs.

Store Layout Optimization: Understanding which items are frequently purchased together can help design the store layout in a way that groups related products together, encouraging customers to make additional purchases.

Targeted Marketing: Retailers can create targeted marketing campaigns based on customer purchasing behavior, offering personalized discounts or promotions based on customers' previous transactions.

7. Challenges and Limitations

While Market Basket Analysis and Association Rule Mining are powerful tools, they do come with challenges:

Scalability: For large datasets, algorithms like Apriori may be computationally expensive and slow. Efficient algorithms like FP-Growth can mitigate this challenge.

Interpretability: Sometimes, the generated rules can be numerous and complex, making them difficult to interpret and act upon effectively.

Overfitting: Setting too low a threshold for support or confidence may result in a large number of weak or uninteresting rules that don't provide meaningful insights.

Market Basket Analysis and Association Rule Mining provide valuable insights into customer behavior by uncovering hidden patterns in transactional data. By applying these techniques, businesses can improve sales, enhance marketing efforts, optimize inventory, and better serve their customers. As technology continues to evolve, new methods and improvements in scalability will further enhance the value of these techniques in a wide variety of industries.

10.4 Apriori and FP-Growth Algorithms

In Market Basket Analysis and Association Rule Mining, identifying frequent itemsets is the first step in discovering useful relationships between products or events. Two of the most popular algorithms for mining frequent itemsets are the Apriori algorithm and the FP-Growth algorithm. These algorithms are foundational to the discovery of association rules and have been widely used in industries such as retail, e-commerce, and healthcare.

In this section, we will explore both algorithms in detail, discussing their working principles, strengths, weaknesses, and how they are used in practice.

1. The Apriori Algorithm

The Apriori algorithm is one of the earliest and most well-known algorithms for mining frequent itemsets in large transactional databases. It uses a breadth-first search strategy to explore all possible item combinations, iteratively generating larger itemsets based on smaller, frequent itemsets. The key feature of the Apriori algorithm is its use of the apriori property, which states that "if an itemset is frequent, then all of its subsets must also be frequent."

How Apriori Works

The Apriori algorithm follows a level-wise approach, which means it generates itemsets of increasing sizes (1-itemsets, 2-itemsets, 3-itemsets, etc.) at each step, and it prunes the search space at every level.

Generate Candidate Itemsets: Start by generating all individual items (1-itemsets). Then, iterate through the dataset and count the frequency (support) of each itemset. Keep only those itemsets whose support meets or exceeds the user-defined minimum support threshold.

Prune Infrequent Itemsets: The Apriori algorithm uses the apriori property to prune infrequent itemsets at each step. If a subset of an itemset is infrequent, then the itemset itself is also infrequent and can be discarded from further consideration.

Generate Larger Itemsets: Once the frequent itemsets of size 1 are identified, the algorithm generates larger itemsets (size 2, size 3, etc.) by combining frequent itemsets found in the previous iteration. This is done using a process called candidate generation.

Repeat: The algorithm repeats the process until no more frequent itemsets can be generated. The final output consists of all the frequent itemsets and the corresponding association rules.

Example of Apriori Algorithm

Consider a small retail dataset with five transactions:

Transaction ID	Items Purchased
1	{milk, bread}
2	{milk, diaper, beer}
3	{milk, bread, diaper}
4	{bread, diaper, beer}
5	{milk, bread, diaper}

Let's assume the minimum support threshold is 60% (i.e., an itemset must appear in at least 3 transactions).

Step 1: Find 1-itemsets:

- **{milk}**: 4/5 = 80% (Frequent)
- **{bread}**: 4/5 = 80% (Frequent)
- **{diaper}**: 4/5 = 80% (Frequent)
- **{beer}**: 2/5 = 40% (Infrequent)

Discard {beer} since its support is below the threshold.

Step 2: Find 2-itemsets by combining frequent 1-itemsets:

- **{milk, bread}**: 3/5 = 60% (Frequent)
- **{milk, diaper}**: 3/5 = 60% (Frequent)
- **{bread, diaper}**: 3/5 = 60% (Frequent)

The itemsets {milk, beer}, {bread, beer}, and {diaper, beer} are discarded because their support is below the threshold.

Step 3: Find 3-itemsets by combining frequent 2-itemsets:

- {milk, bread, diaper}: 2/5 = 40% (Infrequent)

Since no 3-itemsets meet the support threshold, the algorithm terminates here.

The frequent itemsets found are:

- {milk}, {bread}, {diaper}
- {milk, bread}, {milk, diaper}, {bread, diaper}

These itemsets can now be used to generate association rules.

Pros and Cons of the Apriori Algorithm

Pros:

- **Simple and Intuitive**: Apriori is easy to understand and implement, making it a good choice for beginners.
- **Wide Application**: It can be applied to a wide range of domains, such as retail, e-commerce, healthcare, etc.

Cons:

- **Inefficiency**: The algorithm generates a large number of candidate itemsets, especially in large datasets, which leads to high computational cost and memory usage.
- **Multiple Scans of the Dataset**: Apriori requires multiple scans of the dataset, which makes it slower compared to other algorithms.

2. The FP-Growth Algorithm

The FP-Growth (Frequent Pattern Growth) algorithm is an improvement over the Apriori algorithm, designed to be faster and more memory efficient. Unlike Apriori, which generates candidate itemsets and scans the dataset multiple times, FP-Growth uses a compact data structure called the FP-tree to efficiently find frequent itemsets.

How FP-Growth Works

FP-Growth follows a divide-and-conquer approach. It first builds a compact FP-tree, which is a tree-like structure that stores the transaction data in a compressed form. It then recursively mines the FP-tree to find frequent itemsets without generating candidate itemsets.

Build the FP-Tree:

- First, the algorithm scans the dataset once to find frequent 1-itemsets.
- The frequent 1-itemsets are sorted in descending order of their support count.
- Then, an FP-tree is constructed by iterating through the dataset and inserting transactions into the tree. Each path in the tree represents a transaction, and each node represents an item in that transaction.

Mine the FP-Tree:

Once the FP-tree is built, the algorithm mines the tree recursively to find frequent itemsets. Starting from the leaf nodes, FP-Growth recursively explores itemsets and their frequent extensions.

Recursive Mining:

For each frequent item, FP-Growth generates a conditional FP-tree that contains all transactions containing that item, and the process continues recursively until no more frequent itemsets are found.

Example of FP-Growth Algorithm

Let's consider the same dataset:

Transaction ID	Items Purchased
1	{milk, bread}
2	{milk, diaper, beer}
3	{milk, bread, diaper}
4	{bread, diaper, beer}
5	{milk, bread, diaper}

Using the minimum support threshold of 60%, we find that frequent 1-itemsets are:

- {milk}, {bread}, {diaper}

The FP-tree is constructed by sorting items by their support count:

- {milk} → 4
- {bread} → 4
- {diaper} → 4

Then, the transactions are inserted into the FP-tree.

Once the FP-tree is built, the algorithm proceeds to recursively mine the tree, generating frequent itemsets similar to Apriori, but with greater efficiency due to the compact structure of the tree.

Pros and Cons of the FP-Growth Algorithm

Pros:

- **Efficient**: FP-Growth requires only two passes over the dataset, making it faster than Apriori, especially for large datasets.
- **Memory Efficient**: It stores only the compressed FP-tree, reducing memory requirements.

Cons:

- **Complexity**: The algorithm is more complex than Apriori, and the construction of the FP-tree can be difficult to implement.
- **Not Intuitive**: The FP-tree structure can be harder to understand for beginners, making the algorithm less approachable.

3. Comparison of Apriori and FP-Growth

Feature	Apriori	FP-Growth
Algorithm Type	Candidate-based, Level-wise search	Pattern-growth, tree-based search
Data Structure	No special data structure	Uses an FP-tree (compact tree structure)
Scans of Dataset	Multiple scans of dataset	Two passes over the dataset
Efficiency	Less efficient, especially for large datasets	More efficient, especially for large datasets
Memory Usage	Can be memory-intensive for large datasets	Memory-efficient due to FP-tree structure
Complexity	Simple and intuitive	More complex to implement
Speed	Slower due to candidate generation	Faster due to FP-tree compression

Both the Apriori and FP-Growth algorithms are essential tools for frequent itemset mining and association rule generation. Apriori is simple and intuitive, making it a good choice for small datasets or educational purposes. However, for larger datasets, FP-Growth is more efficient, as it avoids the candidate generation step and uses a compact FP-tree to store and mine frequent itemsets.

In practice, FP-Growth is often preferred when working with large-scale data, while Apriori may still be useful in cases where the dataset is smaller or computational efficiency is not a critical factor.

11. Neural Networks & Deep Learning

Artificial Neural Networks (ANNs) are the foundation of deep learning. In this chapter, you'll learn how neurons, activation functions, and backpropagation work together to power intelligent systems, setting the stage for deep learning applications.

11.1 Introduction to Artificial Neural Networks

Artificial Neural Networks (ANNs) are a powerful class of machine learning algorithms inspired by the structure and functioning of the human brain. They have gained significant attention and success in a variety of fields, including image recognition, natural language processing, and autonomous systems. At their core, ANNs are designed to model complex patterns and relationships in data by simulating the way biological neural networks process information.

In this section, we will explore the fundamentals of Artificial Neural Networks, including their structure, how they work, and their applications in modern machine learning.

What are Artificial Neural Networks?

An Artificial Neural Network is a computational model composed of interconnected layers of nodes, which are also called neurons. These neurons are designed to mimic the neurons in the human brain. Just as biological neurons transmit signals and process information, artificial neurons work together to recognize patterns, classify information, and make predictions.

A neural network learns to map input data to output predictions by adjusting the weights of connections between neurons. This learning process is facilitated by training, where the network uses examples from a labeled dataset to refine its understanding of the data. Through this iterative process, an ANN gradually learns the optimal representation of the data and the best model to make accurate predictions.

Basic Structure of an Artificial Neural Network

The architecture of an artificial neural network can be broken down into several layers. These layers are responsible for transforming the input data into the desired output. The most common architecture of an ANN consists of three main types of layers:

Input Layer: The input layer is the first layer of the network and serves as the interface between the external data and the neural network. Each neuron in this layer represents one feature of the input data. For example, if you are working with an image, each pixel might correspond to one input neuron.

Hidden Layers: The hidden layers are the intermediate layers between the input and output layers. Each neuron in a hidden layer is connected to every neuron in the previous layer and the subsequent layer. These neurons process the inputs they receive through weighted connections and apply activation functions to produce an output that is passed to the next layer. Neural networks can have multiple hidden layers, and the depth of these layers can have a significant impact on the network's ability to capture complex patterns in the data. Networks with many hidden layers are often called deep neural networks (DNNs).

Output Layer: The output layer generates the final predictions or classifications based on the learned weights from the hidden layers. The number of neurons in the output layer depends on the type of task. For example, in a binary classification task, there might be a single neuron, while in a multi-class classification task, there could be as many neurons as there are classes.

Each connection between neurons has a weight, which determines the strength and direction of the signal passing from one neuron to another. During the training process, these weights are adjusted to minimize the error between the predicted output and the actual target output.

Neurons and Activation Functions

Each artificial neuron performs a simple computation, taking in a weighted sum of the inputs and passing the result through an activation function. The activation function introduces non-linearity into the network, which allows ANNs to model complex, non-linear relationships in the data.

Weighted Sum: Each neuron calculates the weighted sum of its inputs:

$$z = w_1 x_1 + w_2 x_2 + \ldots + w_n x_n + b$$

Where:

- w_i are the weights of the connections,

- x_i are the input values,

- b is the bias term (which allows the network to adjust the output independently of the inputs).

Activation Function: After calculating the weighted sum, the result is passed through an activation function. Common activation functions include:

Sigmoid: A logistic function that squashes the output to a range between 0 and 1. It is used in binary classification problems.

$$\sigma(z) = \frac{1}{1 + e^{-z}}$$

ReLU (Rectified Linear Unit): A popular activation function that returns 0 for negative values and the input itself for positive values. ReLU is efficient for deep networks as it helps mitigate the vanishing gradient problem.

$$\text{ReLU}(z) = \max(0, z)$$

Tanh (Hyperbolic Tangent): A function that maps the output to a range between -1 and 1. It is similar to the sigmoid but tends to center the data around 0.

$$\tanh(z) = \frac{e^z - e^{-z}}{e^z + e^{-z}}$$

Softmax: Typically used in multi-class classification, it normalizes the output of neurons to represent probabilities that sum to 1.

These activation functions introduce non-linearity into the network, which enables ANNs to learn and represent complex patterns in the data.

How Do Neural Networks Learn?

Neural networks learn through a process called training, where they adjust their internal parameters (weights and biases) to minimize the difference between their predictions and the actual target values. This process is achieved using a method called backpropagation, which is combined with an optimization technique like gradient descent.

Forward Propagation: During forward propagation, input data is passed through the network, layer by layer, to compute the predicted output. This involves calculating the weighted sum of inputs, applying activation functions, and propagating the result to the next layer.

Loss Function: Once the network has made a prediction, the difference between the predicted output and the actual output is calculated using a loss function (or cost function). The loss function quantifies the error made by the model. Common loss functions include Mean Squared Error (MSE) for regression tasks and Cross-Entropy for classification tasks.

Backpropagation: Backpropagation is the process used to update the weights of the network based on the error. It calculates the gradient of the loss function with respect to each weight using the chain rule of calculus. This gradient tells the network how to adjust the weights to reduce the error. The weights are updated using an optimization algorithm like Gradient Descent, which adjusts the weights in the opposite direction of the gradient to minimize the loss.

Gradient Descent: Gradient descent is an optimization algorithm that adjusts the weights of the network in the direction of the negative gradient to minimize the loss function. The learning rate determines the step size taken towards the minimum, and the process is repeated over many iterations (epochs) until the network converges to the optimal set of weights.

Types of Neural Networks

There are various types of neural network architectures, each designed for specific tasks:

Feedforward Neural Networks (FNNs): The simplest type of neural network, where information flows in one direction, from the input layer to the output layer. It is widely used for basic classification and regression tasks.

Convolutional Neural Networks (CNNs): Used primarily for image and video recognition tasks, CNNs are designed to automatically learn spatial hierarchies of features. They use convolutional layers that apply filters (kernels) to the input data to extract important features such as edges, textures, and shapes.

Recurrent Neural Networks (RNNs): RNNs are used for tasks involving sequential data, such as time series prediction or natural language processing. They have connections that allow information to be passed from one time step to the next, enabling them to learn patterns in sequences of data.

Generative Adversarial Networks (GANs): GANs consist of two networks — a generator and a discriminator — that are trained together in a competitive framework. GANs are used for generating realistic images, videos, and other forms of synthetic data.

Applications of Artificial Neural Networks

ANNs are incredibly versatile and have a wide range of applications across various industries:

- **Image Recognition**: CNNs are used in facial recognition, object detection, and medical imaging (such as detecting tumors in X-rays).
- **Natural Language Processing (NLP):** RNNs and their variants (e.g., LSTMs) are used for tasks like language translation, sentiment analysis, and chatbots.
- **Autonomous Systems**: ANNs are crucial in self-driving cars, where they process data from sensors (such as cameras and LiDAR) to make decisions in real-time.
- **Finance**: ANNs are used for predicting stock prices, fraud detection, and credit scoring.
- **Healthcare**: ANNs help in predicting disease outcomes, identifying medical conditions from diagnostic images, and personalized treatment recommendations.

Artificial Neural Networks are a cornerstone of modern machine learning and artificial intelligence. Their ability to model complex relationships, learn from data, and make accurate predictions has led to groundbreaking advancements across various fields. While they are computationally intensive and require large amounts of data to train, ANNs are powerful tools that have transformed industries from healthcare to finance to autonomous systems.

Understanding the basic structure, learning process, and various applications of ANNs sets the foundation for more advanced topics such as deep learning and neural network architectures. By leveraging these techniques, practitioners can build highly efficient models that tackle some of the most challenging problems in AI today.

11.2 Perceptrons and Activation Functions

Artificial Neural Networks (ANNs) are built on the foundation of a single unit known as the perceptron. Perceptrons are the simplest form of a neural network and serve as the building blocks for more complex architectures. They are designed to simulate the basic function of a neuron in the human brain and are used primarily for binary classification tasks. In this section, we will discuss the perceptron, its structure, how it works, and the role of activation functions in artificial neural networks.

What is a Perceptron?

A perceptron is a single-layer neural network that consists of an input layer, weights, a bias term, and an activation function. It takes a set of input values, processes them through weighted connections, and produces an output value. The perceptron model is a linear classifier, meaning it attempts to find a hyperplane that separates data points belonging to different classes. However, it is important to note that a perceptron is only capable of solving linearly separable problems (problems where a straight line or hyperplane can perfectly divide the classes).

Structure of a Perceptron

The perceptron consists of the following components:

1. **Inputs** $(x_1, x_2, ..., x_n)$: These are the features or attributes of the data that are provided as input to the perceptron. For example, if you're classifying an email as spam or not spam, the inputs could represent the frequency of certain keywords in the email.

2. **Weights** $(w_1, w_2, ..., w_n)$: Each input is associated with a weight that determines the importance of that input. Weights are adjustable parameters that the perceptron learns during the training process.

3. **Bias** (b): The bias term is an additional parameter that allows the perceptron to adjust the output independently of the input values. The bias helps the model make predictions even when all input values are zero.

Summation: The perceptron computes the weighted sum of the inputs plus the bias term. The output of the summation is:

$$z = w_1 x_1 + w_2 x_2 + \ldots + w_n x_n + b$$

5. **Activation Function**: The summation result (z) is passed through an activation function, which determines the output of the perceptron. The activation function applies a transformation to the summation result to produce the final output of the perceptron.

How the Perceptron Works

The perceptron operates in the following steps:

1. **Input and Weighting**: The perceptron receives an input vector ($x_1, x_2, \ldots, x_n$) from the dataset. Each input value is multiplied by its corresponding weight ($w_1, w_2, \ldots, w_n$).

2. **Summation**: The perceptron computes the weighted sum of the inputs, along with the bias term, producing a result z.

3. **Activation**: The summation result z is passed through the **activation function** to produce the final output of the perceptron. The output will be a binary value, typically 0 or 1, depending on whether the result of the activation function exceeds a certain threshold.

4. **Decision Rule**: For a binary classification task, the perceptron uses a threshold (often set to zero) to classify the input:

   - If $z > 0$, the output is 1 (one class).

   - If $z \leq 0$, the output is 0 (the other class).

The perceptron learns by adjusting its weights during the training process, using an algorithm like gradient descent or perceptron learning rule, to minimize the error between predicted outputs and actual labels.

Activation Functions in Artificial Neural Networks

An activation function is a crucial component of neural networks, including perceptrons. It introduces non-linearity into the network, which is necessary for learning complex patterns and solving problems that cannot be separated linearly. Without an activation function, the neural network would simply behave like a linear regressor, unable to capture complex relationships in the data.

There are several types of activation functions used in neural networks. Below are the most common activation functions:

1. Step Function (Threshold Function)

The step function is the simplest form of an activation function and is used in the classic perceptron. It produces binary output based on whether the input exceeds a threshold.

$$f(z) = \begin{cases} 1 & \text{if } z \geq 0 \\ 0 & \text{if } z < 0 \end{cases}$$

- **Pros**: It is easy to implement and understand.
- **Cons**: The step function is discontinuous and not differentiable, which makes it unsuitable for gradient-based optimization techniques like backpropagation.

2. Sigmoid Function

The sigmoid function is a smooth, S-shaped curve that squashes the input value into a range between 0 and 1. It is often used in binary classification tasks, where the output can be interpreted as a probability.

$$\sigma(z) = \frac{1}{1 + e^{-z}}$$

- **Pros**: The sigmoid function is smooth and differentiable, making it suitable for optimization using gradient descent. It also maps input to a probability range between 0 and 1, which is useful for binary classification.
- **Cons**: The sigmoid function suffers from the vanishing gradient problem, where gradients become very small for large or small input values, making it difficult to train deep networks.

3. Tanh Function (Hyperbolic Tangent)

The tanh function is similar to the sigmoid function but squashes the output to a range between -1 and 1.

$$\tanh(z) = \frac{e^z - e^{-z}}{e^z + e^{-z}}$$

- **Pros**: The tanh function is also smooth and differentiable. It has a range between -1 and 1, which can help with data centering and convergence.
- **Cons**: Like the sigmoid function, tanh also suffers from the vanishing gradient problem for very large or small inputs.

4. ReLU (Rectified Linear Unit)

The ReLU activation function is currently one of the most popular choices for deep learning models due to its simplicity and efficiency. ReLU outputs the input value if it is positive and zero otherwise.

$$\mathrm{ReLU}(z) = \max(0, z)$$

- **Pros**: ReLU is computationally efficient and allows for faster training of deep networks. It reduces the likelihood of the vanishing gradient problem.
- **Cons**: ReLU can suffer from the dying ReLU problem, where neurons get "stuck" and always output zero, especially when weights are initialized poorly.

5. Leaky ReLU

The Leaky ReLU is a variant of ReLU that allows a small negative slope for negative input values, preventing the issue of neurons getting stuck at zero.

$$\mathrm{Leaky\ ReLU}(z) = \begin{cases} z & \text{if } z > 0 \\ \alpha z & \text{if } z \leq 0 \end{cases}$$

- **Pros**: Leaky ReLU solves the problem of dying ReLUs by allowing a small negative slope.
- **Cons**: It introduces a small amount of non-linearity for negative inputs, but the choice of α can impact performance.

6. Softmax

The Softmax function is used in multi-class classification tasks. It converts the raw output values of the neural network into probabilities by normalizing them so that the sum of the output probabilities equals 1.

$$\text{Softmax}(z_i) = \frac{e^{z_i}}{\sum_j e^{z_j}}$$

- **Pros**: Softmax ensures that the network's outputs are interpreted as probabilities, which is essential for classification problems with multiple classes.
- **Cons**: Softmax can be computationally expensive when dealing with a large number of classes.

Perceptron Training Process

The perceptron learns by adjusting its weights and bias through an iterative process called perceptron learning rule. During training:

- The perceptron processes each training sample.
- If the prediction is incorrect, the weights are adjusted to reduce the error. Specifically, the weights are updated based on the difference between the predicted and actual output.

The update rule for the weights and bias is as follows:

$$w_i \leftarrow w_i + \Delta w_i$$

$$b \leftarrow b + \Delta b$$

Where:

$$\Delta w_i = \eta(y - \hat{y})x_i$$

$$\Delta b = \eta(y - \hat{y})$$

The perceptron is the simplest neural network model, but it is powerful in its ability to perform binary classification. Activation functions are key to enabling neural networks to model complex, non-linear relationships in data. By choosing the appropriate activation function for a given task, the performance of the network can be significantly improved. Whether you are using simple perceptrons for linear problems or more advanced deep neural networks, understanding perceptrons and activation functions is crucial for building effective AI systems.

11.3 Forward and Backpropagation

In this section, we delve into the two key processes that power the training of artificial neural networks: forward propagation and backpropagation. These two concepts are fundamental to understanding how neural networks learn and improve their performance over time. Let's explore each of these steps in detail and how they contribute to training a neural network.

Forward Propagation

Forward propagation is the process by which the input data flows through the layers of the network to generate predictions or outputs. It is the first step in the neural network's operation, where data is passed through the network's neurons, and each neuron applies a mathematical operation to produce an output. The forward propagation process involves two key components:

Input Layer: This is where the raw data enters the network. The features of the dataset (such as pixels in an image, words in a sentence, or other measurable values) are provided as inputs to the network.

Hidden Layers: The data is then passed through one or more hidden layers in the neural network. Each neuron in the hidden layers performs a weighted sum of its inputs, adds a bias term, and applies an activation function to produce the output. This output is then passed on to the next layer. The network learns by adjusting the weights and biases during training to minimize the error in predictions.

Output Layer: After the input data has passed through the hidden layers, it reaches the output layer. The output layer contains neurons that produce the final prediction. For classification tasks, the output could be a probability distribution (using softmax) for each class, and for regression tasks, it could be a continuous value.

The steps in forward propagation are as follows:

For each neuron in a layer, compute the weighted sum of the inputs:

$$z = w_1 x_1 + w_2 x_2 + \dots + w_n x_n + b$$

- Pass the weighted sum through an activation function $f(z)$ to generate the output:

$$a = f(z)$$

At the end of forward propagation, we have the network's output (or prediction). This output is compared with the true label or target value to calculate the loss, which measures the error or discrepancy between the predicted output and the actual label.

Backpropagation

Backpropagation (short for "backward propagation of errors") is the key algorithm for training neural networks. It is the process by which the network adjusts its weights and biases based on the error from the forward pass to minimize the loss. Backpropagation is the cornerstone of supervised learning in deep learning models, and it uses the chain rule of calculus to propagate the error backward through the network.

In backpropagation, we update the weights and biases of the network by computing the gradient of the loss function with respect to each weight and bias. The process involves two main steps: calculating the error and updating the parameters.

Step 1: Calculate the Error (Loss Function)

The first step in backpropagation is to calculate the error (or loss). This is done by comparing the predicted output (from the forward pass) to the actual target value. The most commonly used loss functions are:

Mean Squared Error (MSE): Used for regression problems, it computes the average squared difference between the predicted and actual values.

$$L = \frac{1}{m} \sum_{i=1}^{m} (y_i - \hat{y}_i)^2$$

Cross-Entropy Loss: Used for classification problems, it measures the difference between the predicted probability distribution (output of the softmax function) and the true label.

$$L = -\sum_{i=1}^{n} y_i \log(\hat{y}_i)$$

Where:

- y_i is the true label (either 0 or 1 for binary classification),

- $\hat{y}_i$ is the predicted probability.

Step 2: Compute Gradients Using the Chain Rule

Once the error (or loss) has been computed, backpropagation uses the chain rule of calculus to compute the gradients (derivatives) of the loss function with respect to the weights and biases in the network.

The chain rule allows us to break down the derivative of the loss function into simpler parts. The gradient of the loss with respect to a weight is calculated by tracing the error back through the network, from the output layer to the input layer.

The general process is as follows:

- Calculate the gradient of the loss with respect to the output of the last layer (the final output layer).
- Propagate this gradient backward through the network, layer by layer, using the chain rule to compute the gradient of the loss with respect to the weights and biases at each layer.

Mathematically, for a given weight w, the gradient of the loss with respect to the weight is:

$$\frac{\partial L}{\partial w} = \frac{\partial L}{\partial a} \cdot \frac{\partial a}{\partial z} \cdot \frac{\partial z}{\partial w}$$

Where:

- $\frac{\partial L}{\partial a}$ is the derivative of the loss with respect to the output of the neuron.

- $\frac{\partial a}{\partial z}$ is the derivative of the activation function.

- $\frac{\partial z}{\partial w}$ is the derivative of the weighted sum with respect to the weight.

By applying the chain rule recursively from the output layer to the input layer, we can compute the gradients for each weight and bias in the network.

Step 3: Update Weights Using Gradient Descent

Once the gradients are computed, backpropagation updates the weights and biases in the network to minimize the loss. The weights and biases are adjusted using gradient descent, which moves the parameters in the direction that reduces the error. The update rule is:

$$w_i \leftarrow w_i - \eta \frac{\partial L}{\partial w_i}$$

$$b \leftarrow b - \eta \frac{\partial L}{\partial b}$$

Where:

- η is the **learning rate**, a small constant that controls the size of the step taken in the direction of the gradient.

- $\frac{\partial L}{\partial w_i}$ is the gradient of the loss with respect to the weight.

By iteratively performing forward propagation and backpropagation, the network gradually learns to adjust its weights and biases to minimize the loss function, thereby improving its performance.

Putting Forward and Backpropagation Together

The process of training a neural network involves alternating between forward propagation and backpropagation in multiple iterations (or epochs):

Forward Propagation: The input data is passed through the network, and the predicted output is generated. The loss is then computed by comparing the predicted output to the true label.

Backpropagation: The error is propagated backward through the network, and the weights and biases are adjusted using gradient descent to minimize the loss.

Repeat: This process is repeated for many iterations, and over time, the network improves its ability to make accurate predictions by updating its weights and biases.

Forward and backpropagation are the core mechanisms behind the training of neural networks. Forward propagation allows the network to make predictions, while backpropagation enables the network to learn from its mistakes by adjusting its parameters to reduce errors. Through iterative training, forward and backpropagation work together to help the network learn complex patterns in data, making neural networks a powerful tool for a wide range of machine learning tasks. Understanding these processes is essential for designing, training, and fine-tuning neural networks effectively.

11.4 Training Deep Neural Networks

Training deep neural networks (DNNs) involves optimizing a network's parameters (weights and biases) to minimize the error between the predicted and actual outputs. However, training deep networks can be more challenging compared to shallow networks due to the complexity, large number of parameters, and potential issues like overfitting, vanishing gradients, and slow convergence. This section covers the key aspects of training deep neural networks, the challenges involved, and strategies used to improve performance and efficiency.

Challenges in Training Deep Neural Networks

Before diving into the training process itself, it's important to understand some common challenges that arise when training deep neural networks:

Vanishing Gradient Problem:

- In very deep networks, the gradients of the loss function can become extremely small as they propagate backward through the layers, making it difficult to adjust the weights effectively. This problem is especially prominent when using activation functions like sigmoid or tanh, which squash the outputs into a small range.

- **Solution**: Using ReLU (Rectified Linear Unit) or its variants (like Leaky ReLU) helps mitigate this issue since they allow for larger gradients and prevent vanishing gradients during backpropagation.

Exploding Gradients:

- In contrast to vanishing gradients, exploding gradients occur when gradients grow exponentially as they propagate backward, resulting in large updates to weights. This can lead to unstable training and a network that fails to converge.
- **Solution**: Gradient clipping is a common technique used to limit the size of the gradients, ensuring they don't grow too large and destabilize the network.

Overfitting:

- Overfitting happens when a model learns the training data too well, including the noise and outliers, resulting in poor generalization to new, unseen data. This is a significant problem in deep learning because deep networks have a large number of parameters, which increases the risk of overfitting.
- **Solution**: Regularization techniques such as Dropout, L2 regularization (weight decay), and early stopping help mitigate overfitting by encouraging the model to generalize better.

Computational Complexity:

- Deep neural networks require substantial computational resources for training, especially when dealing with large datasets and numerous layers. The training process can take a long time without efficient hardware (such as GPUs or TPUs) and proper optimization techniques.
- **Solution**: Techniques like mini-batch gradient descent, using GPU acceleration, and utilizing efficient algorithms like Adam for optimization can speed up the training process.

Training Deep Neural Networks: A Step-by-Step Guide

Now that we know the challenges, let's break down the typical steps involved in training a deep neural network.

Step 1: Define the Network Architecture

The first step is to define the structure of the neural network. This includes determining:

- The number of layers (depth of the network),
- The number of neurons in each layer (width of the network),
- The type of layers (fully connected, convolutional, recurrent, etc.),
- The activation functions for each layer (ReLU, Sigmoid, Tanh, etc.).

The architecture depends on the specific problem you're trying to solve. For example, convolutional neural networks (CNNs) are often used for image classification, while recurrent neural networks (RNNs) are better suited for sequential data like text or time series.

Step 2: Initialize Weights and Biases

The network parameters—weights and biases—are typically initialized randomly or using specific initialization schemes such as:

- **Xavier/Glorot Initialization**: Used for sigmoid/tanh activation functions, this method initializes the weights by drawing them from a distribution with zero mean and variance depending on the number of neurons in the previous layer.
- **He Initialization**: This is used for ReLU and its variants, where weights are initialized using a normal distribution with a mean of 0 and variance adjusted based on the number of input neurons.

Good weight initialization is crucial for avoiding problems like vanishing or exploding gradients during training.

Step 3: Define the Loss Function

The loss function is used to measure the difference between the predicted output and the actual target values. For classification tasks, a common loss function is cross-entropy loss, and for regression tasks, mean squared error (MSE) is often used.

The choice of loss function depends on the type of problem:

- **Binary Classification**: Binary cross-entropy loss.
- **Multi-Class Classification**: Categorical cross-entropy loss.
- **Regression**: Mean squared error.

Step 4: Choose the Optimizer

The optimizer is the algorithm that adjusts the network's weights to minimize the loss function during training. Several optimization techniques are commonly used in deep learning:

- **Stochastic Gradient Descent (SGD):** A basic gradient descent algorithm that updates the weights based on the gradient of the loss with respect to the parameters. It's computationally efficient but often requires careful tuning of the learning rate.
- **Momentum**: Adds a fraction of the previous update to the current update to accelerate convergence and smooth out fluctuations.
- **Adam (Adaptive Moment Estimation):** A popular optimizer that combines the benefits of both AdaGrad and RMSProp. It adapts the learning rate based on the moment estimates of the gradients, making it particularly useful for training deep networks.

Step 5: Train the Network Using Mini-Batch Gradient Descent

In mini-batch gradient descent, the training data is divided into small batches (e.g., 32 or 64 samples per batch). For each batch:

- **Forward Propagation**: The inputs are passed through the network, and the output is computed.
- **Loss Calculation**: The loss is computed based on the predicted output and actual label.
- **Backpropagation**: The gradients of the loss with respect to the network's parameters are computed.
- **Parameter Update**: The weights and biases are updated using the optimizer (e.g., Adam or SGD).

This process is repeated for multiple epochs (iterations over the entire dataset), where the parameters are gradually adjusted to minimize the loss function. Training typically continues until the loss reaches an acceptable value or the model's performance on the validation data stops improving (early stopping).

Step 6: Monitor Performance Using Validation Data

While training on the training data, it's important to validate the network's performance using a separate validation dataset. This helps monitor the model's ability to generalize to unseen data and provides an early indication if overfitting is occurring.

If the loss on the validation set starts to increase while the training loss continues to decrease, this may signal overfitting, and techniques such as early stopping, regularization, or cross-validation can be employed.

Advanced Techniques to Improve Training

Several advanced techniques are used to train deep neural networks more effectively and efficiently:

Dropout:

- Dropout is a regularization technique that randomly "drops out" a percentage of neurons during each training iteration. This prevents the model from becoming too reliant on any particular neuron and helps improve generalization.
- For example, during each iteration, neurons may be randomly set to zero with a certain probability (e.g., 0.2 or 0.5).

Batch Normalization:

Batch normalization normalizes the output of each layer so that it has a mean of 0 and variance of 1. This helps stabilize the learning process and can speed up convergence by reducing the internal covariate shift (the change in the distribution of inputs to a layer during training).

Data Augmentation:

In cases where data is limited (e.g., in image classification tasks), data augmentation techniques (like flipping, rotating, or zooming images) can be applied to artificially increase the size of the dataset and make the model more robust.

Transfer Learning:

Transfer learning involves pretraining a deep neural network on a large dataset (e.g., ImageNet for image classification) and then fine-tuning it for a specific task with a smaller dataset. This helps leverage existing knowledge and speeds up training.

Training deep neural networks is a complex but powerful process. While it comes with various challenges, including vanishing gradients, overfitting, and high computational costs, the use of modern techniques such as advanced optimizers, regularization methods, and specialized architectures has made it feasible to train highly effective and efficient deep models. By carefully designing the network architecture, initializing the parameters correctly, and applying the right optimization and regularization strategies, you can train deep neural networks that perform exceptionally well on a wide range of tasks, from image recognition to natural language processing. Understanding these steps and techniques is crucial for building successful deep learning models.

12. Convolutional Neural Networks (CNNs)

CNNs revolutionized computer vision by enabling machines to "see" and recognize images. This chapter explains how convolutional layers, pooling, and feature extraction work, with hands-on coding examples using TensorFlow and PyTorch.

12.1 Introduction to CNNs and How They Work

Convolutional Neural Networks (CNNs) are a specialized class of neural networks that are particularly well-suited for tasks involving grid-like data, such as images, audio, and video. They have been highly successful in computer vision, speech recognition, natural language processing, and even medical image analysis. CNNs are designed to automatically and adaptively learn spatial hierarchies of features, which makes them especially effective for tasks like object recognition, face detection, and scene segmentation.

In this section, we'll break down the core components of CNNs, explain how they work, and explore why they are so powerful for image processing and other applications.

The Inspiration Behind CNNs

CNNs were inspired by the visual processing that happens in the biological brain, particularly how the human visual system works. The primary inspiration came from Hubel and Wiesel's studies in the 1960s, which demonstrated that the brain processes visual information hierarchically—early layers detect simple features like edges and textures, while later layers combine these features into more complex representations such as shapes and objects.

This hierarchical processing is mimicked in CNNs through layers that perform convolutions, pooling, and non-linear transformations, enabling CNNs to automatically learn spatial features from raw input data.

How CNNs Work: A Layered Approach

A Convolutional Neural Network is composed of several layers, each serving a specific purpose to transform the input data into a meaningful output. The key layers in a CNN include:

1. Convolutional Layer

The convolutional layer is the core building block of a CNN. It is responsible for applying convolutional operations to the input data, typically an image. The convolutional layer consists of a set of learnable filters (also called kernels) that slide over the input image, detecting features like edges, corners, and textures.

- **How it works**: Each filter is a small matrix (e.g., 3x3 or 5x5) that scans the image from left to right and top to bottom, computing a weighted sum of the pixel values it is currently covering. The result is a feature map, which represents the activation (or presence) of a feature in different regions of the image.
- **Example**: A 3x3 filter might detect horizontal edges in an image. As the filter slides across the image, it generates a feature map that highlights where these horizontal edges are present.

The convolution operation is mathematically represented as:

$$\text{Output} = \sum (\text{Filter} \times \text{Input})$$

Each filter is learned during the training process, allowing the network to adapt to the specific features relevant to the task (e.g., detecting faces in an image).

2. Activation Layer (ReLU)

After the convolution operation, the activation layer applies a non-linear function to the output, typically using the ReLU (Rectified Linear Unit) activation function. ReLU introduces non-linearity by replacing all negative values in the feature map with zero, while keeping positive values unchanged:

$$\text{ReLU}(x) = \max(0, x)$$

This non-linearity is crucial because it allows the network to learn complex patterns, as linear models alone would be insufficient for tasks like object recognition.

3. Pooling Layer (Subsampling)

The pooling layer reduces the spatial dimensions (height and width) of the feature maps while preserving the most important information. This helps in reducing the number of parameters, computational cost, and potential overfitting.

- **Max Pooling**: The most common pooling technique is max pooling, where a filter (usually 2x2) slides over the feature map and picks the maximum value from each region. This operation effectively reduces the spatial resolution by retaining the strongest features.
- **Average Pooling**: Another option is average pooling, where the average value is taken from each region, but max pooling tends to be more widely used.

For example, if the feature map is of size 8x8, applying 2x2 max pooling will reduce it to 4x4, keeping the most prominent features from each section of the map.

The pooling operation is essential because it makes the model more computationally efficient and less sensitive to small translations or distortions in the input image (translation invariance).

4. Fully Connected Layer (Dense Layer)

Once the feature maps have been extracted and pooled, the data is passed through one or more fully connected layers. In these layers, each neuron is connected to every neuron in the previous layer, and the output from the previous layer is used to make the final decision. These layers are responsible for combining the high-level features learned by the convolutional and pooling layers into a final prediction or classification.

For example, in an image classification task, the fully connected layer might take the high-level features (such as edges, textures, shapes, etc.) learned by the convolutional layers and combine them to recognize specific objects (e.g., a dog, a car, or a person).

5. Output Layer

The final layer in a CNN is the output layer, which produces the network's prediction. This layer often uses a softmax activation function (for multi-class classification) or a sigmoid function (for binary classification) to output probabilities for each class. The network is trained to minimize the cross-entropy loss, which measures the difference between the predicted probabilities and the actual labels.

Softmax: For multi-class classification problems, the softmax function ensures that the output probabilities sum to 1, giving a valid probability distribution over all possible classes.

Why CNNs Are So Powerful

The architecture of CNNs allows them to learn and extract hierarchical features from the input data. This is what makes them so effective, especially for image-related tasks. Let's break down the reasons why CNNs are so powerful:

Automatic Feature Extraction: Unlike traditional machine learning models, which often require handcrafted features (e.g., edges, textures, colors), CNNs automatically learn the relevant features directly from the data. This reduces the need for manual feature engineering.

Parameter Sharing: In a CNN, the same filter is applied across the entire image, which leads to parameter sharing. This drastically reduces the number of parameters in the model and helps prevent overfitting. It also allows the network to recognize features regardless of their position in the image.

Translation Invariance: Due to the pooling layers and convolution operation, CNNs exhibit translation invariance—meaning they can recognize an object in an image regardless of its location. This is particularly useful for tasks like object detection, where the position of the object can vary.

Efficient Use of Parameters: The use of convolutional and pooling layers allows CNNs to use fewer parameters than fully connected networks, making them more computationally efficient and faster to train, even for large datasets.

Applications of CNNs

CNNs have found applications in a variety of domains beyond just image classification. Some notable applications include:

- **Image Classification**: Recognizing objects or categories in an image (e.g., identifying cats vs. dogs).
- **Object Detection**: Locating and identifying objects in an image (e.g., detecting faces or cars).
- **Image Segmentation**: Dividing an image into regions, such as segmenting different organs in medical imaging.

- **Speech Recognition**: Processing and interpreting audio data.
- **Natural Language Processing**: Using CNNs for text classification and sentiment analysis.

Convolutional Neural Networks (CNNs) have revolutionized the field of machine learning, particularly in computer vision, by enabling automatic feature extraction, translation invariance, and computational efficiency. Their architecture, which is based on convolutions, pooling, and fully connected layers, makes them particularly powerful for image recognition and related tasks. By learning hierarchical feature representations, CNNs have become the go-to model for a wide range of applications, from self-driving cars to medical image analysis, and they continue to push the boundaries of what is possible in deep learning.

12.2 Convolution and Pooling Layers

Convolution and pooling layers are the core components of Convolutional Neural Networks (CNNs), playing a crucial role in feature extraction and dimensionality reduction. These layers are designed to work specifically with grid-like data, such as images, and enable CNNs to automatically learn spatial hierarchies of features. In this section, we will delve into the inner workings of convolution and pooling layers, exploring their roles, operations, and why they are integral to the success of CNNs in various applications like image classification and object detection.

1. Convolution Layer: Feature Extraction

The convolutional layer is where the network first starts to extract meaningful features from the input data. Convolution involves sliding a small matrix of weights (called a filter or kernel) across the input image and performing a dot product between the filter and the portion of the image it's covering. This operation results in a feature map, which highlights the presence of specific features in different spatial locations of the image.

How the Convolution Operation Works

Filter (Kernel): A filter is a small matrix, usually of size 3x3 or 5x5, that contains a set of learnable weights. During the convolution operation, this filter slides over the input image, computing the dot product of the filter and the image region it covers at each step.

Stride: The stride refers to how much the filter moves across the image. If the stride is 1, the filter moves by one pixel at a time. A larger stride (e.g., 2) moves the filter by two pixels at a time, which results in a smaller output feature map. Stride helps control the size of the feature map and the computational efficiency of the convolution.

Padding: Padding is the process of adding extra pixels (usually zeros) around the edges of the input image. Padding is often used to ensure that the output feature map has the same spatial dimensions as the input (in the case of "same" padding). It also helps preserve the size of the image when the filter slides across the borders.

Dot Product: At each position of the filter, a dot product is computed between the filter values and the corresponding values in the image region. The result of this operation is a single value, which forms part of the feature map. This process is repeated as the filter slides across the entire image.

The result of applying a filter to an image is a feature map that represents the activation of that particular feature in different locations across the image. For example, a filter might detect edges, corners, or textures, and the feature map highlights where these features appear in the image.

Example

Consider a simple 3x3 filter applied to a 5x5 image with a stride of 1 and no padding:

Image (5x5 matrix):

$$\begin{bmatrix} 1 & 2 & 3 & 4 & 5 \\ 6 & 7 & 8 & 9 & 10 \\ 11 & 12 & 13 & 14 & 15 \\ 16 & 17 & 18 & 19 & 20 \\ 21 & 22 & 23 & 24 & 25 \end{bmatrix}$$

Filter (3x3 matrix):

$$\begin{bmatrix} 1 & 0 & -1 \\ 1 & 0 & -1 \\ 1 & 0 & -1 \end{bmatrix}$$

After applying the filter with a stride of 1, the result would be a smaller feature map that captures the presence of horizontal edges:

$$\begin{bmatrix} -3 & -3 & -3 \\ -3 & -3 & -3 \\ -3 & -3 & -3 \end{bmatrix}$$

This feature map indicates the presence of strong horizontal edges in the image.

Multiple Filters

In practice, CNNs use multiple filters in each convolutional layer. Each filter detects different features, such as edges, textures, or patterns. As the network deepens, the filters learn increasingly complex and abstract features, enabling the CNN to recognize high-level objects and structures.

2. Pooling Layer: Dimensionality Reduction

The pooling layer is typically used after the convolutional layer to reduce the spatial dimensions (height and width) of the feature map. Pooling helps to decrease the number of parameters in the model, reduces the computational cost, and introduces a form of translation invariance, which makes the network more robust to small translations of the image (i.e., objects in different locations).

Types of Pooling

There are two common types of pooling: max pooling and average pooling.

Max Pooling: Max pooling is the most widely used form of pooling in CNNs. It takes a sliding window (typically 2x2) and extracts the maximum value from the region covered by the window. This operation ensures that only the most important feature in each region is retained.

Average Pooling: Average pooling is similar to max pooling but instead of taking the maximum value, it computes the average of the values in the region covered by the window.

Both max pooling and average pooling help reduce the spatial dimensions of the feature map, making the network more computationally efficient.

How Pooling Works

Pooling Window: A pooling window (typically 2x2 or 3x3) slides across the feature map and computes the summary statistic (max or average) for each region. Like convolution, pooling uses a stride to move the window across the feature map.

Stride: The stride in pooling is typically set to 2, meaning the pooling window moves by two pixels at a time. This reduces the size of the output feature map by half.

Example of Max Pooling

Suppose we have the following 4x4 feature map after applying a convolutional layer:

$$\begin{bmatrix} 1 & 3 & 2 & 4 \\ 5 & 6 & 7 & 8 \\ 9 & 10 & 11 & 12 \\ 13 & 14 & 15 & 16 \end{bmatrix}$$

If we apply 2x2 max pooling with a stride of 2, the result would be:

$$\begin{bmatrix} 6 & 8 \\ 14 & 16 \end{bmatrix}$$

In this case, the max pooling operation reduces the spatial size of the feature map by half, while retaining the most important features (i.e., the maximum values from each 2x2 region).

Benefits of Pooling
Dimensionality Reduction: Pooling reduces the spatial dimensions of the feature map, which decreases the number of parameters in the network and speeds up the computation.

Translation Invariance: Pooling provides a form of translation invariance, meaning the model can recognize objects even if they are shifted or translated slightly within the image.

Noise Reduction: By focusing on the most prominent features (e.g., the maximum value), pooling helps remove less important information and noise from the feature maps.

3. Combining Convolution and Pooling Layers

In a typical CNN architecture, multiple convolutional layers and pooling layers are stacked on top of one another. Each convolutional layer learns low-level features, such as edges or textures, while each pooling layer reduces the dimensionality of the feature map. As the network deepens, the layers begin to capture more complex, abstract features, such as shapes and objects.

The combination of convolution and pooling layers allows CNNs to efficiently extract and learn hierarchical features, making them highly effective for tasks like image classification, object detection, and image segmentation.

Convolution and pooling layers are fundamental to the success of Convolutional Neural Networks (CNNs). The convolutional layer extracts local features from the input data using filters, while the pooling layer reduces the spatial dimensions of the feature maps, making the network more computationally efficient and less sensitive to small translations of the input. By stacking these layers, CNNs can automatically learn complex, hierarchical features, making them incredibly effective for image-related tasks and a wide range of other applications. Understanding the operations of convolution and pooling layers is essential to understanding how CNNs work and why they are so powerful for deep learning.

12.3 Building CNNs for Image Classification

Convolutional Neural Networks (CNNs) have revolutionized the field of computer vision, making them the go-to architecture for tasks such as image classification, object detection, and image segmentation. One of the most common applications of CNNs is image classification, where the goal is to assign a label to an image based on its content. In this section, we will discuss how to build a CNN from scratch for image classification, walk through the key steps involved in the process, and explain how each layer works together to achieve high-performance results.

1. Understanding Image Classification

Image classification is the task of categorizing an image into one of several predefined classes. For instance, a model trained to classify images of animals might categorize an image as a "cat," "dog," or "bird" based on the content of the image. The main challenge here is to teach the neural network to recognize and differentiate between these categories by analyzing pixel values and learning spatial patterns in the images.

Given that images are high-dimensional data (e.g., 224x224 pixels for a standard image), traditional machine learning models struggle with this complexity. CNNs, however, are designed to handle this kind of structured data by automatically learning hierarchical features, from low-level details (like edges) to high-level patterns (like object shapes).

2. The Basic Structure of a CNN for Image Classification

To build a CNN for image classification, we will need to define a series of layers that work together to process the image and make predictions. Let's break down the components of a typical CNN architecture for this task:

a. Input Layer

- The input layer of the CNN is where the raw image data is fed into the network. In most cases, the input will be a 3D array, where the dimensions correspond to the height, width, and color channels of the image (e.g., a color image might have 3 channels: Red, Green, and Blue).
- For instance, a 224x224 image with 3 color channels (RGB) would have a shape of 224x224x3.

b. Convolutional Layer

- The convolutional layers are the heart of the CNN. These layers apply multiple filters (kernels) to the input image to extract important features. Each filter is responsible for detecting a specific feature in the image, such as edges, textures, or corners.
- A common practice is to apply several convolutional layers sequentially, each detecting progressively more complex features.
- As the filter slides over the image, it performs convolution operations, producing feature maps that highlight the regions of the image where certain features (like edges or textures) are prominent.

c. Activation Function (ReLU)

- After each convolution operation, an activation function such as ReLU (Rectified Linear Unit) is applied element-wise to the feature map. ReLU introduces non-

linearity by transforming all negative values to zero and keeping the positive ones unchanged.
- This step is crucial because it allows the network to learn complex patterns that linear models can't capture.

d. Pooling Layer

- Pooling layers are used to reduce the spatial dimensions of the feature maps while preserving the important features. The most common type of pooling is max pooling, where the maximum value is taken from a specific region of the feature map (e.g., a 2x2 window).
- Pooling helps to downsample the feature maps, reducing computational complexity and helping to make the network invariant to small translations of the image.

e. Fully Connected Layer (Dense Layer)

- After several convolution and pooling layers, the feature maps are flattened into a 1D vector and passed through one or more fully connected layers (also called dense layers). These layers combine the extracted features into high-level representations of the image.
- The neurons in the fully connected layers are connected to every neuron in the previous layer, making them capable of learning complex relationships between the features.

f. Output Layer

- The final layer in the CNN is the output layer, which produces the model's predictions. For a multi-class image classification task, this layer typically uses a softmax activation function to output a probability distribution over all possible classes.
- The class with the highest probability is chosen as the model's predicted label for the image.

3. Step-by-Step Guide to Building a CNN for Image Classification

Let's now go through a step-by-step approach to building a simple CNN for image classification using Python and TensorFlow/Keras.

Step 1: Import Libraries

We need to import the necessary libraries, including TensorFlow and Keras, which provide high-level APIs for building deep learning models.

```
import tensorflow as tf
from tensorflow.keras import layers, models
from tensorflow.keras.preprocessing.image import ImageDataGenerator
```

Step 2: Load and Preprocess Data

To train our CNN, we need a labeled dataset. For this example, let's assume we're using a dataset like CIFAR-10, which contains images of 10 different classes. The data needs to be loaded and preprocessed before it can be fed into the CNN.

```
# Load CIFAR-10 dataset
(x_train, y_train), (x_test, y_test) = tf.keras.datasets.cifar10.load_data()

# Normalize pixel values to be between 0 and 1
x_train, x_test = x_train / 255.0, x_test / 255.0
```

Step 3: Build the CNN Model

Now, let's build the CNN architecture. We will start with a few convolutional layers, followed by pooling layers, and finish with fully connected layers for classification.

```
# Build CNN model
model = models.Sequential()

# Convolutional layer 1
model.add(layers.Conv2D(32, (3, 3), activation='relu', input_shape=(32, 32, 3)))
model.add(layers.MaxPooling2D((2, 2)))

# Convolutional layer 2
model.add(layers.Conv2D(64, (3, 3), activation='relu'))
model.add(layers.MaxPooling2D((2, 2)))

# Convolutional layer 3
model.add(layers.Conv2D(64, (3, 3), activation='relu'))
```

```
# Flatten the feature maps
model.add(layers.Flatten())

# Fully connected layer
model.add(layers.Dense(64, activation='relu'))

# Output layer
model.add(layers.Dense(10, activation='softmax'))
```

In this architecture:

- The first two convolutional layers use 32 and 64 filters respectively, followed by max-pooling layers to reduce spatial dimensions.
- The third convolutional layer continues the pattern with 64 filters.
- The output layer has 10 neurons (one for each class in CIFAR-10) and uses softmax to output class probabilities.

Step 4: Compile the Model

Next, we need to compile the model by specifying the optimizer, loss function, and metrics.

```
model.compile(optimizer='adam',
        loss='sparse_categorical_crossentropy',
        metrics=['accuracy'])
```

- Adam is a popular optimization algorithm that adapts the learning rate during training.
- Sparse categorical crossentropy is the loss function for multi-class classification problems.
- We are tracking the model's accuracy as the performance metric.

Step 5: Train the Model

Now, we can train the model on the CIFAR-10 dataset using the fit function. We'll specify the number of epochs and batch size.

```
model.fit(x_train, y_train, epochs=10, batch_size=64, validation_data=(x_test, y_test))
```

Step 6: Evaluate the Model

After training, we can evaluate the model's performance on the test data.

```
test_loss, test_acc = model.evaluate(x_test, y_test)
print(f"Test accuracy: {test_acc}")
```

4. Key Considerations When Building CNNs for Image Classification

- **Hyperparameter Tuning**: Experimenting with different hyperparameters, such as the number of filters, filter sizes, and the number of convolutional layers, can significantly affect the model's performance.
- **Data Augmentation**: To avoid overfitting and improve generalization, data augmentation techniques like rotation, flipping, and zooming can be applied to the training data.
- **Transfer Learning**: For more complex tasks, you can leverage pretrained CNNs like VGG16, ResNet, or Inception, which have already been trained on large datasets like ImageNet, and fine-tune them for your specific task.

Building a Convolutional Neural Network for image classification involves stacking convolutional, pooling, and fully connected layers to extract meaningful features from the images and make predictions. By following the steps outlined in this section, you can build and train a CNN from scratch using popular frameworks like TensorFlow and Keras. While this simple architecture can handle basic classification tasks, more complex problems may require deeper or more advanced models, fine-tuning, and the use of techniques like transfer learning. Nonetheless, CNNs remain one of the most powerful tools for image classification and are widely used in modern computer vision applications.

12.4 Transfer Learning in CNNs

Transfer learning has become a cornerstone of deep learning, especially in the realm of Convolutional Neural Networks (CNNs) for tasks such as image classification, object detection, and more. This technique leverages pre-trained models, which have already been trained on large and diverse datasets, to help solve a new but related problem with significantly less data and computational effort.

In this section, we will explore what transfer learning is, how it works, and how to use it effectively within the context of CNNs for image classification tasks. By understanding this process, you can speed up the training process and improve the accuracy of your model, even with limited data.

1. What is Transfer Learning?

Transfer learning is a machine learning technique where a model that has been trained on a large dataset (typically for one task) is reused and fine-tuned for a different but related task. The idea is that the knowledge gained during the initial training on the large dataset (e.g., ImageNet) can be transferred to solve a new problem with smaller datasets.

In the context of Convolutional Neural Networks for image classification, transfer learning takes advantage of the fact that CNNs learn hierarchical features, starting from basic patterns like edges in early layers to more complex structures like objects in deeper layers. These low-level features are often transferable to many different types of image classification tasks.

Key Concepts in Transfer Learning

- **Pre-trained Models**: These are models that have been trained on large-scale datasets like ImageNet, which contains millions of labeled images across 1,000 different categories.
- **Fine-tuning**: Fine-tuning refers to adjusting a pre-trained model on a new dataset, typically by training only the final layers (or a subset of layers) on the new task, while freezing the weights of the earlier layers.
- **Feature Extraction**: Instead of fine-tuning the model, you can use the pre-trained model as a fixed feature extractor by passing the new data through the pre-trained layers and using the output as input to a new classifier.

2. How Transfer Learning Works

In transfer learning, the process typically involves three main stages:

a. Use of a Pre-trained Model

You start by selecting a pre-trained model that has been trained on a large dataset like ImageNet. Popular CNN architectures that are often used for transfer learning include:

- VGG16 and VGG19
- ResNet (Residual Networks)
- Inception
- Xception
- MobileNet

These models are already trained to recognize various patterns and features in images. For example, VGG16 has learned to detect edges, textures, and more abstract features, making it a good starting point for other image classification tasks.

b. Freezing Layers

In most transfer learning approaches, the initial layers (which capture low-level features like edges, colors, and textures) are frozen. Freezing means that the weights of these layers are not updated during training. This is because the low-level features they detect are generally useful for a wide range of image classification tasks and do not need to be retrained.

c. Fine-tuning the Model

Once the initial layers are frozen, the next step is to fine-tune the model for your specific task. This typically involves:

- Replacing the top layers of the pre-trained model (i.e., the fully connected layers or the classifier part) to suit your new problem.
- Training the new layers on your dataset while keeping the early layers frozen.
- Optionally, you can also choose to unfreeze some of the earlier layers and continue training them alongside the new layers if your new task is sufficiently different from the pre-trained model's original task.

d. Feature Extraction

An alternative to fine-tuning is to use the pre-trained model purely for feature extraction. In this case, you:

- Pass your new dataset through the pre-trained layers of the model.
- Extract the feature maps or output activations from these layers.
- Use these features as input to a new classifier (e.g., a fully connected layer or a support vector machine) to perform the classification task.

3. Why Use Transfer Learning in CNNs?

a. Reduced Training Time

Training deep neural networks from scratch on large datasets can take a tremendous amount of time, especially for image classification tasks where millions of images are involved. Transfer learning reduces this time by using a pre-trained model that already knows how to recognize low-level patterns in images. You can focus your efforts on fine-tuning the model to suit your specific task.

b. Better Performance with Less Data

Training deep learning models from scratch often requires large amounts of labeled data. In many cases, such data may not be available for specific tasks. Transfer learning helps overcome this limitation because the pre-trained model already has learned useful features. This means you can achieve good performance on your task even with a smaller dataset.

c. Improved Accuracy

Transfer learning allows models to achieve better accuracy by starting with weights that already encode knowledge about general image features. This often leads to higher performance compared to training a model from scratch, especially for complex tasks that require a deep understanding of visual data.

4. How to Implement Transfer Learning in CNNs

Let's walk through how you can implement transfer learning for image classification using a pre-trained CNN model, such as VGG16 or ResNet, with TensorFlow/Keras.

Step 1: Import Libraries and Load Pre-trained Model

You first need to import the necessary libraries and load a pre-trained model. We'll use VGG16 as an example, but this method applies to other models as well.

```
import tensorflow as tf
from tensorflow.keras import layers, models
from tensorflow.keras.applications import VGG16
from tensorflow.keras.preprocessing.image import ImageDataGenerator
```

Now, load the pre-trained VGG16 model without the top classification layers (this is crucial for fine-tuning):

```
# Load the pre-trained VGG16 model without the fully connected layers (top)
base_model = VGG16(weights='imagenet', include_top=False, input_shape=(224,
224, 3))
weights='imagenet': This specifies that the weights of the model should come from
ImageNet.
include_top=False: We exclude the fully connected layers at the top, as we will add our
own classifier for the new task.
```

Step 2: Freeze the Base Model

Next, freeze the layers of the pre-trained model so that their weights are not updated during training.

```
base_model.trainable = False
```

Step 3: Add Custom Layers

After freezing the base model, we add our own classifier. This classifier will learn to classify the features extracted by the pre-trained model.

```
# Create a new model on top of the base model
model = models.Sequential([
    base_model,
    layers.GlobalAveragePooling2D(),  # Global Average Pooling to reduce spatial
dimensions
    layers.Dense(1024, activation='relu'),
    layers.Dense(10, activation='softmax')  # Assuming we have 10 classes
])
```

Step 4: Compile the Model

Now compile the model with an appropriate optimizer and loss function for multi-class classification.

```
model.compile(optimizer='adam',
        loss='sparse_categorical_crossentropy',
        metrics=['accuracy'])
```

Step 5: Train the Model

You can now train the model using the training data. Only the newly added layers (not the base model) will be trained in the beginning, as the pre-trained layers are frozen.

```
model.fit(train_data, epochs=10, validation_data=val_data)
```

Step 6: Fine-tune the Model (Optional)

Once the new classifier layers have been trained, you can unfreeze some of the base model layers and fine-tune them. This step is optional and depends on how much data you have and how similar your task is to the pre-trained model's original task.

```
# Unfreeze some layers of the base model
base_model.trainable = True

# Re-compile the model with a lower learning rate
model.compile(optimizer=tf.keras.optimizers.Adam(learning_rate=1e-5),
        loss='sparse_categorical_crossentropy',
        metrics=['accuracy'])

# Fine-tune the model
model.fit(train_data, epochs=5, validation_data=val_data)
```

Transfer learning is a powerful technique that allows you to build high-performing CNNs for image classification tasks with significantly less data and computational resources. By leveraging pre-trained models, you can take advantage of the knowledge they have gained from large-scale datasets like ImageNet, allowing you to focus on fine-tuning the model for your specific task.

Through transfer learning, you can achieve better accuracy and reduce training time, making it an essential tool in practical deep learning applications, especially when dealing with smaller datasets. The process of fine-tuning pre-trained models and using them for feature extraction has made CNNs even more accessible for solving complex image classification problems in fields like healthcare, autonomous driving, and retail, among many others.

13. Recurrent Neural Networks (RNNs) & LSTMs

Time-series data, speech recognition, and chatbots rely on sequential learning models like RNNs and LSTMs. This chapter explores how these networks process sequences and retain memory, enabling AI to understand context in text and speech.

13.1 Understanding Sequential Data

In the world of machine learning, sequential data refers to any type of data where the order of the elements matters. Unlike traditional tabular data, where each feature is independent of others, sequential data is interdependent, meaning that the arrangement or sequence of the data points plays a crucial role in interpreting the overall meaning or prediction. Understanding and handling sequential data effectively is key to solving problems in various domains, including natural language processing (NLP), speech recognition, time series forecasting, and more.

In this section, we'll explore what sequential data is, why it's important, and how it differs from other types of data. We will also look at key characteristics and examples of sequential data, and understand why specialized models are necessary for processing such data.

1. What is Sequential Data?

Sequential data is a collection of data points that are ordered or indexed in a specific sequence. The relationship between each data point depends on its position in the sequence, and often, the data points that precede or follow an element have significant influence on its interpretation. In other words, the context provided by surrounding elements is essential for understanding each data point.

Sequential data can be one-dimensional, like a sequence of words in a sentence, or multi-dimensional, like a time series dataset where multiple measurements are taken over time.

Examples of Sequential Data:

- **Text and Language**: In natural language processing (NLP), a sentence or document is a sequence of words or characters, and the meaning of each word depends on its surrounding context.

- **Speech and Audio**: In speech recognition, a sequence of sound waves or phonemes needs to be processed in the correct order to understand the spoken words.
- **Time Series**: A time series, such as stock prices, weather data, or sensor readings, consists of data points collected sequentially over time. The patterns in these data points can provide valuable insights when analyzed in order.
- **DNA Sequences**: In bioinformatics, DNA or RNA sequences are made up of ordered nucleotides (A, T, C, G), and the sequence of these nucleotides is crucial for understanding genetic information.

2. Why is Sequential Data Important?

The main reason sequential data is important is because the order of the data carries valuable information. For example:

- In language, the meaning of a word depends on the words around it. For instance, the word "bank" means something completely different in "river bank" compared to "bank account."
- In time series analysis, past values of a dataset help predict future values. For example, the stock price of a company today can depend on the price changes from previous days.

Sequential data is ubiquitous in real-world applications and is critical for tasks where context and temporal dependencies matter. Without considering the sequence of data points, it would be nearly impossible to make accurate predictions or interpretations in many fields, such as weather forecasting, language translation, and medical diagnosis.

3. Key Characteristics of Sequential Data

To work with sequential data effectively, it's important to understand its main characteristics:

a. Temporal Dependencies

Sequential data often exhibits temporal dependencies, meaning that each data point is influenced by or dependent on its predecessor(s). These dependencies could be short-term or long-term, and understanding them is key to making accurate predictions. For example:

- In a time series dataset of monthly sales data, the sales in one month could depend on the sales from the previous month.
- In language, the meaning of a word in a sentence might depend on the words that come before or after it.

b. Sequential Patterns

Sequential data often contains patterns or trends that emerge over time. These patterns could be periodic (e.g., daily, weekly cycles) or irregular (e.g., long-term trends). Identifying these patterns is important for making predictions. For instance:

- In financial markets, stock prices may follow certain patterns based on time of day, week, or season.
- In speech recognition, certain phonemes or words tend to occur in predictable patterns.

c. Variable-Length Sequences

Sequential data often comes in variable lengths, meaning not all sequences have the same number of elements. For instance, in NLP, sentences or paragraphs can vary in length, and in time series data, some sequences might contain fewer or more observations. Dealing with such sequences can be tricky, as models need to handle varying sequence lengths effectively.

d. Temporal or Spatial Ordering

In sequential data, order matters. Reversing the sequence or changing the order of events can lead to very different interpretations. For example:

- In video data, the sequence of frames is crucial for understanding the motion and context in the video.
- In language, the order of words in a sentence is crucial for meaning (e.g., "The dog chased the cat" vs. "The cat chased the dog").

4. Types of Sequential Data

Sequential data can come in various forms, depending on the domain and context. Here are a few common types of sequential data:

a. Time Series Data

Time series is a type of sequential data where the order of the data points is determined by time. This type of data is common in applications like:

- **Financial markets**: Stock prices, currency exchange rates, and bond yields are examples of time series data.
- **Weather forecasting**: Temperature, rainfall, humidity, and other environmental measurements taken at regular intervals are examples of time series data.
- **IoT data**: Sensor readings over time, such as monitoring a machine's performance or tracking environmental conditions.

Time series data can exhibit patterns like trends, seasonality, and noise. Techniques like moving averages, ARIMA models, and neural networks like LSTMs (Long Short-Term Memory networks) are often used to model such data.

b. Text and Natural Language Data

In natural language processing (NLP), text is naturally sequential. Words, phrases, and sentences form sequences that need to be processed in order to understand meaning, context, and intent. Examples of sequential data in NLP include:

- **Sentences**: Each word in a sentence depends on the preceding words.
- **Documents**: The entire structure and meaning of a document depend on the ordering of sentences, paragraphs, and ideas.
- **Speech**: Spoken words are also a form of sequential data, where each sound depends on the previous one to form coherent words and sentences.

c. Audio and Speech Data

Audio and speech data is another form of sequential data. It can be used for tasks such as speech recognition, music generation, and sound classification. In speech recognition, each spoken word is a sequence of audio features that needs to be processed in order.

d. Video Data

Video is a form of sequential data in which each frame in the video is ordered in time to create motion and context. In computer vision tasks, each frame is often treated as part of a larger sequence, and understanding the sequence of frames is essential for tasks like action recognition and video summarization.

e. Biological Data

In the field of bioinformatics, DNA, RNA, and protein sequences are examples of sequential data. The order of nucleotides (A, T, C, G) in a DNA sequence, for example, contains genetic information that needs to be processed in sequence to understand biological processes.

5. Challenges with Sequential Data

Working with sequential data presents several challenges:

- **Handling dependencies**: Since each data point is dependent on others, we need models that can capture these dependencies effectively. Traditional machine learning algorithms are often not equipped to handle this kind of dependency, requiring specialized models like Recurrent Neural Networks (RNNs) and Long Short-Term Memory (LSTM) networks.
- **Varying sequence lengths**: Sequences of different lengths require models that can handle variable-length input, such as padding sequences or using dynamic architectures.
- **Long-term dependencies**: Sequential data often involves long-term dependencies, which can be difficult for models to capture, especially when sequences are very long (e.g., in time series forecasting or long documents). LSTMs and GRUs (Gated Recurrent Units) are designed to handle such dependencies.
- **Noise and missing data**: Sequential data can often be noisy or have missing values, especially in time series data. Proper preprocessing and handling of such issues are crucial for effective modeling.

Sequential data plays a pivotal role in many machine learning tasks, especially in domains such as natural language processing, time series analysis, and speech recognition. Unlike traditional data types, where each feature is independent of others, the order and context in sequential data are crucial for making accurate predictions and classifications. To handle sequential data, specialized models such as Recurrent Neural Networks (RNNs), Long Short-Term Memory networks (LSTMs), and Gated Recurrent Units (GRUs) are commonly used. These models are designed to capture dependencies over time or across sequences, making them ideal for processing sequential data in a variety of real-world applications.

13.2 Introduction to RNNs

Recurrent Neural Networks (RNNs) are a class of neural networks designed specifically for processing sequential data. They are unique because they have an internal memory, which allows them to maintain information from previous steps in a sequence and use that information to influence predictions at later steps. This makes RNNs particularly well-suited for tasks where context or temporal dependencies between elements in the sequence are crucial.

In this section, we will introduce you to RNNs, explain how they work, discuss their key components, and highlight why they are particularly suited for handling sequential data.

1. What is an RNN?

An RNN is a type of neural network designed to process sequences of data by maintaining an internal state (or memory) that captures information about previous inputs in the sequence. In a typical feedforward neural network, each input is treated as an independent entity. However, RNNs treat inputs as part of a sequence and use the information from prior steps to inform the current output.

The key feature of an RNN is its ability to loop back on itself. This means that the output from the previous step is fed back into the network, along with the current input, to inform the next step. This feedback mechanism gives RNNs the ability to retain information across time steps, making them ideal for tasks involving sequences such as speech, text, and time series data.

2. How RNNs Work

In an RNN, each element in a sequence is processed one at a time, and the network has a loop in the architecture that allows it to "remember" information from previous elements. Here's a breakdown of how this works:

a. Basic RNN Architecture

A simple RNN processes an input sequence step by step, updating its internal state at each time step based on both the previous state and the current input. At each time step t, the RNN updates its state h_t and computes an output y_t.

- **Input:** x_t (input at time step t)

- **State:** h_t (the hidden state or memory at time step t)

- **Output:** y_t (the output at time step t)

Mathematically, the operations can be described as:

$$h_t = f(W_h x_t + W_s h_{t-1} + b_h)$$

$$y_t = g(W_y h_t + b_y)$$

Where:

- x_t is the input at time step t,

- h_{t-1} is the hidden state from the previous time step,

- W_h, W_s, and W_y are weight matrices,

- b_h and b_y are bias terms,

- f and g are activation functions (e.g., tanh, ReLU, sigmoid).

The key point here is that the hidden state h_t is influenced by both the current input and the previous hidden state. This gives RNNs the ability to **carry forward information** from previous time steps, allowing them to capture temporal dependencies and context.

b. Unrolling the RNN

When processing a sequence, we can "unroll" the RNN across time steps to represent it as a series of computations. For a sequence of length T, the RNN is unrolled as follows:

- At time step 1: The input x_1 is processed to generate the hidden state h_1, which then influences the output y_1.

- At time step 2: The input x_2 is processed, and the hidden state h_2 is generated based on both x_2 and h_1, which was calculated in the previous step. This results in output y_2.

- This process continues for all time steps $t = 1, 2, ..., T$.

The unrolling of the RNN across time steps helps to understand how information flows from one step to the next, with the network's memory being updated at each stage.

c. The Role of the Hidden State

The hidden state h_t in an RNN is its memory. It holds information about the sequence up to the current time step. As the sequence progresses, the RNN continually updates this memory to reflect the information contained in the sequence. This memory is what allows RNNs to process sequential data and make predictions based on past context.

For example:

- In language modeling, the hidden state helps capture the context of previously seen words, which is necessary to predict the next word in a sentence.
- In time series forecasting, the hidden state captures trends and patterns from previous time points, enabling the model to predict future values.

3. Limitations of Basic RNNs

While RNNs are powerful for handling sequential data, they have some limitations that arise from the difficulty of modeling long-range dependencies.

a. Vanishing Gradient Problem

When training RNNs using backpropagation through time (BPTT), gradients can shrink exponentially as they are propagated back through the network. This is known as the vanishing gradient problem. As a result, RNNs often struggle to learn long-term dependencies, since the gradients needed to update weights become too small to have any meaningful impact during training.

b. Exploding Gradient Problem

On the flip side, RNNs can also face the exploding gradient problem, where gradients grow exponentially during backpropagation, leading to very large weight updates that can destabilize the training process.

c. Difficulty with Long Sequences

RNNs may struggle to retain information over long sequences. While they are designed to capture dependencies over time, the strength of those dependencies decays rapidly as the sequence grows, making it hard for basic RNNs to handle long-range dependencies effectively.

4. Improving RNNs: LSTMs and GRUs

Due to the limitations of basic RNNs, two major improvements have been introduced: Long Short-Term Memory (LSTM) networks and Gated Recurrent Units (GRU). Both LSTMs and GRUs are designed to overcome the vanishing gradient problem and allow the network to retain information over longer sequences.

a. LSTMs (Long Short-Term Memory)

LSTMs are a special type of RNN that incorporates a more complex architecture designed to preserve long-term dependencies. LSTMs use gates to control the flow of information, including:

- **Forget Gate**: Decides what information from the past should be forgotten.
- **Input Gate**: Controls how much new information should be stored in the memory.
- **Output Gate**: Controls how much of the memory is used to generate the current output.

By learning how to regulate the flow of information across these gates, LSTMs can effectively maintain long-term dependencies in the data.

b. GRUs (Gated Recurrent Units)

GRUs are similar to LSTMs but have a simpler structure, combining the forget and input gates into a single gate. Despite their simplicity, GRUs can also handle long-range dependencies and are often faster to train than LSTMs.

5. Applications of RNNs

RNNs, LSTMs, and GRUs have been successfully applied in a variety of domains:

Natural Language Processing (NLP): RNNs are widely used in text generation, machine translation, speech recognition, and sentiment analysis. In NLP, RNNs can capture dependencies between words in a sentence, allowing for more accurate understanding and prediction of textual data.

Speech Recognition: RNNs are employed to convert audio waveforms into text, where the sequence of audio frames is mapped to a sequence of words.

Time Series Forecasting: RNNs are used to predict future values in time series data, such as stock prices, weather conditions, or sensor data.

Music Generation: RNNs can be used to generate sequences of musical notes, creating original compositions based on patterns learned from a training dataset.

Video Processing: RNNs are also used for tasks like action recognition in videos, where understanding the sequence of frames is essential to recognize actions or behaviors.

Recurrent Neural Networks (RNNs) are a powerful tool for working with sequential data, allowing models to maintain context and temporal dependencies between data points. While basic RNNs are limited by challenges such as vanishing gradients, advancements like LSTMs and GRUs have made it possible to capture long-range dependencies effectively. These improvements have enabled RNNs to be applied successfully to a wide range of tasks, including natural language processing, time series forecasting, speech recognition, and more. As you dive deeper into sequential data, understanding RNNs is crucial to mastering the ability to model and predict complex temporal patterns.

13.3 Long Short-Term Memory (LSTM) Networks

Long Short-Term Memory (LSTM) networks are a type of Recurrent Neural Network (RNN) specifically designed to overcome the limitations of traditional RNNs, particularly in learning long-range dependencies. Unlike regular RNNs, which suffer from the vanishing gradient problem, LSTMs are capable of learning and retaining information over long sequences of data, making them highly effective for tasks like time series forecasting, machine translation, speech recognition, and natural language processing.

In this section, we'll dive into the inner workings of LSTM networks, explore their key components, understand how they handle long-term dependencies, and discuss their practical applications.

1. What is an LSTM?

LSTM is a special type of RNN designed to capture long-range dependencies in sequential data. The main advantage of LSTMs over regular RNNs is their ability to retain information for long periods of time, allowing them to effectively handle tasks that involve sequences where information from earlier steps in the sequence is essential for making predictions at later steps.

LSTMs accomplish this through a unique architecture that introduces several key components, known as gates, which control the flow of information and help manage long-term memory.

2. Key Components of an LSTM

The architecture of an LSTM consists of four key components: the cell state, the input gate, the forget gate, and the output gate. These gates regulate the information that flows through the network at each time step, allowing LSTMs to learn what to remember, what to forget, and when to output relevant information.

a. Cell State (Memory)

The cell state is the central component of an LSTM and functions as the memory of the network. It carries information across time steps, allowing the LSTM to remember long-term dependencies. At each time step, the cell state is updated based on the input data and the previous cell state, ensuring that relevant information is retained while unnecessary data is discarded.

b. Forget Gate

The forget gate decides what information from the previous cell state should be discarded. It takes the current input and the previous hidden state as input and outputs a number between 0 and 1 (using a sigmoid activation function). This output determines how much of the previous cell state should be "forgotten" or discarded. A value of 0 means "forget completely," while a value of 1 means "retain completely."

Mathematically, the forget gate output is computed as:

$$f_t = \sigma(W_f[h_{t-1}, x_t] + b_f)$$

Where:

- f_t is the forget gate output,

- σ is the sigmoid activation function,

- h_{t-1} is the previous hidden state,

- x_t is the current input,

- W_f is the weight matrix for the forget gate,

- b_f is the bias term.

c. Input Gate

The input gate controls how much of the new input information should be added to the cell state. It has two parts:

- A sigmoid layer that decides which values to update (similar to the forget gate).
- A tanh layer that generates a vector of new candidate values to be added to the cell state.

The input gate's goal is to filter which information should be updated based on the current input and the previous hidden state.

Mathematically, the input gate is computed as:

$$i_t = \sigma(W_i[h_{t-1}, x_t] + b_i)$$

$$\tilde{C}_t = \tanh(W_C[h_{t-1}, x_t] + b_C)$$

Where:

- i_t is the input gate output,

- $\tilde{C}_t$ is the candidate cell state (new information),

- σ is the sigmoid activation function,

- tanh is the hyperbolic tangent activation function,

- W_i, W_C are weight matrices,

- b_i, b_C are bias terms.

d. Output Gate

The output gate determines what information from the cell state should be passed to the output (the hidden state) of the network. This gate filters the information that needs to be passed to the next time step or used for prediction. The output is determined by the current input, the previous hidden state, and the updated cell state.

Mathematically, the output gate is computed as:

$$o_t = \sigma(W_o[h_{t-1}, x_t] + b_o)$$

$$h_t = o_t \cdot \tanh(C_t)$$

Where:

- o_t is the output gate output,

- h_t is the hidden state (output of the LSTM),

- C_t is the current cell state.

3. LSTM in Action: How It Works

To understand how an LSTM processes data, let's look at a step-by-step overview of how information flows through the network at each time step:

1. **Forget Gate:** At each time step t, the forget gate looks at the previous hidden state h_{t-1} and the current input x_t to decide which information from the previous cell state C_{t-1} should be discarded. This is achieved by generating a value between 0 and 1, with 0 indicating complete forgetfulness and 1 indicating complete retention.

2. **Input Gate:** The input gate then decides which new information should be stored in the cell state. The input gate is controlled by a combination of the current input x_t and the previous hidden state h_{t-1}. A set of candidate values $\tilde{C}_t$ is generated, and the input gate determines how much of this new information should be added to the cell state.

3. **Cell State Update:** The cell state C_t is updated by combining the previous cell state C_{t-1} and the new candidate values, filtered by the forget gate and the input gate. The new cell state is a combination of the retained information from the previous state and the newly added information.

4. **Output Gate:** Finally, the output gate decides what information should be passed to the output. It looks at the current cell state and produces the hidden state h_t, which will be used as the output for the current time step and as the input for the next time step.

4. Advantages of LSTM Networks

LSTMs have several key advantages over traditional RNNs, which make them ideal for tasks that involve learning long-term dependencies:

a. Ability to Learn Long-Term Dependencies

Unlike regular RNNs, which struggle with learning long-term dependencies due to the vanishing gradient problem, LSTMs have a structure that allows them to store information over long periods. This makes them highly effective for tasks where the model needs to "remember" important information from earlier in the sequence.

b. Mitigating the Vanishing Gradient Problem

LSTMs solve the vanishing gradient problem by using their gating mechanisms (input, forget, and output gates) to control the flow of gradients during backpropagation. This enables LSTMs to maintain a stable gradient even during long sequences, allowing the model to learn from long-range dependencies.

c. Flexibility in Sequence Length

LSTMs are capable of handling sequences of varying lengths, making them versatile for tasks like natural language processing (where sentences vary in length) or time series forecasting (where the number of time steps can differ).

d. Improved Performance on Sequential Tasks

LSTMs excel at tasks like speech recognition, text generation, machine translation, and time series forecasting, where the model must learn the context and temporal dependencies between elements in the sequence.

5. Applications of LSTMs

LSTMs are widely used across various domains that involve sequential data, including:

a. Natural Language Processing (NLP)

LSTMs are used in NLP tasks like:

- **Machine translation**: Translating sentences from one language to another by capturing the context and dependencies between words.
- **Speech recognition**: Converting speech into text by capturing the temporal dependencies in sound waves.
- **Text generation**: Generating coherent text, such as poetry or story writing, based on a given prompt.
- **Sentiment analysis**: Understanding the sentiment expressed in text by analyzing the relationships between words.

b. Time Series Forecasting

LSTMs are used to predict future values in time series data, such as:

- **Stock market prediction**: Predicting future stock prices based on historical data.
- **Weather forecasting**: Predicting future weather patterns using past temperature, humidity, and pressure data.

- **Demand forecasting**: Predicting the demand for products based on historical sales data.

c. Video Processing

LSTMs are also employed in tasks like:

- **Action recognition**: Recognizing actions in a video by analyzing sequences of frames.
- **Video captioning**: Generating descriptive captions for video content.

Long Short-Term Memory (LSTM) networks are a powerful tool for processing sequential data, especially when long-term dependencies are crucial for making accurate predictions. By introducing gates that regulate the flow of information, LSTMs overcome the limitations of traditional RNNs and are capable of learning from sequences of varying lengths and complexities. With applications ranging from natural language processing to time series forecasting and video processing, LSTMs have become a cornerstone of modern machine learning, enabling more accurate and robust predictions in real-world tasks.

13.4 Time Series Forecasting with RNNs

Time series forecasting involves predicting future values based on previously observed values in a sequence over time. These tasks are commonly seen in fields like finance (e.g., stock prices), meteorology (e.g., temperature predictions), and supply chain management (e.g., inventory forecasting). Recurrent Neural Networks (RNNs), and specifically their more advanced forms like Long Short-Term Memory (LSTM) networks, have shown great promise in addressing the complexities of time series forecasting.

In this section, we will discuss how RNNs can be applied to time series forecasting, explain the steps involved in building an RNN model for time series predictions, and highlight best practices for optimizing performance.

1. Why RNNs for Time Series Forecasting?

Traditional machine learning models often struggle with sequential data where the order of data points matters, as they are unable to effectively capture the temporal dependencies between past observations and future predictions. RNNs, on the other hand, are designed to handle this type of data by processing it in a sequence. They have an internal memory that allows them to "remember" important information from past time steps, which is crucial when working with time series data, where future values depend on historical context.

Key reasons why RNNs are well-suited for time series forecasting:

a. Sequential Data Handling

RNNs are inherently suited to handle sequential data because of their ability to keep track of information from previous time steps. This allows them to recognize patterns, trends, and dependencies over time.

b. Memory of Past Events

RNNs can "remember" previous data points using their hidden state. This memory is important when there are long-term dependencies in the data. However, traditional RNNs can struggle with long-range dependencies, which is where Long Short-Term Memory (LSTM) networks come in to overcome this limitation.

c. Flexible Prediction Horizons

RNNs can handle multiple types of forecasting tasks, such as predicting future values one time step ahead or making multi-step forecasts (predicting several future time points at once).

2. Steps for Time Series Forecasting with RNNs

Let's break down the steps involved in building an RNN-based time series forecasting model:

a. Data Preparation

Time series forecasting with RNNs begins with preparing the data in a way that is compatible with the model's sequential nature. Time series data typically involves a sequence of observations over time, and for the RNN to understand the temporal structure, the data must be formatted properly:

Sequence Generation: In time series forecasting, the model doesn't simply take the entire dataset as input; it requires splitting the data into overlapping sequences, where each sequence represents a fixed window of time. For example, if we want to predict the next value based on the last 10 time steps, the data would be split into sequences of length 10, and each sequence would be used as input to predict the next time step in the sequence.

Normalization: It's crucial to scale the data, as neural networks perform better when input features are on a similar scale. Time series data can often have large variations, so normalization techniques like Min-Max scaling or Z-score normalization are commonly used.

b. Building the RNN Model

The next step is to define the architecture of the RNN. While traditional RNNs are effective in modeling sequential data, they suffer from limitations in learning long-term dependencies. To overcome this, many time series forecasting models use LSTMs or GRUs (Gated Recurrent Units), which are more effective in capturing long-term relationships.

The architecture for a typical RNN or LSTM model for time series forecasting includes:

Input Layer: The model receives a sequence of past time steps as input. Each sequence is used to predict the next time step or future values.

RNN/LSTM Layer: The core of the model is a recurrent layer that processes the input data sequentially, maintaining a memory of previous time steps.

Dense Layer: After processing through the recurrent layer(s), a dense (fully connected) layer is often used to map the output of the RNN/LSTM to the desired output (i.e., the predicted future value).

Output Layer: The output layer produces the predicted value. For single-step forecasting, this could be a single value representing the forecasted value for the next time step. For multi-step forecasting, it could be a vector representing multiple future values.

c. Training the Model

Training an RNN or LSTM model for time series forecasting involves using historical data to learn the patterns and relationships between past and future values. The training process consists of the following steps:

Loss Function: The most common loss function for time series forecasting tasks is Mean Squared Error (MSE) or Mean Absolute Error (MAE), as they measure the difference between predicted and actual values.

Backpropagation Through Time (BPTT): In RNNs and LSTMs, backpropagation is adapted to handle sequences by applying backpropagation through time. This is how the model updates its weights based on the error between predictions and actual outcomes.

Epochs and Batch Size: Training is performed over several epochs, with each epoch consisting of multiple iterations where the model processes batches of data. The batch size determines how many sequences are used in each iteration, while the number of epochs refers to how many times the entire dataset is passed through the network.

d. Model Evaluation and Testing

Once the model is trained, it's important to evaluate its performance using appropriate metrics. In time series forecasting, the most common evaluation metrics include:

Mean Absolute Error (MAE): Measures the average magnitude of errors in predictions.

Mean Squared Error (MSE): Similar to MAE, but it gives higher weight to larger errors.

Root Mean Squared Error (RMSE): The square root of MSE, providing a more interpretable measure of model accuracy.

R-squared (R^2): Measures how well the model's predictions match the actual values. An R^2 close to 1 indicates that the model explains most of the variance in the data.

Additionally, it is important to visualize the predicted vs. actual values on a plot to understand how well the model is performing over time.

3. Example Use Cases for Time Series Forecasting with RNNs

Here are some practical examples where RNNs, and specifically LSTM networks, can be applied to time series forecasting:

a. Stock Price Prediction

In stock market analysis, RNNs are used to predict future stock prices based on past trends. While predicting stock prices accurately is a complex task due to volatility, RNN-based models can capture patterns in stock movements, identify market trends, and help traders make more informed decisions.

b. Weather Forecasting

Meteorologists use historical weather data (e.g., temperature, humidity, wind speed) to predict future weather conditions. RNNs can capture seasonal patterns and weather trends to improve short-term weather forecasts.

c. Energy Consumption Forecasting

Energy providers use time series forecasting to predict future energy demand and optimize power generation. RNNs can analyze patterns in energy consumption, accounting for factors like time of day, seasonality, and other external factors, to help utilities predict demand more accurately.

d. Demand Forecasting in Retail

Retailers use time series forecasting to predict the demand for products over time. By analyzing sales data from previous periods, RNNs can predict future demand, helping businesses optimize their inventory levels, reduce waste, and ensure product availability.

4. Challenges in Time Series Forecasting with RNNs

While RNNs and LSTMs are powerful tools for time series forecasting, they come with their challenges:

Data Preprocessing: Time series data can be noisy and may require significant preprocessing before it can be used for training. Missing values, outliers, and seasonality need to be handled carefully.

Overfitting: RNNs, especially deep ones, can be prone to overfitting, especially when the model becomes too complex. Regularization techniques, such as dropout, and early stopping are often used to mitigate this problem.

Computational Resources: Training RNNs, especially on long sequences or large datasets, can be computationally intensive. Using GPUs and other hardware accelerators can speed up the training process.

Time series forecasting with RNNs, particularly LSTMs, has revolutionized how we make predictions based on temporal data. By leveraging their ability to capture sequential patterns and dependencies, RNN-based models are highly effective for tasks such as stock price prediction, weather forecasting, and demand forecasting. However, these models come with challenges such as data preprocessing, overfitting, and computational complexity, which require careful consideration and optimization. With the right preprocessing, model design, and evaluation, RNNs can provide valuable insights and accurate predictions for various time-sensitive applications.

14. Machine Learning with Python

Python is the go-to language for ML. This chapter walks you through using Scikit-learn, TensorFlow, and PyTorch for ML development, covering essential libraries, tools, and frameworks needed to implement models effectively.

14.1 Introduction to Python Libraries for ML

Python has become one of the most popular programming languages for machine learning (ML) due to its simplicity, readability, and the vast number of libraries available that facilitate data analysis, modeling, and deployment. Whether you are just starting with ML or are an experienced practitioner, knowing the right libraries to use can make your ML journey much smoother and more efficient.

In this chapter, we'll provide an overview of the most widely-used Python libraries for machine learning, explaining their core functionalities, and how they can be leveraged to solve real-world ML problems.

1. Why Python for Machine Learning?

Before diving into the specific libraries, it's important to understand why Python is the language of choice for many machine learning practitioners:

- **Ease of Use**: Python is easy to learn and use, making it accessible even to those with little programming experience.
- **Large Community and Support**: Python has a massive global community. Whether you need help solving a problem or want to learn best practices, chances are you'll find resources, tutorials, and active discussion forums.
- **Rich Ecosystem of Libraries**: Python's extensive ecosystem includes libraries for data manipulation, statistical analysis, deep learning, visualization, and more. These libraries can speed up the development process and help you implement machine learning algorithms more effectively.
- **Integration**: Python integrates well with other technologies, including web development frameworks, databases, and cloud services, allowing ML models to be deployed and scaled effectively in production environments.

2. Key Python Libraries for Machine Learning

Here's a breakdown of the most popular and essential Python libraries for machine learning:

a. NumPy

NumPy is the fundamental library for numerical computing in Python. It provides support for multidimensional arrays and matrices, along with a large collection of high-level mathematical functions to operate on these arrays.

Key Features:

- **Arrays and Matrices**: NumPy's ndarray object provides efficient storage and manipulation of large arrays and matrices.
- **Linear Algebra Functions**: NumPy contains functions for performing operations like matrix multiplication, eigenvalues, and matrix inversion.
- **Broadcasting**: This feature allows NumPy to perform arithmetic operations on arrays of different shapes, making it highly versatile.

Use Cases in ML:

- Data preprocessing and manipulation (e.g., transforming data into a format suitable for machine learning algorithms).
- Performing numerical operations during model training (e.g., calculating gradients, performing matrix multiplication).

b. Pandas

Pandas is an open-source library built for data manipulation and analysis. It provides data structures such as DataFrames and Series, which are perfect for working with tabular data. This makes it the go-to library for data wrangling and preprocessing.

Key Features:

- **DataFrames and Series**: Pandas' DataFrame allows you to represent and manipulate tabular data (e.g., CSV, Excel files), and the Series is perfect for one-dimensional data.
- **Data Cleaning**: Pandas makes it easy to handle missing data, remove duplicates, and filter or aggregate data.
- **Integration with NumPy**: Pandas is built on top of NumPy, which makes it highly efficient for numerical operations.

Use Cases in ML:

- Importing and cleaning datasets.
- Exploring and analyzing data (e.g., checking correlations, basic statistical summaries).
- Preparing and transforming data for machine learning models.

c. Matplotlib & Seaborn

Both Matplotlib and Seaborn are libraries used for data visualization, which is a crucial step in understanding and interpreting machine learning models and their performance.

Matplotlib is a widely-used library for creating static, interactive, and animated plots in Python. It's highly customizable and can create virtually any kind of plot, from simple line graphs to complex 3D plots.

Seaborn is built on top of Matplotlib and provides a higher-level interface for creating visually appealing statistical graphics. It integrates well with Pandas and makes it easy to plot data directly from DataFrames.

Key Features:

- **Matplotlib**: Basic plotting, subplots, customization of plots, and 3D plotting.
- **Seaborn**: Statistical plotting (e.g., boxplots, violin plots, pair plots), built-in themes for more attractive visuals.

Use Cases in ML:

- Visualizing data distributions and trends.
- Creating diagnostic plots to evaluate model performance.
- Displaying relationships between variables (e.g., scatter plots, heatmaps of correlations).

d. Scikit-Learn

Scikit-Learn is one of the most widely used Python libraries for machine learning. It provides simple and efficient tools for data mining and data analysis. Scikit-learn is built on NumPy, SciPy, and Matplotlib, making it highly compatible with other libraries.

Key Features:

- **Algorithms**: Scikit-learn includes a wide range of supervised and unsupervised learning algorithms, such as linear regression, decision trees, support vector machines (SVM), k-means clustering, and more.
- **Preprocessing Tools**: It provides utilities for feature scaling, encoding categorical variables, and imputing missing values.
- **Model Selection**: Tools for cross-validation, hyperparameter tuning (e.g., GridSearchCV), and model evaluation (e.g., confusion matrix, classification report).

Use Cases in ML:

- Building traditional machine learning models (e.g., regression, classification, clustering).
- Evaluating model performance using cross-validation and performance metrics.
- Data preprocessing tasks like scaling features, handling missing values, and encoding categorical features.

e. TensorFlow & Keras

TensorFlow is an open-source deep learning framework developed by Google, and it is one of the most popular tools for building neural networks. Keras is an API built on top of TensorFlow that provides a high-level interface for defining and training deep learning models. While TensorFlow itself is highly flexible and powerful, Keras offers a simpler, user-friendly way to define deep learning models.

Key Features:

- **TensorFlow**: Provides low-level APIs for defining custom models, layers, and optimization functions. It supports distributed computing and can be deployed to different hardware accelerators like GPUs and TPUs.
- **Keras**: High-level API with easy-to-use functions for defining layers, optimizers, and loss functions. It helps with rapid prototyping.

Use Cases in ML:

- Building deep learning models such as convolutional neural networks (CNNs), recurrent neural networks (RNNs), and generative adversarial networks (GANs).
- Implementing complex neural architectures in a modular and efficient manner.

- Deploying models to production environments with TensorFlow Serving or TensorFlow Lite.

f. XGBoost

XGBoost (Extreme Gradient Boosting) is a popular machine learning library that implements gradient boosting algorithms. It is highly efficient and works well for structured/tabular data, often outperforming other models in terms of accuracy and speed.

Key Features:

- **Gradient Boosting**: XGBoost implements the gradient boosting algorithm, which builds strong predictive models by combining the outputs of many weak models.
- **Tree Boosting**: It builds decision trees in a sequential manner, with each new tree improving the model by correcting the errors of the previous ones.
- **Speed and Scalability**: XGBoost is optimized for speed, with support for parallel processing and distributed computing.

Use Cases in ML:

- Structured data problems, including classification and regression tasks.
- Kaggle competitions and other real-world ML challenges.

g. SciPy

SciPy is a scientific computing library that builds on NumPy and provides additional functionality for advanced mathematical operations, optimization, and statistical analysis.

Key Features:

- **Optimization**: SciPy provides functions for optimization and root finding, which are often needed when fine-tuning machine learning models.
- **Statistics**: It includes a variety of statistical tests, distributions, and hypothesis testing functions.
- **Signal Processing**: SciPy contains tools for filtering, interpolation, and Fourier transforms, which can be useful in pre-processing time-series data.

Use Cases in ML:

- Statistical analysis of model results.

- Optimizing parameters and hyperparameters.
- Handling advanced mathematical operations that go beyond NumPy.

Python's rich ecosystem of libraries makes it an ideal language for building machine learning models and performing data analysis. Libraries like NumPy, Pandas, and Matplotlib serve as the foundation for data manipulation and visualization, while more specialized libraries like Scikit-Learn, TensorFlow, and XGBoost enable the development and training of machine learning models. Understanding these libraries and how to use them effectively will greatly enhance your ability to tackle a wide range of machine learning tasks. By becoming proficient with these tools, you'll be well-equipped to handle everything from basic data analysis to building state-of-the-art machine learning models.

14.2 Using Scikit-learn for Basic Models

Scikit-learn is one of the most widely used libraries in Python for machine learning tasks, especially for traditional models such as regression, classification, clustering, and dimensionality reduction. Its simplicity, ease of use, and wide range of algorithms make it a powerful tool for both beginners and advanced practitioners. In this section, we'll walk through the process of using Scikit-learn to build and evaluate basic machine learning models.

1. Installing and Importing Scikit-learn

Before we start building machine learning models, we need to install and import Scikit-learn. You can install it using pip if you don't already have it:

```
pip install scikit-learn
```

Once installed, you can import it into your Python script or Jupyter notebook as follows:

```
import numpy as np
import pandas as pd
from sklearn.model_selection import train_test_split
from sklearn.preprocessing import StandardScaler
from sklearn.linear_model import LogisticRegression, LinearRegression
from sklearn.metrics import accuracy_score, mean_squared_error
```

Scikit-learn provides a range of tools for preprocessing data, building models, and evaluating performance, making it an ideal choice for a variety of tasks.

2. Basic Workflow with Scikit-learn

The general workflow when using Scikit-learn for building machine learning models consists of the following steps:

- **Data Loading and Preprocessing**: Load your dataset and perform any necessary preprocessing (e.g., handling missing values, feature scaling).
- **Splitting the Data**: Divide the dataset into a training set and a test set to evaluate the model's performance.
- **Model Selection and Training**: Choose a machine learning algorithm, instantiate the model, and train it on the training data.
- **Prediction**: Use the trained model to make predictions on the test data.
- **Evaluation**: Evaluate the model's performance using appropriate evaluation metrics.

We'll go through this process using both a classification and regression example.

3. Example 1: Logistic Regression for Classification

Let's start with a classification problem using Logistic Regression. This algorithm is commonly used for binary classification tasks (e.g., predicting whether an email is spam or not).

a. Loading the Data

We'll use the famous Iris dataset, which is included in Scikit-learn. It contains data about different iris flowers, and the task is to predict the species of the flower based on features such as petal length, petal width, and sepal width.

```
from sklearn.datasets import load_iris

# Load the iris dataset
data = load_iris()
X = data.data  # Features (sepal length, sepal width, petal length, petal width)
y = data.target  # Target variable (species)
```

b. Splitting the Data

Now, we'll split the data into a training set and a test set. Typically, we use 70-80% of the data for training and the rest for testing.

```
X_train, X_test, y_train, y_test = train_test_split(X, y, test_size=0.3, random_state=42)
```

c. Building and Training the Model

Next, we'll create a Logistic Regression model and train it on the training data.

```
# Instantiate the logistic regression model
model = LogisticRegression(max_iter=200)

# Train the model on the training data
model.fit(X_train, y_train)
```

d. Making Predictions

Once the model is trained, we can use it to make predictions on the test set.

```
y_pred = model.predict(X_test)
```

e. Evaluating the Model

To evaluate the model's performance, we will use accuracy as the evaluation metric (i.e., the proportion of correct predictions).

```
accuracy = accuracy_score(y_test, y_pred)
print(f"Accuracy: {accuracy * 100:.2f}%")
```

Logistic regression is often used for simple classification tasks and can be implemented easily using Scikit-learn. In this case, we were able to train a model on the Iris dataset and evaluate its performance using accuracy.

4. Example 2: Linear Regression for Regression

Now, let's move to a regression task using Linear Regression, which is used to predict continuous values.

a. Loading the Data

For this example, we'll use the Boston housing dataset, which contains information about various factors influencing housing prices in Boston. We'll predict the median value of homes (target variable).

```
from sklearn.datasets import load_boston

# Load the Boston housing dataset
data = load_boston()
X = data.data  # Features (e.g., average number of rooms, crime rate)
y = data.target  # Target variable (median home value)
```

b. Splitting the Data

Just as in the classification example, we'll split the data into training and testing sets.

```
X_train, X_test, y_train, y_test = train_test_split(X, y, test_size=0.3, random_state=42)
```

c. Feature Scaling (Optional but Recommended)

It's a good practice to scale the features when using models like linear regression, especially when the features have different scales. We can use StandardScaler from Scikit-learn to standardize the features so that they have zero mean and unit variance.

```
scaler = StandardScaler()

# Fit the scaler on the training data and transform both training and testing sets
X_train_scaled = scaler.fit_transform(X_train)
X_test_scaled = scaler.transform(X_test)
```

d. Building and Training the Model

We'll now instantiate a Linear Regression model and fit it to the training data.

```
# Instantiate the linear regression model
regressor = LinearRegression()

# Train the model on the scaled training data
regressor.fit(X_train_scaled, y_train)
```

e. Making Predictions

After the model has been trained, we can use it to predict the housing prices on the test set.

```
y_pred = regressor.predict(X_test_scaled)
```

f. Evaluating the Model

For regression tasks, we typically use metrics like Mean Squared Error (MSE) or R-squared to evaluate the model's performance. Let's calculate the Mean Squared Error (MSE) and R-squared score for this model.

```
mse = mean_squared_error(y_test, y_pred)
r2 = regressor.score(X_test_scaled, y_test)

print(f"Mean Squared Error: {mse:.2f}")
print(f"R-squared: {r2:.2f}")
```

Linear regression is a powerful and simple model for predicting continuous values. By applying it to the Boston housing dataset, we were able to predict housing prices and evaluate the model using MSE and R-squared.

5. Other Basic Models in Scikit-learn

In addition to Logistic Regression and Linear Regression, Scikit-learn offers a wide range of other machine learning models, including:

Decision Trees: For both classification and regression tasks. Decision trees work by recursively splitting the data based on feature values, making them interpretable but prone to overfitting.

K-Nearest Neighbors (KNN): A simple, instance-based learning algorithm used for both classification and regression. KNN makes predictions based on the labels or values of the nearest data points.

Support Vector Machines (SVM): A powerful classification technique that finds the optimal hyperplane that separates the classes.

Naive Bayes: A probabilistic model based on Bayes' Theorem, commonly used for text classification and spam detection.

Each of these models can be used similarly in Scikit-learn with the fit(), predict(), and score() methods.

Scikit-learn simplifies the process of building, training, and evaluating machine learning models. In this section, we covered how to use Scikit-learn to implement basic models such as Logistic Regression for classification and Linear Regression for regression tasks. The process generally involves data loading, preprocessing, model selection, training, prediction, and evaluation, which can be accomplished in just a few lines of code.

By mastering these basic models, you'll have a solid foundation for tackling more complex machine learning problems. Scikit-learn's easy-to-use API and wide range of models make it an indispensable tool for machine learning practitioners.

14.3 Introduction to TensorFlow and PyTorch

As machine learning and deep learning become increasingly powerful tools for a wide variety of applications, frameworks such as TensorFlow and PyTorch have emerged as the two dominant libraries for building and deploying neural networks. Both of these frameworks provide highly flexible and efficient ways to develop complex models, especially deep learning models such as Convolutional Neural Networks (CNNs), Recurrent Neural Networks (RNNs), and Transformers. This chapter will introduce these two frameworks, highlighting their key features, differences, and use cases.

1. What are TensorFlow and PyTorch?

TensorFlow

TensorFlow is an open-source machine learning library developed by Google. It was released in 2015 and quickly became one of the most popular deep learning frameworks.

TensorFlow is particularly known for its scalability, and it is widely used for both research and production.

- **Core Concept**: TensorFlow's core concept is based on a dataflow graph that defines the computational operations. This makes it particularly efficient for tasks involving large amounts of data, where operations can be executed in parallel across multiple processors.
- **Flexibility**: Initially, TensorFlow was considered less flexible compared to PyTorch, as it required users to define a static computational graph. However, with TensorFlow 2.0, dynamic execution (eager execution) was introduced, making it more user-friendly.
- **Ecosystem**: TensorFlow also offers an extensive ecosystem, including tools like TensorFlow Lite for mobile devices, TensorFlow.js for JavaScript, and TensorFlow Serving for deploying models in production environments.

PyTorch

PyTorch is an open-source deep learning library developed by Facebook's AI Research lab. It was first released in 2016 and has quickly gained popularity due to its ease of use and flexibility. PyTorch is widely used by researchers and data scientists for prototyping and experimenting with new architectures.

- **Core Concept**: PyTorch is designed around dynamic computation graphs, which are created on-the-fly during execution. This makes PyTorch more intuitive and flexible, especially for experimentation and debugging.
- **Flexibility and Debugging**: Since PyTorch operates with dynamic computation graphs, it is often considered easier to debug and more pythonic than TensorFlow (prior to TensorFlow 2.0).
- **Ecosystem**: PyTorch has a rich ecosystem, including libraries such as TorchVision (for computer vision), TorchText (for natural language processing), and TorchAudio (for audio processing).

2. Key Features of TensorFlow and PyTorch

TensorFlow Features

Static and Dynamic Graphs: TensorFlow 1.x was known for its static computational graph, which made optimization and deployment easier but less flexible for rapid prototyping. TensorFlow 2.0 introduced eager execution, allowing dynamic graphs for more intuitive programming.

Scalability: TensorFlow excels at handling large datasets and distributed computing. It can run on CPUs, GPUs, and TPUs (Tensor Processing Units, Google's custom hardware). This makes it highly scalable for both research and production applications.

TensorFlow Serving: TensorFlow's ecosystem includes TensorFlow Serving, a high-performance system for serving machine learning models in production. It can handle real-time inference and is highly scalable.

TensorFlow Lite: For mobile applications, TensorFlow Lite allows you to convert models to run efficiently on mobile devices, with reduced computational resources.

Keras Integration: TensorFlow integrates seamlessly with Keras, a high-level neural networks API. This makes it easier to build and train models with simpler code while still leveraging TensorFlow's backend.

PyTorch Features

Dynamic Computation Graphs (Define-by-Run): PyTorch uses dynamic computation graphs, where the graph is built during runtime. This means the graph is not defined before the execution, which makes it more intuitive for developers to experiment and debug models.

TorchScript: PyTorch introduced TorchScript for model optimization and deployment, allowing users to convert their dynamic models into a static representation that can be run in a high-performance environment.

Better Debugging: PyTorch's dynamic nature allows you to use standard Python debugging tools such as pdb. This makes it easy to inspect variables and outputs during runtime, providing a more intuitive debugging experience compared to static graph-based systems like TensorFlow (pre-2.0).

CUDA Support: PyTorch provides seamless support for CUDA, NVIDIA's parallel computing architecture, enabling the efficient use of GPUs during training and inference.

Ecosystem: PyTorch also has several tools and libraries for specific tasks:

- TorchVision for computer vision tasks like image classification and segmentation.
- TorchText for natural language processing (NLP).
- PyTorch Lightning to simplify research code and improve productivity.

- ONNX (Open Neural Network Exchange) for model interchangeability between frameworks like PyTorch, TensorFlow, and others.

3. Comparison: TensorFlow vs. PyTorch

While both TensorFlow and PyTorch are powerful frameworks, they each have their unique strengths. Here's a comparison based on various factors:

Feature	TensorFlow	PyTorch
Computational Graph	Static (1.x), Dynamic (2.x)	Dynamic (define-by-run)
Ease of Use	Slightly more complex (pre-2.0), easier post-2.0 with Keras integration	More intuitive and flexible, easier for rapid prototyping
Performance	Optimized for large-scale production	Optimized for research, but also good for production
Model Deployment	TensorFlow Serving, TensorFlow Lite, TensorFlow.js	TorchServe, TorchScript, ONNX for cross-framework deployment
Community Support	Larger community, extensive resources	Growing rapidly, especially in research communities
Popularity	More popular in production environments, especially in industry	More popular in research, particularly in academia
Debugging	Eager execution (TensorFlow 2.0+) improves debugging	Excellent debugging with Python's standard tools
Learning Curve	Steeper learning curve (pre-2.0), easier post-2.0	Easier to learn and implement

4. When to Use TensorFlow or PyTorch?

When to Use TensorFlow

- **Production Deployment**: TensorFlow is a great choice for production environments due to its ability to scale and deploy models across platforms, including mobile, web, and cloud. If you need a model to run efficiently in a high-scale environment, TensorFlow's integration with tools like TensorFlow Serving and TensorFlow Lite will be helpful.

- **Large-Scale Data**: TensorFlow excels in handling large datasets and can easily run on distributed systems and hardware like GPUs and TPUs. If you are working with big data, TensorFlow is a powerful framework to use.
- **Cross-Platform Support**: TensorFlow's ability to run on multiple platforms (servers, mobile devices, web) with tools like TensorFlow.js and TensorFlow Lite makes it an excellent choice for cross-platform machine learning.

When to Use PyTorch

- **Research and Prototyping**: PyTorch is the go-to framework for researchers and developers who need flexibility, ease of use, and fast iteration. Its dynamic nature allows you to experiment with models more intuitively.
- **Fast Debugging**: PyTorch's dynamic computation graph makes it easier to debug models, especially when using standard Python debugging tools.
- **Cutting-Edge Research**: PyTorch is widely used in academia, making it ideal for staying up-to-date with the latest research. Many cutting-edge deep learning techniques and papers are implemented in PyTorch first.

5. Example: Building a Simple Neural Network in PyTorch and TensorFlow

PyTorch Example (Neural Network for Classification)

```
import torch
import torch.nn as nn
import torch.optim as optim

# Sample data (X: features, y: target labels)
X = torch.tensor([[0.1, 0.2], [0.3, 0.4], [0.5, 0.6]], dtype=torch.float32)
y = torch.tensor([0, 1, 0], dtype=torch.long)

# Define a simple neural network model
class SimpleNN(nn.Module):
    def __init__(self):
        super(SimpleNN, self).__init__()
        self.fc1 = nn.Linear(2, 2)
        self.fc2 = nn.Linear(2, 2)

    def forward(self, x):
        x = torch.relu(self.fc1(x))
        x = self.fc2(x)
```

```
      return x

# Initialize model, loss function, and optimizer
model = SimpleNN()
criterion = nn.CrossEntropyLoss()
optimizer = optim.SGD(model.parameters(), lr=0.01)

# Training loop
for epoch in range(100):
    optimizer.zero_grad()
    outputs = model(X)
    loss = criterion(outputs, y)
    loss.backward()
    optimizer.step()
    if (epoch+1) % 20 == 0:
        print(f"Epoch [{epoch+1}/100], Loss: {loss.item():.4f}")
```

TensorFlow Example (Neural Network for Classification)

```
import tensorflow as tf
from tensorflow.keras.models import Sequential
from tensorflow.keras.layers import Dense
from tensorflow.keras.optimizers import SGD

# Sample data (X: features, y: target labels)
X = [[0.1, 0.2], [0.3, 0.4], [0.5, 0.6]]
y = [0, 1, 0]

# Define a simple neural network model
model = Sequential([
    Dense(2, activation='relu', input_dim=2),
    Dense(2, activation='softmax')
])

# Compile the model
model.compile(optimizer=SGD(learning_rate=0.01),
loss='sparse_categorical_crossentropy', metrics=['accuracy'])

# Train the model
```

```
model.fit(X, y, epochs=100, verbose=2)
```

TensorFlow and PyTorch are both powerful frameworks that serve different needs. TensorFlow is often preferred for production and deployment in large-scale environments, whereas PyTorch shines in research and experimentation due to its flexibility and ease of use. Both frameworks have evolved significantly over time, making it easier for users to choose between them depending on their specific use case. Whether you're working on cutting-edge research or deploying models to production, both TensorFlow and PyTorch provide the tools necessary to build and scale deep learning applications.

14.4 Hands-on Data Processing with Pandas & NumPy

Data processing and manipulation are crucial steps in the machine learning pipeline. Before any model training can occur, data must be gathered, cleaned, transformed, and often enriched to ensure the best possible performance. In Python, Pandas and NumPy are the two most widely used libraries for these tasks. Together, they provide the tools necessary to manage, process, and analyze data efficiently.

In this section, we will cover the essentials of working with Pandas for data manipulation and NumPy for numerical computations, providing practical hands-on examples to demonstrate their power and versatility.

1. Introduction to Pandas

Pandas is an open-source library that provides easy-to-use data structures and data analysis tools for Python. It is particularly well-suited for structured data (i.e., data in tabular form like CSV files, Excel sheets, SQL databases, etc.).

Key Features of Pandas

- **DataFrames**: The primary data structure in Pandas is the DataFrame, which is essentially a two-dimensional table (like a spreadsheet). It allows for row and column operations.
- **Series**: A one-dimensional array-like object, often used for individual columns of data.
- **Data Cleaning**: Pandas provides powerful tools for cleaning data, including handling missing data, filtering out irrelevant data, and performing transformations.

- **Data Aggregation**: It has built-in functions for grouping, aggregating, and summarizing data.

Installing Pandas

You can install Pandas using pip:

```
pip install pandas
```

Basic DataFrame Operations

Let's start by loading a simple CSV dataset using Pandas.

```python
import pandas as pd

# Load a dataset (example dataset is 'iris.csv')
df = pd.read_csv('iris.csv')

# Show the first 5 rows of the DataFrame
print(df.head())
```

This would output the first 5 rows of the DataFrame, allowing you to preview the data.

DataFrame Slicing and Indexing

You can access rows, columns, and subsets of the data with Pandas.

```python
# Accessing a specific column
sepal_length = df['sepal_length']

# Accessing multiple columns
subset = df[['sepal_length', 'species']]

# Filtering rows based on a condition
setosa = df[df['species'] == 'setosa']
```

Handling Missing Data

Missing data is common in real-world datasets. Pandas provides several ways to handle missing values.

```
# Checking for missing values
print(df.isnull().sum())

# Filling missing values with a specific value (e.g., mean)
df['sepal_length'] = df['sepal_length'].fillna(df['sepal_length'].mean())

# Dropping rows with missing values
df = df.dropna()
```

2. Introduction to NumPy

NumPy (Numerical Python) is a library for numerical computing in Python. It provides support for large, multi-dimensional arrays and matrices, as well as a collection of mathematical functions to operate on these arrays.

Key Features of NumPy

- **ndarray**: The core object in NumPy is the ndarray, a powerful n-dimensional array.
- **Vectorized Operations**: NumPy supports element-wise operations on arrays, allowing for fast, efficient computation.
- **Broadcasting**: NumPy can perform operations on arrays of different shapes, and it automatically aligns dimensions in a process known as broadcasting.
- **Mathematical Functions**: NumPy provides a wide array of mathematical operations such as matrix multiplication, summation, statistics, linear algebra, and more.

Installing NumPy

You can install NumPy with the following pip command:

```
pip install numpy
```

Creating NumPy Arrays

Let's create and manipulate some arrays using NumPy.

```
import numpy as np

# Creating a 1D NumPy array
arr = np.array([1, 2, 3, 4, 5])

# Creating a 2D NumPy array (Matrix)
matrix = np.array([[1, 2, 3], [4, 5, 6]])

# Array with zeros
zeros_array = np.zeros((3, 4))  # 3x4 matrix of zeros

# Array with ones
ones_array = np.ones((2, 3))  # 2x3 matrix of ones

# Random array
random_array = np.random.rand(3, 3)  # 3x3 matrix with random values between 0 and 1
```

Array Operations

You can perform mathematical operations directly on NumPy arrays.

```
# Element-wise addition
arr = np.array([1, 2, 3])
result = arr + 5  # Adding 5 to each element
print(result)  # Output: [6, 7, 8]

# Element-wise multiplication
arr2 = np.array([2, 3, 4])
result = arr * arr2  # Multiplying corresponding elements
print(result)  # Output: [2, 6, 12]

# Matrix multiplication
mat1 = np.array([[1, 2], [3, 4]])
mat2 = np.array([[5, 6], [7, 8]])
result = np.dot(mat1, mat2)  # Matrix multiplication
print(result)
```

3. Combining Pandas & NumPy for Data Processing

Combining Pandas for data manipulation and NumPy for numerical computations allows for more efficient data processing and analysis. Let's go through a hands-on example where we combine these two libraries to preprocess and analyze a dataset.

Example: Data Analysis with Pandas & NumPy

Let's assume we have a dataset of customer transactions with columns like "Age," "Salary," "Purchase Amount," and "Gender." We'll go through the steps of processing this data:

Loading the Data:

```python
import pandas as pd
import numpy as np

# Load the customer transactions data
df = pd.read_csv('customer_data.csv')

# Show the first few rows
print(df.head())
```

Data Cleaning (Handling Missing Values):

```python
# Check for missing values
print(df.isnull().sum())

# Fill missing 'Salary' values with the median salary
df['Salary'] = df['Salary'].fillna(df['Salary'].median())

# Drop rows with missing 'Age'
df = df.dropna(subset=['Age'])
```

Feature Engineering:

```python
# Creating a new feature: "Age Group"
df['Age Group'] = np.where(df['Age'] > 40, 'Senior', 'Junior')
```

```
# Encoding 'Gender' column (Male = 0, Female = 1)
df['Gender'] = np.where(df['Gender'] == 'Male', 0, 1)
```

Statistical Analysis:

```
# Calculate the mean salary for each age group
age_group_salary = df.groupby('Age Group')['Salary'].mean()
print(age_group_salary)

# Get the correlation matrix for numerical features
correlation_matrix = df[['Age', 'Salary', 'Purchase Amount']].corr()
print(correlation_matrix)
```

Data Visualization (Using Pandas built-in plotting functionality):

```
import matplotlib.pyplot as plt

# Plotting the distribution of ages
df['Age'].plot(kind='hist', bins=10, alpha=0.7, color='blue')
plt.title('Age Distribution')
plt.xlabel('Age')
plt.show()

# Scatter plot of Age vs. Purchase Amount
df.plot(kind='scatter', x='Age', y='Purchase Amount', alpha=0.7, color='green')
plt.title('Age vs Purchase Amount')
plt.xlabel('Age')
plt.ylabel('Purchase Amount')
plt.show()
```

In this section, we've explored the core features of Pandas and NumPy for data processing and analysis. These libraries form the backbone of data manipulation in Python, and mastering them will significantly streamline your workflow, especially when preparing data for machine learning.

- Pandas excels at handling structured data and performing operations like filtering, grouping, and aggregating.

- NumPy is essential for numerical operations and working with multi-dimensional arrays, enabling fast computations that are often required during model training.

Together, these two libraries make data manipulation, cleaning, and transformation an easy and efficient process, laying the groundwork for building and deploying machine learning models.

15. Building Your First ML Model

Time to put theory into practice! In this chapter, you'll build your first end-to-end ML model, covering everything from data preprocessing to model training, evaluation, and deployment using real-world datasets.

15.1 Problem Definition & Data Selection

In the journey of building a machine learning (ML) model, the most critical starting point is problem definition and data selection. The success of any machine learning project hinges on how well you define the problem you're trying to solve and how appropriate your data is for solving that problem. In this section, we will dive deep into these foundational steps, exploring how to clearly define a problem and select the right data for machine learning.

1. Understanding Problem Definition

Problem definition is the first and most important step in any machine learning project. It determines the direction of your work and ensures that you are solving the right problem with the appropriate tools. This step helps you establish clear objectives and provides focus throughout the modeling process.

Why is Problem Definition Crucial?

- **Focuses efforts on relevant aspects**: A well-defined problem will highlight the key objectives and drive you to collect and analyze data that directly pertains to those goals.
- **Improves model selection**: The type of machine learning model you choose depends heavily on the problem at hand. Whether it's a classification, regression, or clustering problem influences how the data is used.
- **Establishes metrics for evaluation**: The way you define the problem will help in deciding what success looks like. This is often in the form of performance metrics, such as accuracy, precision, recall, or others depending on the task.

Steps to Define the Problem:

Identify the Goal: Understand what you are trying to achieve with the data. Do you need to classify something, predict future values, or identify patterns?

Example: Predict whether a customer will churn based on their usage patterns (classification problem).

Understand the Business Context: You must consider the context of the problem to ensure the solution you are building provides business value. Discuss with domain experts to identify the key factors impacting the outcome.

Example: In a retail business, predicting customer churn can help create targeted marketing strategies to retain customers.

Specify Input and Output: Clearly define what the inputs (features) and outputs (labels or predictions) are for the model.

Example: For predicting customer churn, inputs could include customer demographics, usage history, customer support interactions, etc. The output would be whether the customer churned (yes/no).

Decide on the Problem Type: Based on the data and the goal, determine the type of problem:

Supervised Learning: If you have labeled data and are predicting an output (e.g., classification, regression).

Unsupervised Learning: If you are identifying patterns or groups in data without labels (e.g., clustering, anomaly detection).

Reinforcement Learning: If the problem involves learning through interaction with an environment (e.g., game AI, robotics).

Clarify Constraints: Identify any constraints or limitations, such as time, computational resources, or data privacy issues.

Example: Defining a Problem

Let's consider an example of predicting house prices. The goal is to predict the price of a house based on features like its size, location, age, etc.

Goal: Predict the price of a house.

Input: Features like square footage, number of bedrooms, neighborhood, age of the house, etc.

Output: A continuous numerical value representing the price.

Type of Problem: This is a regression problem since the output is a continuous variable (price).

2. Data Selection

Once you have a clear problem definition, the next step is selecting the right data. The quality and quantity of data you use directly impact the performance of your machine learning model. Good data selection ensures that the model learns meaningful patterns and can generalize well to unseen data.

Key Factors in Data Selection:

Relevance: The data must be relevant to the problem at hand. Irrelevant features or data that do not have a clear relationship with the outcome will confuse the model and lead to poor performance.

Example: For a house price prediction model, features like the house's color would be irrelevant, whereas features like the number of bedrooms or location would be highly relevant.

Quality: The data needs to be clean, accurate, and complete. Data quality issues like missing values, errors, or duplicates must be addressed before the model is trained.

Example: Missing values in critical features such as the square footage or number of bedrooms can drastically reduce model accuracy, so these need to be handled properly.

Quantity: Sufficient data must be available to train a model effectively. Too little data can lead to overfitting (model performs well on the training set but poorly on unseen data). However, having more data is generally beneficial as it enables the model to learn more patterns.

Example: If you're predicting house prices for a specific city, having data from only a few houses might not allow the model to generalize well. A larger, more diverse dataset would be better.

Data Sources: Identify where your data will come from. There are various sources of data:

Internal Data: Data collected within an organization (e.g., customer transaction logs, product sales data).

External Data: Public datasets, web scraping, third-party data providers, etc.

Feature Selection: Select the most relevant features to predict the target variable. Too many features can make the model overly complex, while too few features may leave out critical information.

Example: For predicting house prices, features like the house's location, size, and condition may be more important than less relevant ones like the type of flooring.

Data Collection Process:

Identify Data Sources: Whether the data comes from existing databases, third-party APIs, or sensors, clearly identify where it will be sourced from.

Example: Data for a house price prediction model can be sourced from real estate websites or public government data.

Preprocessing the Data: Clean the data by handling missing values, outliers, and duplicates. Standardize the format and ensure consistency across the dataset.

Example: If one column uses a different unit (e.g., square feet vs. square meters), convert it to a common unit.

Splitting the Data: Typically, the dataset is split into three parts:

- **Training Set**: The data used to train the model.
- **Validation Set**: Used to tune the hyperparameters of the model.
- **Test Set**: Used to evaluate the performance of the model after training.

Augmenting Data: Sometimes, the available data is not sufficient. In such cases, you may need to augment the data by generating synthetic data or leveraging techniques like data augmentation (especially in image-based models).

Example: In an image recognition task, you can rotate, flip, or adjust images to create new training examples.

Example: Selecting Data for the Problem

For the house price prediction model:

- **Data Sources**: Public real estate listings, government databases, or proprietary internal sales data.
- **Features to Include**: Square footage, number of bedrooms, neighborhood, year built, proximity to amenities, etc.
- **Data Cleaning**: Remove rows with missing house prices or features, handle missing values in the location field by imputing with the most common location, and remove any duplicates.
- **Splitting the Data**: Split the data into 70% training, 15% validation, and 15% test.

In this section, we have discussed the importance of problem definition and data selection in building machine learning models. These two steps lay the groundwork for a successful ML project and directly influence the outcome of your model. Here's a quick recap of the key points:

- **Problem Definition**: Establishes the goal, input/output, problem type, and constraints. It guides you toward selecting the appropriate data and machine learning techniques.
- **Data Selection**: Ensures that you have high-quality, relevant, and sufficient data to solve the problem. Proper data selection involves identifying key features, addressing missing values, and preparing the data for model training.

By mastering problem definition and data selection, you're well on your way to developing effective machine learning solutions that solve real-world problems.

15.2 Training a Simple Model from Scratch

Once you've defined the problem and selected your data, the next step is to start building a machine learning model. While there are many libraries available to train models (such as Scikit-learn, TensorFlow, or PyTorch), sometimes it's useful to train a model from scratch to understand the underlying principles and gain deeper insights into how machine learning works. In this section, we will walk through the process of training a simple model from scratch using Python.

We'll start by training a linear regression model, which is one of the simplest and most widely used algorithms in machine learning. Linear regression aims to predict a continuous target variable based on one or more features.

1. What is Linear Regression?

Linear regression is a statistical method used for modeling the relationship between a dependent variable (the target) and one or more independent variables (the features). The relationship is modeled using a linear equation:

$$y = w_1 x_1 + w_2 x_2 + ... + w_n x_n + b$$

Where:

- y is the predicted output.

- $w_1, w_2, ..., w_n$ are the model's weights (coefficients) for the features.

- $x_1, x_2, ..., x_n$ are the input features.

- b is the bias term, which helps adjust the output.

The goal of linear regression is to find the optimal values of $w_1, w_2, ..., w_n$ and b that minimize the error between the predicted and actual outputs.

2. Steps for Training a Model from Scratch

Step 1: Import Libraries

First, we need to import the necessary libraries. We will be using NumPy for numerical computations and matplotlib for visualization.

```
import numpy as np
import matplotlib.pyplot as plt
```

Step 2: Generate Data (or Use an Existing Dataset)

For simplicity, let's generate some synthetic data. In real-world scenarios, you would load your data using Pandas or another method.

```
# Generate synthetic data for linear regression
# X is the feature (independent variable), and y is the target (dependent variable)
np.random.seed(42)  # For reproducibility
X = 2 * np.random.rand(100, 1)  # 100 random data points between 0 and 2
y = 4 + 3 * X + np.random.randn(100, 1)  # y = 4 + 3*X + noise
```

In this case, the underlying true model is $y = 4 + 3x + \epsilon$, where ϵ is the noise term.

Step 3: Define the Model and Loss Function

We'll train a linear regression model by minimizing the Mean Squared Error (MSE) between the predicted and actual values. The MSE is defined as:

$$MSE = \frac{1}{m} \sum_{i=1}^{m} (y_i - \hat{y}_i)^2$$

Where:

- m is the number of data points.

- y_i is the actual value.

- $\hat{y}_i$ is the predicted value.

For the linear regression model, the prediction is given by:

$$\hat{y} = X \cdot w + b$$

Where:

- X is the input feature.

- w is the weight (slope).

- b is the bias (intercept).

We need to compute the gradient of the loss function to update our weights during training. We'll use Gradient Descent for optimization.

```
# Initialize weights (w) and bias (b) to random values
w = np.random.randn(1, 1)  # Weight (slope)
b = np.random.randn(1)     # Bias (intercept)

# Learning rate and number of iterations
learning_rate = 0.1
iterations = 1000

# Number of training examples
m = len(X)
```

Step 4: Implement Gradient Descent

Gradient Descent is an optimization algorithm used to minimize the loss function. We update the parameters (weights and bias) in the opposite direction of the gradient of the loss function to find the minimum.

The gradients for the weights and bias are computed as follows:

- Gradient of the loss with respect to w (weight):

$$\frac{\partial MSE}{\partial w} = -\frac{2}{m} \sum_{i=1}^{m} X_i(y_i - \hat{y}_i)$$

- Gradient of the loss with respect to b (bias):

$$\frac{\partial MSE}{\partial b} = -\frac{2}{m} \sum_{i=1}^{m} (y_i - \hat{y}_i)$$

```
# Gradient Descent loop
for i in range(iterations):
    # Predictions
    y_pred = X.dot(w) + b
```

```
# Compute the loss (MSE)
loss = (1/m) * np.sum((y_pred - y) ** 2)

# Compute the gradients
dw = -(2/m) * np.sum(X * (y - y_pred))
db = -(2/m) * np.sum(y - y_pred)

# Update the parameters (weights and bias)
w -= learning_rate * dw
b -= learning_rate * db

# Print the loss every 100 iterations for monitoring progress
if i % 100 == 0:
    print(f"Iteration {i}, Loss: {loss}")
```

At each iteration, the model's weights w and bias b are updated using the gradients. This process continues until the loss stops decreasing significantly or the set number of iterations is reached.

Step 5: Visualizing the Results

Once the model is trained, we can visualize the fitted line along with the original data.

```
# Visualize the results
plt.scatter(X, y, color='blue', label='Data points')
plt.plot(X, X.dot(w) + b, color='red', label='Fitted line')
plt.title('Linear Regression - Fitting a Line')
plt.xlabel('X')
plt.ylabel('y')
plt.legend()
plt.show()
```

This will show the scatter plot of the data points and the fitted line from the trained model.

Step 6: Evaluate the Model

To evaluate how well our model performs, we can compute the Mean Squared Error (MSE) on a test set. In this case, we're using the training data as both the training and test set for simplicity.

```
# Test the model
y_pred_test = X.dot(w) + b
mse = np.mean((y_pred_test - y) ** 2)
print(f"Final MSE: {mse}")
```

In this section, we trained a simple linear regression model from scratch using Python and NumPy. The steps we covered are:

- **Data Generation**: We created synthetic data that follows a linear pattern with some added noise.
- **Model Definition**: We defined the model, loss function, and the optimization technique (gradient descent).
- **Training the Model**: We used gradient descent to optimize the model's weights and bias.
- **Visualization**: We visualized the model's predictions alongside the data points to see how well the model fits the data.
- **Evaluation**: We computed the MSE on the training set to evaluate the model's performance.

Training a model from scratch like this helps you understand how machine learning algorithms work under the hood. While libraries like Scikit-learn provide high-level APIs for training models, knowing how to implement algorithms from scratch strengthens your foundation in machine learning.

15.3 Evaluating & Improving Model Performance

After training your machine learning model, the next critical step is to evaluate its performance and determine whether it meets the required criteria. Evaluating your model helps you understand how well it performs on new, unseen data and provides insights into areas where it can be improved. In this section, we'll discuss how to evaluate a model's performance, common evaluation metrics, and strategies for improving your model.

1. Evaluating Model Performance

The evaluation process depends on the type of machine learning problem you're solving—whether it's regression or classification. Different metrics help assess how well the model is generalizing to new data and how close its predictions are to the actual values.

A. Evaluation Metrics for Regression Models

For regression tasks (where the output is continuous), such as predicting house prices or stock prices, we typically use the following metrics:

Mean Absolute Error (MAE):

MAE measures the average absolute differences between predicted and actual values. It's easy to understand and gives a clear picture of how far off predictions are, on average, from the true values.

Formula:

$$MAE = \frac{1}{n} \sum_{i=1}^{n} |y_i - \hat{y}_i|$$

Where:

- y_i is the true value
- $\hat{y}_i$ is the predicted value
- n is the number of predictions

Mean Squared Error (MSE):

MSE gives a higher penalty for larger errors, as the differences are squared. It's more sensitive to large deviations between predicted and actual values.

- Formula:

$$MSE = \frac{1}{n} \sum_{i=1}^{n} (y_i - \hat{y}_i)^2$$

- MSE is commonly used in **regression** tasks.

Root Mean Squared Error (RMSE):

RMSE is the square root of MSE and provides the error in the same units as the target variable. It's useful when the cost of large errors is significant.

- Formula:

$$RMSE = \sqrt{\frac{1}{n}\sum_{i=1}^{n}(y_i - \hat{y}_i)^2}$$

4. R-squared (R^2):

- R^2 represents the proportion of the variance in the dependent variable that is predictable from the independent variables. It provides a measure of how well the regression model fits the data.

- Formula:

$$R^2 = 1 - \frac{\sum_{i=1}^{n}(y_i - \hat{y}_i)^2}{\sum_{i=1}^{n}(y_i - \bar{y})^2}$$

Where $\bar{y}$ is the mean of the actual values. An R^2 value close to 1 indicates a good fit, while a value close to 0 indicates poor predictive performance.

B. Evaluation Metrics for Classification Models

For classification tasks (where the output is categorical, such as determining whether an email is spam or not), the following metrics are commonly used:

Accuracy:

Accuracy is the simplest and most commonly used metric for classification tasks. It measures the percentage of correct predictions.

- Formula:

$$Accuracy = \frac{TP + TN}{TP + TN + FP + FN}$$

Where:

- TP: True Positives (correctly predicted positive instances)

- TN: True Negatives (correctly predicted negative instances)

- FP: False Positives (incorrectly predicted as positive)

- FN: False Negatives (incorrectly predicted as negative)

Precision:

Precision measures the accuracy of positive predictions. It is the ratio of true positive predictions to the total predicted positives.

- Formula:

$$Precision = \frac{TP}{TP + FP}$$

- Precision is especially useful in scenarios where false positives are costly (e.g., detecting fraudulent transactions).

Recall (Sensitivity or True Positive Rate):

Recall measures the model's ability to detect positive instances. It is the ratio of true positive predictions to the total actual positives.

- Formula:

$$Recall = \frac{TP}{TP + FN}$$

- Recall is important when false negatives are costly (e.g., in medical diagnoses, where missing a positive case can be dangerous).

F1-Score:

The F1-Score is the harmonic mean of precision and recall. It provides a single metric that balances both precision and recall, especially useful when you need to strike a balance between the two.

- Formula:

$$F1 = 2 \times \frac{Precision \times Recall}{Precision + Recall}$$

Confusion Matrix:

A confusion matrix is a table that summarizes the performance of a classification model by showing the counts of true positives, false positives, true negatives, and false negatives. It provides more detailed information on how the model is performing.

2. Improving Model Performance

After evaluating your model, you may find areas for improvement. There are several techniques to enhance the performance of machine learning models.

A. Feature Engineering

Feature Selection:

Sometimes, models underperform because irrelevant or redundant features are included. By carefully selecting the most important features, you can reduce the complexity of the model and improve performance.

Techniques:

- **Filter Methods**: Use statistical tests to rank features based on their relevance to the target variable.
- **Wrapper Methods**: Train models with different feature subsets and evaluate their performance.
- **Embedded Methods**: Use algorithms that perform feature selection as part of the training process (e.g., decision trees).

Feature Transformation:

Transform features to better capture the underlying patterns in the data. For example, using log transformations for highly skewed features can help linear models perform better.

Interaction Features:

Create new features that capture interactions between existing features. For example, multiplying two features might capture an important relationship not immediately apparent.

B. Model Selection

Try Different Models:

Different models have different strengths. If your current model isn't performing well, consider trying other algorithms. For example, try switching from linear regression to decision trees or support vector machines for more complex relationships in the data.

Ensemble Methods:

Combine multiple models to improve overall performance. Common ensemble methods include:

- **Bagging (e.g., Random Forests):** Reduces variance by training multiple models on different subsets of the data.
- **Boosting (e.g., Gradient Boosting Machines, XGBoost):** Focuses on correcting the errors of previous models to reduce bias.
- **Stacking**: Combines different types of models by training a meta-model on their outputs.

C. Hyperparameter Tuning

Grid Search:

Grid search involves training a model using various combinations of hyperparameters and selecting the one that yields the best performance. It's a brute-force method that tries all possible combinations.

Random Search:

Random search is less exhaustive than grid search. It randomly selects hyperparameters from a defined range and evaluates the model's performance. It's often faster and can find better solutions than grid search, especially when there are many hyperparameters to tune.

Bayesian Optimization:

Bayesian optimization is a more advanced method that builds a probabilistic model to guide the search for the best hyperparameters. It tries to intelligently select hyperparameters that are likely to improve performance based on past results.

D. Regularization

L1 and L2 Regularization:

Regularization methods such as L1 (Lasso) and L2 (Ridge) are used to penalize large coefficients in regression models. They prevent overfitting by reducing the model's complexity, ensuring the model does not fit the noise in the training data.

Dropout (for Neural Networks):

In deep learning models, dropout is a regularization technique where random units (nodes) in the neural network are "dropped" (i.e., set to zero) during training to prevent overfitting.

E. Cross-Validation

K-Fold Cross-Validation:

- The dataset is divided into k folds.
- For each fold, the model is trained on $k-1$ folds and tested on the remaining fold.
- This process repeats k times, with each fold being used as the test set once.

The advantage of k-fold cross-validation is that it helps ensure that each data point gets used for both training and testing, providing a more robust estimate of the model's performance.

Leave-One-Out Cross-Validation (LOOCV):

LOOCV is an extreme form of cross-validation where each data point is used once as a test set. While computationally expensive, it can provide a more accurate estimate of the model's generalization ability.

Evaluating and improving model performance is an ongoing process that is essential for developing robust machine learning models. Key steps include:

- **Evaluating Model Performance**: Choose appropriate metrics for your problem, such as MSE for regression or accuracy, precision, recall, and F1-score for classification.
- **Improving Model Performance**: Focus on feature engineering, selecting the right model, hyperparameter tuning, and applying regularization techniques to prevent overfitting.
- **Cross-Validation**: Use techniques like K-Fold Cross-Validation to assess the generalizability of your model.

By following these steps, you can continually improve your model and ensure that it performs well not just on training data but also on unseen, real-world data.

15.4 Deploying a Model for Real-World Use

Once you've trained and evaluated your machine learning model, the next essential step is to deploy it so that it can be used in a real-world environment. This stage of the process involves taking your model from a development environment and integrating it into a live system where it can make predictions on new data. Proper deployment ensures that your model is scalable, reliable, and performs well over time. In this section, we'll cover the various steps involved in deploying a machine learning model, from setting up the infrastructure to monitoring the model's performance post-deployment.

1. Preparing the Model for Deployment

Before deploying a machine learning model, it's important to ensure that it's ready for production. This includes finalizing the model, ensuring it's well-optimized, and preparing it to handle real-world data.

A. Finalizing the Model

Model Serialization (Saving the Model):

Once your model is trained and tuned, you need to save it so that it can be reused without retraining. This process is called serialization. Common methods for saving models include:

- **Pickle (Python):** A Python module used to serialize and deserialize objects. You can save the entire model or only specific parts of it (e.g., the model weights or parameters).
- **Joblib (Python):** Similar to Pickle but optimized for handling large numerical arrays. Joblib is a good choice for saving models with large datasets or complex parameters.
- **TensorFlow SavedModel**: For TensorFlow models, the SavedModel format provides a robust way to store models, including their architecture, weights, and metadata.

Model Optimization:

Optimize your model to ensure it runs efficiently in a production environment. Optimization can include:

- **Reducing Model Size**: Compressing the model size without compromising accuracy, such as pruning unnecessary neurons or quantizing model weights.
- **Model Pruning**: Removing redundant neurons or layers from the neural network to reduce its complexity and improve inference speed.
- **Quantization**: Reducing the precision of model weights (e.g., from float32 to int8) to make the model faster and more memory-efficient, particularly in resource-constrained environments like mobile devices.

B. Environment Preparation

Before you deploy your model, ensure that the environment it will run in is ready. This involves setting up the infrastructure, selecting the appropriate deployment platform, and preparing the system to handle the model's input and output.

Environment Setup:

- Set up a production environment where your model will run. This can be done using containerization technologies like Docker, which allows you to create a portable and consistent environment for your model.

- Docker: Docker is a popular tool that enables you to package your model and its dependencies into a container that can be easily deployed to various platforms. This ensures that your model runs consistently across different environments.

Cloud vs. On-Premise:

- Decide where to deploy your model: in the cloud or on-premise. Cloud services like Amazon Web Services (AWS), Google Cloud Platform (GCP), and Microsoft Azure offer specialized tools for model deployment, including infrastructure, auto-scaling, and monitoring. On-premise deployment is an option when data privacy or latency is a concern.

Choosing the Right Deployment Platform:

Several platforms cater specifically to deploying machine learning models:

- **AWS SageMaker, Google AI Platform, Azure ML**: These platforms provide end-to-end machine learning model deployment services, including model hosting, scaling, and monitoring.
- **TensorFlow Serving**: If you're using TensorFlow, you can use TensorFlow Serving to deploy models in production environments.
- **Flask/FastAPI**: For custom deployment, particularly in small-scale applications or when building REST APIs for your models, frameworks like Flask or FastAPI in Python allow you to serve models as APIs that can receive requests and return predictions.

2. Deploying the Model

Now that your model is prepared, it's time to deploy it for real-world use. There are several common methods to deploy machine learning models depending on the type of application and infrastructure.

A. Model Deployment as a Service (API)

One of the most common methods for deploying a model is to expose it as a REST API (Representational State Transfer). In this approach, your model is hosted on a server and can receive requests, process input data, and return predictions.

Building the API:

Use web frameworks like Flask or FastAPI in Python to create an API that serves your model. The basic flow is as follows:

- Set up a web server that listens for incoming HTTP requests.
- Preprocess the incoming data.
- Pass the data to your model to get predictions.
- Postprocess the results and return them in a suitable format (e.g., JSON).

Containerization with Docker:

Package your model and API into a Docker container to make it easier to deploy. Docker containers allow you to bundle all the dependencies (e.g., Python libraries, model files, etc.) required to run your model into one unit. This makes it easy to deploy the model on any machine with Docker installed, whether on-premise or in the cloud.

Deploying to the Cloud:

Deploy your containerized application to cloud services like AWS EC2, Google Cloud Run, or Azure App Service. These services allow you to run your application with minimal setup, and they automatically scale to handle varying traffic loads.

B. Batch Processing

If real-time predictions are not required, you can deploy the model for batch processing. In this scenario, data is collected over time, and the model processes it in bulk periodically, rather than handling individual requests in real-time.

For example, you can deploy your model to run periodically using Apache Airflow or AWS Lambda for scheduled execution. This is often used for cases like periodic predictions or batch updates to databases.

C. Model Deployment in Edge Devices

In some scenarios, you might want to deploy your model directly onto edge devices, such as smartphones, IoT devices, or embedded systems. This is often required in use cases where low latency or offline access to predictions is important.

Optimizing for Edge Deployment:

Models deployed on edge devices need to be highly optimized to work within the constraints of the device's processing power and memory. Techniques like quantization, pruning, and model distillation can help reduce the size of the model and make it more efficient for real-time inference.

Frameworks for Edge Deployment:

There are several frameworks and platforms designed for deploying machine learning models to edge devices:

- **TensorFlow Lite**: A lightweight version of TensorFlow designed for mobile and embedded devices.
- **ONNX Runtime**: Open Neural Network Exchange (ONNX) allows you to deploy models across a wide range of platforms, including edge devices.
- **CoreML**: A framework for deploying models on Apple devices like iPhones, iPads, and Macs.

3. Monitoring and Maintaining the Model

Once the model is deployed, continuous monitoring and maintenance are essential to ensure it continues to perform well in the real world. Over time, models may degrade in performance due to data drift, concept drift, or other factors, and they may need to be retrained.

A. Monitoring Model Performance

Tracking Model Metrics:

Continuously track key performance metrics such as accuracy, precision, recall, and other relevant metrics, depending on the model type. Setting up automatic alerts for when performance drops can help catch problems early.

Data Drift Detection:

Data drift occurs when the distribution of incoming data changes over time. For instance, if customer behavior changes significantly, a model trained on old data might not be relevant anymore. Detecting data drift allows you to retrain the model using more recent data.

Concept Drift Detection:

Concept drift refers to changes in the relationship between inputs and outputs. For example, if you are predicting sales based on historical data, changes in market conditions might affect the relationship between input features and sales. Detecting concept drift helps ensure the model remains accurate as new trends emerge.

B. Model Retraining

Retraining the Model:

Depending on the type of drift or degradation in model performance, you may need to retrain your model periodically with new data. Automation tools like MLflow, Kubeflow, or AWS SageMaker provide workflows to automate model retraining and redeployment.

A/B Testing:

To ensure that the updated model performs better than the previous version, you can perform A/B testing, where different versions of the model are served to different subsets of users, and the performance of each model is compared.

C. Handling Model Updates

Rolling Updates:

When updating a deployed model, use rolling updates to minimize disruptions. Gradually deploy the new version while monitoring its performance, ensuring that the old model is still available in case issues arise.

Versioning:

Maintain different versions of the model to track changes and rollback to previous versions if necessary. This is important for debugging and understanding how the model's performance has changed over time.

Deploying a machine learning model for real-world use is a complex but crucial part of the ML lifecycle. It involves preparing the model for deployment, selecting the right deployment method (API, batch processing, or edge devices), and ensuring that the system is scalable, reliable, and robust. Monitoring the model's performance post-deployment is equally important to maintain its accuracy and relevance over time. By following the right practices, you can successfully deploy and maintain a machine learning model that provides valuable insights and makes accurate predictions in a real-world context.

16. ML in the Real World

Machine Learning is shaping industries like healthcare, finance, and e-commerce. This chapter explores case studies where ML is driving innovation, demonstrating its impact on business, automation, and everyday life.

16.1 ML in Finance (Fraud Detection, Algorithmic Trading)

Machine learning (ML) has rapidly become an essential tool in the finance industry, transforming how financial institutions, traders, and investors make decisions. From detecting fraudulent activity to automating trading strategies, ML offers the potential to uncover insights, optimize operations, and enhance decision-making processes in the world of finance. In this section, we will explore two critical applications of ML in the financial sector: fraud detection and algorithmic trading.

1. Fraud Detection

Fraud detection is one of the most crucial applications of machine learning in finance. Financial institutions, including banks, credit card companies, and payment systems, face significant challenges in identifying fraudulent activities. Traditional rule-based systems often struggle to adapt to new types of fraud, making it difficult to detect suspicious activities in real-time. This is where machine learning comes into play.

A. The Role of ML in Fraud Detection

Machine learning models can process vast amounts of transaction data and learn patterns associated with both legitimate and fraudulent behavior. By identifying subtle anomalies in transaction history, ML algorithms can detect fraud at a much earlier stage than traditional systems.

Anomaly Detection:

- Anomaly detection is a primary technique used in fraud detection. It involves training machine learning models to recognize normal behavior patterns of users or accounts. When a transaction deviates from these patterns, it is flagged as potentially fraudulent.
- For example, a sudden large withdrawal from an account located in a different country or an abnormal spending pattern on a credit card could trigger an alert.

Supervised Learning:

- In supervised learning for fraud detection, historical data containing labeled instances of both fraudulent and non-fraudulent transactions is used to train a classifier. The model learns to distinguish between the two categories and predicts the likelihood that a given transaction is fraudulent.
- Algorithms such as Logistic Regression, Random Forests, Support Vector Machines (SVM), and Gradient Boosting Machines (e.g., XGBoost) are frequently employed for this purpose.

Unsupervised Learning:

- When labeled data is unavailable, unsupervised learning methods are used for fraud detection. Clustering algorithms like K-Means or DBSCAN can group transactions with similar characteristics. Transactions that do not fit into any cluster are flagged as potential fraud cases.
- Isolation Forests and Autoencoders are also popular unsupervised techniques for detecting anomalies and unusual behavior patterns that might indicate fraud.

B. Key Features Used for Fraud Detection

Several features are important in identifying potential fraudulent activities. These can be extracted from transaction data and account behavior:

Transaction Amount: Larger or unusual transactions, especially when they occur outside regular spending patterns, can be a red flag for fraud.

Transaction Location: A sudden change in location, such as a credit card being used in a country far from the user's typical geographical area, can indicate unauthorized usage.

Time of Transaction: Fraudulent activity may occur at odd hours or during times when the account holder would not normally be making transactions.

Transaction Frequency: A spike in the frequency of transactions or sudden bursts of activity can indicate fraudulent behavior.

Device Information: Information about the device or IP address used for the transaction can help detect fraud, especially when used inconsistently or from unknown devices.

Account History: The history of the account, such as long periods of inactivity followed by sudden activity, can be a strong signal for fraud.

C. Real-World Example: Credit Card Fraud Detection

Credit card companies use machine learning to analyze cardholder transactions in real-time. They can identify if a transaction is likely fraudulent by comparing the transaction details (location, amount, time) with the cardholder's usual patterns. If the model identifies a significant deviation, it can trigger a flag or require further verification from the cardholder.

A popular example of an ML model used for fraud detection in credit card transactions is Random Forests. This algorithm can handle large datasets with multiple features and detect complex relationships between transaction features that may not be apparent with simpler algorithms.

2. Algorithmic Trading

Algorithmic trading involves the use of computer algorithms to automate trading decisions based on predefined criteria. In financial markets, speed, precision, and accuracy are critical, and machine learning plays a key role in improving these factors. By leveraging historical market data, news, and other factors, ML models can develop complex trading strategies that continuously adapt to market conditions.

A. The Role of ML in Algorithmic Trading

Machine learning enables traders to create and execute algorithms that analyze market trends and predict future movements. These algorithms can react to new information faster and more accurately than human traders, making them highly valuable in the fast-paced world of finance.

Price Prediction and Forecasting:

ML models, particularly Regression Models and Time Series Models (such as LSTMs), are used to predict future asset prices or market trends. These predictions are often based on historical price data, market sentiment, and other relevant features such as volume or volatility.

Sentiment Analysis:

Sentiment analysis is a subfield of natural language processing (NLP) that can be used to analyze financial news, reports, social media, and other unstructured data sources. By understanding market sentiment, ML models can predict how market participants will react to news, earnings reports, or geopolitical events.

For example, if a company announces a positive earnings report, the model can analyze the sentiment of the news articles and social media to predict a potential increase in the company's stock price.

Feature Engineering:

ML in algorithmic trading relies heavily on feature engineering to identify patterns that indicate profitable trading opportunities. Some features that can be used include moving averages, momentum indicators, relative strength indices (RSI), and other technical indicators.

B. Common Algorithms Used in Algorithmic Trading

Various machine learning techniques are applied to algorithmic trading, each serving different purposes depending on the strategy:

Supervised Learning:

Linear Regression, Random Forests, and Gradient Boosting Machines (GBM) are commonly used for predicting asset prices based on historical data.

Reinforcement Learning:

Reinforcement learning (RL) has gained significant popularity in algorithmic trading. In RL, an agent (the trading algorithm) learns optimal trading strategies by interacting with the environment and receiving feedback (rewards or penalties) based on the performance of trades. The agent adapts its strategy over time to maximize its long-term profits.

Algorithms like Deep Q-Learning and Proximal Policy Optimization (PPO) are widely used in RL-based trading strategies.

Neural Networks:

Deep Learning techniques, including Convolutional Neural Networks (CNNs) and Recurrent Neural Networks (RNNs), are used to model complex patterns and time-dependent structures in financial markets.

LSTM Networks are particularly useful for time series forecasting, as they can capture long-term dependencies in sequential data, making them a popular choice for stock price prediction and financial time series analysis.

Genetic Algorithms and Evolutionary Strategies:

Genetic algorithms are used to evolve optimal trading strategies through simulated evolution. By combining randomness and selection, genetic algorithms can generate and refine trading strategies over multiple iterations.

C. High-Frequency Trading (HFT) and Machine Learning

High-frequency trading (HFT) refers to algorithmic trading strategies that involve executing a large number of orders in fractions of a second. In HFT, speed is of the essence, and ML techniques can be used to optimize decision-making and execution strategies. HFT systems often use ML models to predict small price movements, identify liquidity opportunities, and improve trade execution algorithms.

Machine learning's role in HFT is to identify market inefficiencies that can be exploited for profit, analyze vast amounts of market data in real-time, and automatically adjust strategies based on market conditions.

3. Challenges and Ethical Considerations in ML in Finance

While ML has significant potential to revolutionize finance, there are some challenges and ethical considerations to address:

Model Interpretability:

Machine learning models, especially deep learning models, are often seen as "black boxes." In finance, where decisions can have major consequences, it's critical to ensure that models are interpretable and their decisions can be explained.

Bias and Fairness:

Machine learning models can inadvertently learn biases from historical data, leading to unfair outcomes in areas like credit scoring or loan approval. Ensuring fairness and preventing bias is essential in financial applications.

Market Manipulation:

Algorithmic trading and ML-driven systems may unintentionally cause market manipulation or exacerbate volatility. Regulators are working on frameworks to monitor and prevent unethical practices.

Data Privacy:

Financial institutions must ensure that sensitive customer data used in ML models is protected and handled in compliance with privacy regulations, such as GDPR or CCPA.

Machine learning has become an indispensable tool in modern finance, significantly enhancing fraud detection and algorithmic trading capabilities. In fraud detection, ML models help identify suspicious patterns and prevent financial crime, while in algorithmic trading, they enable traders to make data-driven decisions and execute strategies at high speeds. However, as these technologies continue to evolve, it's essential to address challenges such as model transparency, fairness, and regulatory compliance. As the financial industry continues to embrace machine learning, its applications will likely expand, offering new opportunities and efficiencies for both financial institutions and their customers.

16.2 ML in Healthcare (Disease Prediction, Drug Discovery)

The application of machine learning (ML) in healthcare has revolutionized the way medical professionals approach diagnostics, treatment, and the discovery of new therapies. By harnessing the power of large datasets, machine learning models can recognize patterns, make predictions, and optimize decision-making in ways that were not possible before. In this section, we will explore two significant applications of ML in healthcare: disease prediction and drug discovery.

1. Disease Prediction

Disease prediction refers to the process of using machine learning algorithms to analyze data and predict the likelihood of a person developing a specific disease or health condition in the future. By analyzing patient data, including medical history, lifestyle factors, and genetic information, ML models can help healthcare providers identify individuals at high risk of developing diseases, enabling earlier interventions and better patient outcomes.

A. The Role of ML in Disease Prediction

Machine learning models are particularly well-suited for disease prediction because of their ability to analyze large, complex datasets and learn intricate relationships between variables that might be too subtle for human experts to detect. These models can recognize patterns in patient records and correlate them with disease outcomes, which is invaluable in preventive healthcare.

Data Sources:

ML models rely on diverse data sources, including electronic health records (EHRs), genomic data, medical imaging, patient-reported outcomes, and lifestyle information.

The vast amount of data available today enables the development of more accurate predictive models, but it also requires sophisticated algorithms to extract meaningful patterns and avoid overfitting.

Supervised Learning:

Disease prediction typically involves supervised learning, where the model is trained on historical data with labeled outcomes (e.g., whether a patient developed a disease or not). The goal is to learn the relationship between patient characteristics and disease occurrence, and then predict the likelihood of disease for new, unseen patients.

For instance, models can predict the likelihood of conditions such as diabetes, heart disease, cancer, stroke, and Alzheimer's disease based on factors such as blood pressure, cholesterol levels, family history, age, and lifestyle habits.

B. Examples of Disease Prediction Applications

Cardiovascular Disease Prediction:

Cardiovascular disease (CVD) is one of the leading causes of death worldwide. Machine learning algorithms are used to predict the likelihood of heart disease by analyzing patient data, such as age, blood pressure, cholesterol levels, physical activity, smoking status, and family medical history.

Algorithms like Logistic Regression, Random Forests, and Support Vector Machines (SVM) are often employed to predict whether a patient is at risk of developing CVD in the near future. These models can identify high-risk individuals, allowing for early intervention with lifestyle changes or medication.

Cancer Diagnosis and Prediction:

ML is widely used in oncology to predict the likelihood of cancer based on factors such as genetic information, biomarkers, and medical imaging.

For example, ML models can analyze mammograms and biopsy images to detect early signs of breast cancer or lung cancer. Convolutional Neural Networks (CNNs), a type of deep learning model, are highly effective for processing medical images and identifying tumors in imaging data.

In addition, genetic sequencing data can be used to predict a patient's risk of developing specific types of cancer, as well as personalize their treatment options.

Diabetes Prediction:

Machine learning is widely used to predict the onset of Type 2 diabetes by analyzing patient data, such as age, body mass index (BMI), family history, blood sugar levels, and lifestyle habits.

Models can predict whether a person is likely to develop diabetes, allowing for early intervention to prevent or delay the disease through lifestyle modifications, such as improving diet and increasing physical activity.

Neurological Disease Prediction:

In the case of Alzheimer's disease or Parkinson's disease, machine learning models can analyze a patient's cognitive test results, brain scans (such as MRI), and genetic data to predict the likelihood of developing these conditions.

ML techniques such as Support Vector Machines (SVM), Random Forests, and Recurrent Neural Networks (RNNs) have shown promise in early detection, helping to identify patients who may benefit from early-stage interventions or therapies.

C. Benefits and Challenges of Disease Prediction in Healthcare

Benefits:

- **Early Detection and Prevention**: By identifying high-risk individuals early, machine learning models enable timely interventions, which can prevent or mitigate the severity of diseases.
- **Personalized Treatment**: Disease prediction models can help tailor treatment plans based on individual risk profiles, improving the efficacy of treatments and reducing unnecessary interventions.
- **Improved Healthcare Efficiency**: Automated predictions reduce the workload of healthcare providers and allow them to focus on high-risk patients who require immediate attention.

Challenges:

- **Data Quality and Availability**: Disease prediction models require high-quality, accurate, and comprehensive data. Incomplete or biased data can lead to inaccurate predictions.
- **Model Interpretability**: While complex ML models may provide high accuracy, their "black-box" nature can make it difficult to understand how decisions are made, which is a concern in healthcare where transparency is important.
- **Ethical Concerns**: There are ethical issues around the use of personal health data. Ensuring patient privacy and data security is paramount when implementing ML models in healthcare.

2. Drug Discovery

The process of discovering new drugs is long, costly, and uncertain. Machine learning is transforming drug discovery by enabling researchers to analyze vast amounts of data to predict which drug compounds will be most effective in treating specific diseases. By utilizing ML, researchers can accelerate the identification of potential drug candidates, design more efficient clinical trials, and minimize the risks and costs associated with traditional drug development.

A. The Role of ML in Drug Discovery

Machine learning can optimize various stages of drug discovery, from initial compound screening to preclinical and clinical testing. By using ML, pharmaceutical companies and research institutions can identify promising drug candidates faster, predict their interactions with target proteins, and optimize dosing regimens. ML models can also help identify potential side effects and predict how patients will respond to different drugs.

Drug Target Identification:

- Identifying the biological target (e.g., protein or gene) that a drug should interact with is one of the first steps in drug discovery. Machine learning algorithms can analyze large datasets from genomics, proteomics, and metabolomics to identify potential drug targets.
- Deep learning and unsupervised learning methods can find hidden patterns in biological data, leading to the discovery of new therapeutic targets.

Compound Screening and Virtual Screening:

- Traditional drug discovery methods involve testing thousands of compounds in the lab to identify those that show therapeutic potential. Machine learning can speed up this process by analyzing the chemical structure of compounds and predicting their likelihood of interacting with a target protein.
- Quantitative Structure-Activity Relationship (QSAR) models are widely used in virtual screening to predict the biological activity of molecules based on their chemical structure.
- Models like Random Forests and Deep Neural Networks have been successfully applied to predict which drug molecules are most likely to bind to a specific protein target, helping to narrow down the list of potential candidates for further testing.

Clinical Trial Optimization:

- Machine learning is also used to optimize the design and execution of clinical trials by predicting patient responses, identifying optimal dosing schedules, and reducing trial failures.
- Reinforcement learning algorithms can simulate clinical trial scenarios and suggest optimal strategies for patient enrollment, trial monitoring, and adaptive trial designs.

Drug Repurposing:

- Drug repurposing, or repositioning, refers to the process of finding new uses for existing drugs. ML models can identify similarities between diseases and drugs, helping to discover new therapeutic applications for drugs that are already approved for other conditions.

- For example, Deep Learning and Graph Neural Networks can be used to mine databases of existing drugs and their known interactions to find potential new indications.

B. Examples of ML in Drug Discovery

Predicting Drug-Drug Interactions:

ML algorithms can predict potential interactions between drugs, helping to identify harmful combinations that may lead to adverse reactions. This can be achieved by analyzing chemical structures, biological data, and clinical data on drug interactions.

Optimizing Drug Dosage:

ML models can predict the optimal dosage of a drug for different patient populations based on factors such as age, weight, genetic factors, and drug metabolism rates. Personalized dosing recommendations help maximize therapeutic efficacy and minimize side effects.

Cancer Drug Discovery:

ML is playing a key role in the discovery of cancer therapies. By analyzing genomic and proteomic data, ML models can predict which cancer mutations are most likely to respond to specific drugs, enabling personalized cancer treatment regimens.

3. Challenges and Ethical Considerations in Drug Discovery

Data Quality and Bias:

Like disease prediction, the quality of data used in drug discovery is paramount. If the data is biased or incomplete, the resulting models may not yield accurate or safe predictions.

Regulatory Approval:

While ML models can significantly speed up drug discovery, regulatory agencies like the FDA must assess the safety and efficacy of drugs through rigorous clinical trials. ML predictions should be viewed as a tool to aid decision-making, not a substitute for clinical validation.

Ethical Concerns:

As with any application of ML in healthcare, ethical considerations regarding patient privacy, data security, and fairness are crucial. Data used for drug discovery should be anonymized, and the models should be transparent and interpretable to avoid unethical use of patient information.

Machine learning has become an invaluable tool in healthcare, enabling earlier disease detection, personalized treatment plans, and faster, more efficient drug discovery. The ability of ML models to process and analyze vast amounts of data has the potential to revolutionize the way diseases are predicted, diagnosed, and treated, as well as accelerate the development of life-saving drugs. However, challenges remain in ensuring data quality, model interpretability, and ethical considerations in both disease prediction and drug discovery. As ML continues to advance, its impact on healthcare will only grow, offering new opportunities for improving patient outcomes and optimizing medical practices.

16.3 ML in E-Commerce (Recommendation Systems, Customer Segmentation)

The e-commerce industry has seen an exponential rise in recent years, driven by the increasing use of the internet and advancements in technology. As the volume of data generated by consumers continues to grow, machine learning (ML) has emerged as a game-changer in optimizing e-commerce operations. From personalizing user experiences to enhancing operational efficiency, ML plays a pivotal role in shaping the future of online shopping. In this section, we will explore two key applications of machine learning in e-commerce: Recommendation Systems and Customer Segmentation.

1. Recommendation Systems

Recommendation systems are one of the most widely used applications of machine learning in e-commerce. These systems aim to provide personalized product suggestions to users based on their preferences, behaviors, and past interactions with the platform. By making relevant recommendations, e-commerce businesses can improve user experience, increase sales, and build customer loyalty.

A. How Recommendation Systems Work

Recommendation systems typically rely on historical data about users and items (products, services, or content) to make predictions about what a user may like. These systems can be broadly classified into three categories: Collaborative Filtering, Content-Based Filtering, and Hybrid Approaches.

Collaborative Filtering (CF):

- Collaborative filtering is based on the idea that users who have agreed on past preferences will continue to agree in the future. It predicts the products a user may be interested in by leveraging the preferences of similar users.
- User-based collaborative filtering involves finding users with similar tastes and recommending products that those similar users have liked.
- Item-based collaborative filtering focuses on recommending items that are similar to items the user has interacted with. For instance, if a user bought product A, the system will recommend product B, which has been purchased by users who bought A.

Content-Based Filtering:

- In content-based filtering, the system recommends items based on their features and the user's past interactions with similar items. For example, if a user has previously purchased running shoes, the system will recommend other products with similar features, such as athletic wear or running accessories.
- The algorithm uses metadata such as product descriptions, tags, and categories to match items with user preferences.

Hybrid Recommendation Systems:

- Hybrid models combine the strengths of collaborative filtering and content-based filtering. By blending both approaches, hybrid recommendation systems can overcome the limitations of each individual method (e.g., cold-start problem in collaborative filtering or overspecialization in content-based filtering).
- For instance, a hybrid approach may use collaborative filtering to suggest items based on user similarity and content-based filtering to refine those recommendations by considering product characteristics.

B. Applications of Recommendation Systems in E-Commerce

Product Recommendations:

The most common use of recommendation systems in e-commerce is suggesting products to customers based on their past behavior, such as previous purchases, browsing history, or search queries. For example, Amazon's recommendation engine is known for displaying items like "Customers who bought this also bought" or "Inspired by your browsing history."

Personalized Marketing:

ML algorithms analyze customer behavior and segment users based on their interests, enabling personalized email marketing campaigns or special promotions. For instance, e-commerce platforms can send personalized product recommendations via email or push notifications based on user browsing or purchase patterns.

Content Recommendations:

Platforms like Netflix, YouTube, and Spotify use recommendation systems to suggest movies, TV shows, or music based on user preferences. The underlying principles of these recommendation systems are similar to e-commerce product recommendations, leveraging both collaborative filtering and content-based filtering to tailor suggestions.

Dynamic Pricing and Offers:

Recommendation systems can be used to suggest personalized pricing or discount offers to customers. By analyzing user purchasing patterns, these systems can predict when a customer is more likely to make a purchase and offer targeted discounts or time-limited deals.

Cross-Selling and Upselling:

E-commerce platforms can use recommendation systems to suggest complementary or higher-value products. For example, when a customer adds a laptop to their shopping cart, the system may recommend accessories such as laptop bags, headphones, or extended warranties.

C. Benefits and Challenges of Recommendation Systems

Benefits:

- **Improved User Experience**: Personalized recommendations enhance the shopping experience by helping customers find products that align with their preferences and needs.
- **Increased Sales**: By suggesting relevant products, recommendation systems can increase the likelihood of purchase, leading to higher conversion rates and average order values.
- **Customer Retention**: Tailored recommendations can boost customer loyalty, as customers feel that the platform understands their preferences and offers a more personalized experience.

Challenges:

- **Cold-Start Problem**: One of the challenges with collaborative filtering is the cold-start problem, where new users or new items with limited data may not receive accurate recommendations.
- **Data Privacy Concerns**: The use of customer data to generate personalized recommendations raises privacy concerns, and e-commerce platforms must ensure they comply with regulations such as the General Data Protection Regulation (GDPR).
- **Overfitting**: Recommendation models can sometimes become too focused on past behavior, leading to overfitting. As a result, users may receive overly repetitive suggestions, preventing them from discovering new products.
- **Bias in Recommendations**: Algorithms can inadvertently perpetuate biases present in historical data. If a recommendation system is trained on biased data, it may result in unfair or skewed recommendations that favor certain groups or products.

2. Customer Segmentation

Customer segmentation is the process of dividing a customer base into distinct groups based on common characteristics, such as demographics, behaviors, and purchasing patterns. By identifying and understanding these segments, e-commerce businesses can create targeted marketing campaigns, improve product offerings, and optimize customer service.

Machine learning techniques are particularly useful for customer segmentation because they can automatically identify patterns and create segments based on large and complex datasets.

A. How Customer Segmentation Works

Customer segmentation typically involves clustering similar customers based on multiple variables. Machine learning algorithms are used to analyze customer data and group customers who exhibit similar behaviors or characteristics. The most common ML techniques for customer segmentation include:

K-Means Clustering:

- K-means clustering is a popular unsupervised learning algorithm used for grouping customers based on similar attributes. It works by partitioning the dataset into K clusters, with each cluster representing a group of similar customers.
- The algorithm assigns each customer to a cluster based on factors such as purchase history, frequency, and amount spent, and then iteratively adjusts the cluster centers to minimize the distance between customers and their respective centroids.

Hierarchical Clustering:

Hierarchical clustering builds a tree of customer segments by iteratively merging or splitting clusters based on similarity. This method does not require specifying the number of clusters in advance and can provide more nuanced insights into customer segmentation.

DBSCAN (Density-Based Spatial Clustering of Applications with Noise):

DBSCAN is another clustering algorithm that groups customers based on density. It is particularly useful for identifying segments of varying shapes and sizes, as well as handling outliers (customers who don't fit into any particular group).

Principal Component Analysis (PCA):

PCA is often used for dimensionality reduction in customer segmentation tasks. It reduces the number of features in the dataset while preserving the most important information. PCA is helpful when working with high-dimensional customer data, such as when combining demographic and behavioral information.

Latent Class Analysis (LCA):

LCA is a statistical method used to identify unobserved subgroups within a population. In customer segmentation, LCA can reveal hidden patterns in customer behaviors, such as differences in shopping habits that are not immediately apparent.

B. Applications of Customer Segmentation in E-Commerce

Targeted Marketing Campaigns:

By segmenting customers into meaningful groups, e-commerce businesses can create targeted marketing campaigns tailored to the needs and preferences of each segment. For example, a fashion retailer could send personalized emails to customers based on their preferred clothing styles or past purchasing behavior.

Personalized Product Recommendations:

Customer segmentation allows e-commerce platforms to group customers based on similar tastes, enabling them to recommend products that are more likely to be of interest to each segment.

Dynamic Pricing:

Businesses can use segmentation to implement dynamic pricing strategies that vary according to customer segments. For instance, loyal customers or high-value customers may receive discounts or special offers, while new customers may be offered introductory prices.

Customer Retention and Churn Prediction:

Machine learning-based customer segmentation can help identify at-risk customer groups who are likely to churn. By offering personalized incentives, e-commerce businesses can retain these customers and improve lifetime value.

Product Development and Inventory Management:

Understanding customer segments can guide product development decisions, ensuring that the products offered cater to the needs and desires of specific groups. It also helps with inventory management by highlighting which products are popular with particular segments.

C. Benefits and Challenges of Customer Segmentation

Benefits:

- **Improved Customer Targeting**: E-commerce businesses can create more precise and effective marketing campaigns by targeting specific customer segments.
- **Increased Revenue**: Personalized offerings and promotions result in higher conversion rates, increased customer lifetime value, and higher sales.
- **Better Customer Retention**: By understanding customer needs and preferences, businesses can enhance their relationships with customers and improve retention.

Challenges:

- **Data Quality**: The accuracy of segmentation depends on the quality of the data used. Incomplete or inaccurate data can result in misleading segments.
- **Oversegmentation**: Too many customer segments may lead to overly complex marketing strategies, diluting efforts and making it harder to manage.
- **Customer Privacy**: As with recommendation systems, customer segmentation often involves the analysis of personal data, raising privacy concerns. Businesses must ensure that segmentation processes comply with data protection regulations.

Machine learning has become integral to the success of e-commerce businesses. Recommendation systems and customer segmentation are two of the most impactful applications of ML in this domain. By leveraging these technologies, businesses can provide personalized experiences, increase sales, optimize marketing efforts, and improve customer retention. However, the key to successful implementation lies in effectively managing data quality, addressing ethical concerns, and continually refining ML models to adapt to changing customer behaviors. As the e-commerce landscape continues to evolve, ML will remain a vital tool in driving innovation and enhancing customer experience.

16.4 ML for Social Good

Machine learning (ML) has shown incredible promise in solving complex problems across a variety of industries, but its impact extends far beyond commercial use cases. As the world faces critical challenges such as climate change, health crises, poverty, and inequality, machine learning has emerged as a powerful tool for addressing some of the most pressing issues in society. In this section, we will explore how ML can be leveraged for social good, discussing its role in healthcare, disaster response, environmental protection, education, and humanitarian aid.

1. ML in Healthcare: Improving Lives and Saving Lives

Healthcare is one of the sectors where ML is having a profound impact, revolutionizing both preventative care and treatment. ML techniques are being used to analyze vast amounts of medical data to improve diagnostics, optimize treatment plans, and even discover new drugs.

A. Early Disease Detection

Machine learning algorithms can analyze medical data, such as imaging scans, genetic information, and patient history, to detect diseases in their early stages. For example:

- **Cancer Detection**: ML models are trained to detect abnormalities in medical imaging, such as X-rays, CT scans, and MRIs, to help radiologists identify early signs of cancer, such as breast cancer or lung cancer.
- **Diabetes Prediction**: Machine learning can analyze patient data to predict the likelihood of developing diabetes, enabling doctors to recommend preventative measures early on.
- **Heart Disease Risk**: By examining factors such as medical history, lifestyle, and genetic predisposition, ML can predict the risk of heart disease and provide actionable insights for early intervention.

B. Personalized Medicine and Treatment Plans

ML is also making strides in tailoring treatment plans to individual patients. By analyzing patient data, including genetic profiles and medical histories, machine learning models can help doctors recommend the most effective treatments for each patient. This personalized approach leads to better outcomes, fewer side effects, and lower healthcare costs.

C. Epidemic Monitoring and Response

Machine learning can be applied to track, predict, and manage disease outbreaks. For example:

- **Predicting Disease Spread**: During outbreaks like the COVID-19 pandemic, ML models were used to predict how the disease would spread, helping public health officials allocate resources and implement containment strategies.
- **Vaccine Distribution**: ML can help optimize vaccine distribution, ensuring that doses reach the most vulnerable populations first, based on real-time data.

2. ML for Disaster Response and Crisis Management

Natural disasters, such as hurricanes, earthquakes, and wildfires, require rapid and efficient response efforts to save lives and reduce damage. Machine learning can help improve disaster prediction, preparedness, and response strategies.

A. Disaster Prediction and Early Warning Systems

Machine learning can be used to predict natural disasters by analyzing historical data, environmental factors, and real-time monitoring. For example:

- **Earthquake Prediction**: ML models can analyze seismic data to predict the likelihood of an earthquake occurring in specific regions, helping to mitigate damage through early warnings.
- **Hurricane Tracking**: By processing satellite data, ML models can track the formation and movement of hurricanes, providing more accurate forecasts and early warnings for vulnerable areas.
- **Flooding Prediction**: ML algorithms can analyze rainfall patterns, river levels, and topographical data to predict potential flooding events and alert communities in advance.

B. Optimizing Disaster Response

Once a disaster occurs, machine learning can help optimize the allocation of resources such as medical aid, food, and shelter:

- **Resource Allocation**: ML models can analyze real-time data, such as damage reports, population density, and infrastructure availability, to allocate resources where they are most needed.
- **Search and Rescue Operations**: Drone technology and machine learning can work together to analyze aerial images and identify areas where search and rescue teams should focus their efforts, potentially saving lives more efficiently.

3. ML in Environmental Conservation: Protecting the Planet

Machine learning has become an essential tool in the fight against climate change and environmental degradation. From monitoring ecosystems to predicting environmental threats, ML is being used to conserve biodiversity and promote sustainability.

A. Wildlife Monitoring and Conservation

One of the most important applications of ML in environmental conservation is in monitoring wildlife populations and preserving endangered species. For example:

- **Wildlife Tracking**: Machine learning can be used to analyze data from GPS collars and camera traps to track the movements of animals, helping conservationists better understand migration patterns, behavior, and habitat preferences.
- **Poaching Detection**: ML algorithms can analyze patterns of activity in protected areas to identify potential poaching activity, alerting authorities to intervene before animals are harmed.
- **Biodiversity Monitoring**: Using image recognition, ML can identify and classify species in the wild, providing insights into biodiversity and population health in real-time.

B. Climate Change Prediction and Mitigation

Machine learning is also helping scientists predict the impact of climate change and develop strategies for mitigation:

- **Climate Modeling**: ML algorithms can analyze climate data to improve weather forecasts and predict future climate patterns, helping governments and organizations plan for extreme weather events such as heatwaves, storms, and rising sea levels.
- **Energy Efficiency**: ML models are being used to optimize energy consumption in buildings, industries, and transportation, leading to reductions in greenhouse gas emissions and promoting sustainable practices.
- **Carbon Footprint Reduction**: ML can analyze industrial processes and supply chains to identify inefficiencies and suggest ways to reduce the carbon footprint, encouraging businesses to adopt greener practices.

4. ML in Education: Enhancing Learning and Access

Education is another area where machine learning has the potential to make a significant impact. ML can help provide personalized learning experiences, improve educational outcomes, and bridge the gap between students from different socio-economic backgrounds.

A. Personalized Learning

Machine learning can be used to create adaptive learning systems that adjust the curriculum based on the individual needs of each student:

- **Tailored Learning Plans**: By analyzing student performance, ML algorithms can generate personalized learning plans that target specific areas of weakness and adjust the difficulty of exercises to match the student's learning pace.
- **Real-Time Feedback**: ML-powered systems can provide students with instant feedback on their assignments, quizzes, and exercises, helping them improve and master subjects more effectively.
- **Tutoring and Assistance**: AI-driven chatbots and virtual tutors powered by machine learning can assist students with questions and guide them through complex topics, providing support outside of regular classroom hours.

B. Expanding Access to Education

Machine learning can also be used to expand access to quality education, particularly in underserved or remote areas:

- **Language Translation**: ML algorithms can break down language barriers by providing real-time translation of educational content, enabling students from diverse linguistic backgrounds to access materials in their native languages.
- **Automated Content Creation**: ML can assist educators in creating content, from lesson plans to quizzes, by analyzing vast amounts of educational materials and identifying relevant resources for specific topics.
- **Distance Learning**: During the COVID-19 pandemic, machine learning-powered tools allowed for more effective remote learning by providing students with customized educational experiences, tracking engagement, and identifying areas for improvement.

5. ML for Humanitarian Aid: Improving Crisis Relief Efforts

Humanitarian organizations are using machine learning to address the needs of vulnerable populations and optimize relief efforts during humanitarian crises, such as refugee situations, armed conflicts, and economic instability.

A. Refugee Assistance and Resource Distribution

Machine learning can help improve the efficiency and effectiveness of aid distribution in refugee camps and conflict zones:

- **Predicting Refugee Movements**: ML can analyze historical migration patterns to predict the flow of refugees and help organizations allocate resources such as food, shelter, and healthcare to the areas of greatest need.
- **Optimizing Resource Distribution**: By analyzing data from refugees, including their location, needs, and demographic profiles, ML can optimize the distribution of resources, ensuring that supplies reach the most vulnerable populations.

B. Crisis Monitoring and Response

ML can help humanitarian organizations track the status of crises in real-time, enabling them to respond faster and more effectively:

- **Real-Time Crisis Mapping**: By analyzing satellite images, news reports, and social media, ML models can create real-time crisis maps that help aid organizations understand the scope of the problem and deploy resources more effectively.
- **Sentiment Analysis**: Machine learning models can be used to analyze social media content for sentiment, helping organizations understand the needs and concerns of affected populations and prioritize responses accordingly.

Machine learning holds tremendous potential for addressing societal challenges and driving positive change across various sectors, including healthcare, disaster response, environmental conservation, education, and humanitarian aid. By applying ML to these critical areas, we can solve complex problems more efficiently, improve lives, and create a more equitable and sustainable world. As we continue to develop more advanced ML algorithms and techniques, it is essential to keep in mind the ethical implications and ensure that these technologies are used responsibly for the greater good of society.

17. Ethics & Bias in AI

AI should be fair, transparent, and ethical. This chapter discusses biases in machine learning, responsible AI development, and how to design models that prioritize fairness, inclusivity, and accountability.

17.1 The Problem of Bias in ML Models

Machine learning (ML) has revolutionized a variety of industries, from healthcare and finance to retail and transportation. As more organizations rely on ML models to make important decisions, the challenge of bias in these models has become increasingly prominent. Bias in ML models refers to systematic errors that favor certain groups or outcomes over others, leading to unfair or discriminatory results. Addressing bias in ML is essential for ensuring that these technologies are equitable, trustworthy, and effective in their real-world applications.

This chapter will explore the different types of bias that can emerge in machine learning models, their potential impacts, and strategies for detecting and mitigating bias to create fairer and more ethical AI systems.

1. What is Bias in Machine Learning?

Bias in machine learning refers to the presence of skewed or unequal representation of data in the training set, or an inherent bias introduced during the development, testing, or deployment of the model. This can result in machine learning algorithms making unfair predictions or decisions based on characteristics such as race, gender, age, socio-economic status, or other demographic attributes.

In simple terms, bias occurs when a model's predictions are systematically skewed in favor of certain groups or outcomes, which can lead to unjust outcomes for those who are not represented adequately in the data. Bias can manifest in different stages of the ML lifecycle, including data collection, feature selection, model training, and deployment.

2. Types of Bias in Machine Learning

Bias in ML models can take many forms, and understanding its types is crucial for addressing the issue effectively. Below are some common types of bias that can affect machine learning models:

A. Data Bias

Data bias arises when the data used to train the model does not accurately represent the population or scenario the model is intended to predict. This is perhaps the most common source of bias in machine learning models.

- **Sampling Bias**: This occurs when the data collected is not representative of the entire population. For example, if an ML model for facial recognition is trained predominantly on images of light-skinned people, it will likely perform poorly on people with darker skin tones.
- **Label Bias**: In supervised learning, the training labels themselves can be biased. If human annotators are labeling data based on their own prejudices, the model will learn these biases and reproduce them in its predictions. For example, a sentiment analysis model trained on biased reviews may learn to associate certain words with positive or negative sentiments based on the biases of the annotators.
- **Measurement Bias:** This occurs when the features used in the model are measured inaccurately or inconsistently, leading to skewed predictions. For instance, if a health insurance model uses height as a feature to predict health risks, but the data collection method for height is flawed, the model may make incorrect assumptions.

B. Algorithmic Bias

Algorithmic bias occurs when the design or decision-making process behind a model itself introduces bias. Even if the data is unbiased, the way the algorithm processes it can cause disparities in outcomes.

- **Feature Selection Bias**: If the features selected for the model are not representative or are chosen based on flawed assumptions, the model may make biased predictions. For example, a hiring algorithm might be biased toward candidates from certain schools if the feature selection process inadvertently prioritizes educational background over other, more relevant qualifications.
- **Model Bias**: Some machine learning algorithms have inherent biases based on how they are structured. For example, decision trees tend to favor features with more categories, which can result in biased outcomes if the feature space is not carefully balanced. Similarly, neural networks may become biased if not properly regularized or trained with diverse data.

C. Confirmation Bias

Confirmation bias happens when models are developed or trained to confirm preconceived notions or hypotheses rather than objectively exploring all possibilities. This bias is often introduced by the developers themselves, consciously or unconsciously.

For instance, when a company builds a model to predict loan approval, and the historical data already reflects discriminatory lending practices, the model may reinforce and perpetuate those biases, rather than challenging or changing them. If developers don't critically analyze the biases in the data, they may end up amplifying existing prejudices.

D. Deployment Bias

Even if a model is trained without bias, issues can still arise during the deployment phase. Deployment bias happens when the model is applied in contexts that it was not trained for, or when its performance is disproportionately better for one group over another due to external factors.

For example, a facial recognition model trained in a controlled environment with uniform lighting and limited diversity in backgrounds may perform poorly when deployed in real-world scenarios with varied lighting and demographic diversity.

3. The Consequences of Bias in ML Models

The consequences of bias in machine learning models can be severe, particularly in high-stakes applications such as hiring, criminal justice, lending, healthcare, and law enforcement. Some of the key consequences include:

A. Discrimination and Inequality

Bias can result in certain groups being unfairly discriminated against. For example, biased recruitment algorithms may systematically reject qualified candidates from underrepresented groups, or biased healthcare models might provide subpar treatment recommendations to certain populations. Over time, this can lead to a reinforcement of societal inequalities and exacerbate existing disparities.

B. Erosion of Trust

When machine learning models make biased or unfair decisions, they can erode trust in AI systems and their developers. This is particularly problematic in applications where decisions have real-world consequences, such as criminal justice or finance. If people believe that AI systems are biased, they may be less likely to trust or use them, which can stifle innovation and hinder adoption.

C. Legal and Ethical Risks

The use of biased ML models can also lead to legal consequences. Discriminatory practices in hiring, lending, or criminal justice may violate anti-discrimination laws and lead to lawsuits, fines, or reputational damage. Additionally, there are growing concerns about the ethical implications of deploying biased AI systems that perpetuate social inequalities.

4. Detecting and Mitigating Bias in ML Models

Addressing bias in machine learning models requires a proactive approach that includes understanding the sources of bias, detecting its presence, and implementing strategies to mitigate it.

A. Bias Detection

- **Fairness Metrics**: There are several fairness metrics that can be used to detect bias in models, such as demographic parity, equal opportunity, and disparate impact. These metrics help assess whether the model's predictions are consistent across different demographic groups.
- **Explaining Model Decisions**: Model interpretability techniques, such as SHAP (Shapley Additive Explanations) or LIME (Local Interpretable Model-Agnostic Explanations), allow developers to understand which features are driving the model's decisions. By analyzing the decisions, developers can spot whether certain features are contributing to biased outcomes.

B. Bias Mitigation Techniques

- **Preprocessing Techniques**: Before training a model, data preprocessing steps can be used to balance the dataset and reduce bias. For example, reweighting the data to ensure that underrepresented groups are adequately represented can help prevent biased predictions.
- **Fair Algorithms**: Some algorithms are specifically designed to reduce bias by optimizing for fairness alongside accuracy. For instance, adversarial debiasing is an approach where an adversarial network is trained to counteract bias in the predictions made by the primary model.

- **Postprocessing Adjustments**: After the model has been trained, postprocessing techniques can be applied to adjust the model's outputs to ensure fairness. This may involve adjusting thresholds for different groups or re-ranking the predicted outcomes.

C. Diverse and Representative Data

To combat bias, it is essential to ensure that the training data is diverse and representative of the populations the model is intended to serve. This means considering factors such as race, gender, socioeconomic status, and geographical location when gathering and labeling data.

D. Ongoing Monitoring

Bias mitigation is not a one-time task; it is an ongoing process. Once a model is deployed, continuous monitoring is necessary to ensure that it remains fair and equitable as new data is introduced. This involves tracking the model's performance across different demographic groups and adjusting as necessary to address any emerging biases.

Bias in machine learning models is a complex and significant challenge that has the potential to perpetuate discrimination, inequality, and unfairness in AI-driven systems. Addressing this issue requires a multi-faceted approach that includes detecting bias, understanding its sources, and implementing techniques to mitigate it. By prioritizing fairness and equity in the design and deployment of machine learning models, we can create more trustworthy and inclusive AI systems that benefit society as a whole. The responsibility lies with developers, data scientists, and organizations to ensure that AI technologies are used ethically and responsibly, without reinforcing existing biases.

17.2 Ethical Considerations in AI Decision-Making

The rapid advancement of artificial intelligence (AI) has made it an integral part of various sectors, from healthcare and finance to law enforcement and transportation. AI systems are now capable of making decisions in environments where human judgment once prevailed, such as diagnosing diseases, approving loans, recommending content, and even determining criminal sentences. However, as AI systems take on more decision-making responsibilities, they raise important ethical concerns that must be addressed to ensure these technologies are deployed responsibly and fairly.

Ethical considerations in AI decision-making involve evaluating the impact of AI on individuals and society, ensuring fairness, accountability, transparency, and maintaining human rights. This chapter will explore the key ethical issues that arise in AI decision-making and discuss approaches to ensure that AI technologies are designed, deployed, and monitored in ways that align with ethical principles.

1. The Importance of Ethics in AI Decision-Making

AI's ability to make decisions autonomously, based on vast amounts of data and complex algorithms, can have far-reaching implications. While AI has the potential to enhance productivity, improve services, and optimize outcomes, its unchecked use could lead to harmful consequences, including bias, discrimination, privacy violations, and job displacement. The ethical implications of AI are particularly important because these systems can affect people's lives in significant ways, such as who gets hired for a job, which criminal justice sentences are imposed, or how healthcare resources are allocated.

Therefore, ensuring that AI is used ethically is not just a matter of fairness but also about maintaining public trust in these technologies. Ethical AI promotes responsible decision-making and seeks to minimize the negative consequences of automation.

2. Key Ethical Principles in AI Decision-Making

When designing, deploying, and using AI systems, it is essential to consider several key ethical principles. These principles help guide developers, organizations, and governments in ensuring AI is used in ways that are beneficial to individuals and society as a whole.

A. Fairness

Fairness is one of the most discussed ethical considerations in AI. It relates to ensuring that AI systems make decisions that are free from bias and discrimination. A fair AI system should treat all individuals or groups equally and should not favor one group over another based on characteristics such as race, gender, age, or socio-economic status.

Achieving fairness in AI requires addressing the biases in data, models, and algorithms that may disproportionately affect underrepresented groups. For example, a hiring algorithm that favors candidates from specific educational backgrounds might inadvertently discriminate against qualified candidates from different socio-economic backgrounds. Thus, fairness in AI decision-making requires careful consideration of how data is collected, how features are selected, and how models are evaluated.

B. Transparency and Explainability

Transparency refers to the ability to understand how and why AI systems make decisions. As AI models become more complex, especially deep learning models, they can act as "black boxes," meaning that even their developers may not fully understand how the models arrive at their predictions or decisions. This lack of transparency can be problematic, especially in high-stakes domains like healthcare, finance, and criminal justice, where understanding the rationale behind decisions is essential for ensuring accountability.

Explainability, a related concept, refers to the degree to which an AI model's decision-making process can be interpreted and understood by humans. Transparent and explainable AI systems allow users to understand how a model works, which factors influenced its decision, and whether the decision-making process was fair. Techniques like LIME (Local Interpretable Model-Agnostic Explanations) and SHAP (Shapley Additive Explanations) are becoming increasingly popular to help explain complex AI models.

In many contexts, especially in regulated sectors like healthcare and finance, explainable AI is not just an ethical preference but a legal requirement. For instance, the European Union's General Data Protection Regulation (GDPR) grants individuals the "right to explanation" when automated decisions are made about them.

C. Accountability

Accountability in AI decision-making refers to the responsibility that developers, organizations, and policymakers have for the outcomes of AI systems. As AI systems make more decisions autonomously, determining who is accountable for the consequences becomes a critical ethical issue. If an AI system makes a mistake, causes harm, or results in unintended consequences, it is important to know who is responsible—whether it is the developers who created the system, the organization that deployed it, or other stakeholders.

In high-risk applications, such as autonomous vehicles or healthcare AI, clear accountability mechanisms are essential. For example, if an autonomous vehicle causes an accident, it may be difficult to assign blame to the AI itself. Is the manufacturer responsible? The developer of the algorithms? The owner of the vehicle? Having clear accountability frameworks is vital for ensuring that any negative outcomes are addressed and that there is recourse for those affected.

D. Privacy and Data Protection

AI systems often rely on large datasets, many of which include personal information about individuals. This raises significant concerns about privacy, data protection, and the potential misuse of sensitive information. For example, AI systems used for targeted advertising or facial recognition might collect and process personal data without individuals' explicit consent or knowledge. This could lead to violations of privacy rights and even identity theft or other malicious activities.

Ethical AI requires strict adherence to data protection regulations, such as the GDPR in the European Union and the California Consumer Privacy Act (CCPA) in the U.S. These regulations place limitations on the use of personal data and ensure that individuals have control over their data. In addition to complying with legal frameworks, ethical AI should prioritize transparency in data usage, obtain informed consent from users, and ensure that data is anonymized or pseudonymized whenever possible to protect individuals' privacy.

E. Human-Centered Design

Human-centered design is a principle that emphasizes the importance of designing AI systems that align with human values, needs, and goals. AI should be developed to augment human capabilities, not replace them. This principle involves designing systems that prioritize human welfare, well-being, and dignity. Human-centered AI focuses on ensuring that the technology enhances the lives of users while being sensitive to their social, cultural, and ethical contexts.

AI systems, particularly those that interact with people directly (such as virtual assistants or autonomous vehicles), should be designed with empathy and consideration for the impact they have on people's lives. Developers should consider the potential societal impact of AI, and involve stakeholders, including marginalized communities, in the design and testing processes to ensure the systems serve everyone equitably.

3. Ethical Challenges in AI Decision-Making

Despite the principles outlined above, applying ethics to AI decision-making is not always straightforward. Several challenges arise when attempting to create ethical AI systems, including:

A. Balancing Efficiency and Fairness

In some cases, AI systems designed for efficiency (such as maximizing profits or reducing operational costs) can conflict with ethical principles such as fairness and equity. For example, an AI system used to predict customer churn in a business might prioritize high-value customers and exclude lower-value ones, even if the lower-value customers are from disadvantaged or marginalized groups. Balancing business objectives with ethical considerations can be a difficult task for organizations, but it is essential for ensuring that AI benefits society at large.

B. Global and Cultural Differences

AI systems that are deployed globally must navigate a diverse set of cultural norms, legal frameworks, and ethical standards. What is considered ethical in one country may not be viewed the same way in another. For instance, privacy expectations vary significantly between cultures, and what is acceptable in terms of data usage may differ from region to region. Ensuring that AI systems are adaptable to these differences and respect local ethical standards is a major challenge for global AI deployment.

C. The Risk of Autonomy vs. Human Oversight

AI decision-making systems are increasingly being deployed in environments where human oversight is minimal or nonexistent. In cases like autonomous vehicles, AI may need to make split-second decisions with life-or-death consequences. Balancing AI's autonomy with the need for human oversight raises critical ethical issues. If an autonomous vehicle makes an error, who is responsible—the AI or the human operator? How can we ensure that AI systems make decisions in ways that align with human values?

Ethical considerations in AI decision-making are crucial to ensuring that AI systems are used responsibly, transparently, and fairly. By adhering to principles such as fairness, accountability, transparency, privacy, and human-centered design, we can build AI systems that enhance human capabilities while respecting individual rights and societal values. As AI continues to evolve and take on more decision-making roles, it is essential for developers, organizations, and governments to prioritize ethics in the development and deployment of AI systems. Only through ethical decision-making can AI reach its full potential for good without compromising the values that define us as a society.

17.3 Privacy and Data Security in ML

As machine learning (ML) becomes more integrated into various applications, the privacy and security of data used in training models have become significant concerns. Machine learning algorithms rely on vast amounts of data to identify patterns and make predictions, and this data often includes sensitive or personal information about individuals. While ML has the potential to drive innovation and provide valuable insights, it also raises serious ethical and legal questions related to privacy, data security, and the protection of personal information.

This chapter will explore the intersection of privacy and data security in machine learning, focusing on the risks associated with the use of personal data, strategies to protect privacy, and methods to ensure that data is handled securely throughout the ML lifecycle.

1. The Importance of Privacy and Data Security in Machine Learning

The effectiveness of machine learning models depends largely on the data they are trained on. For models to be accurate and robust, they require large and diverse datasets, often containing personal or sensitive information, such as health records, financial transactions, and demographic details. The use of such data raises important privacy concerns because:

- **Sensitive Information**: Personal data like names, addresses, medical histories, and financial transactions can be used to build models that influence critical decisions in healthcare, finance, and other sectors. Misuse or leakage of this information can have devastating consequences for individuals.
- **Data Sharing**: ML systems often require data to be shared across organizations or entities. This sharing can introduce risks if data is not adequately protected or if it is exposed during transfer.
- **Model Inference**: The very nature of machine learning means that sensitive information can be inadvertently learned or exposed by the model. In some cases, an attacker could infer personal details from the model itself, leading to potential privacy violations.

Because of these concerns, both privacy and data security must be top priorities when working with machine learning systems. Without proper safeguards, sensitive data may be exposed to unauthorized parties or used in ways that violate privacy rights.

2. Privacy Challenges in Machine Learning

Machine learning introduces several unique privacy challenges that need to be addressed to protect individuals' data.

A. Data Collection and Usage

In order to train an effective machine learning model, large datasets are often required. This data can be collected from a variety of sources, including online interactions, user activity, sensors, and surveys. The challenge lies in ensuring that this data is collected ethically and that users' privacy is respected.

- **Informed Consent**: One of the main privacy concerns is whether users are fully aware of how their data is being collected and used. In many cases, users may not know that their data is being used to train machine learning models, or they may not fully understand the implications of such data usage. Informed consent is a crucial aspect of respecting privacy.
- **Data Minimization**: Data should only be collected when necessary for a specific purpose. Over-collection or the use of irrelevant data increases the risk of privacy violations and data misuse. The principle of data minimization emphasizes collecting only the data that is needed and ensuring that it is used responsibly.
- **Data Retention**: Another issue is how long data is retained. Storing data for longer than necessary can increase the risk of unauthorized access or exposure. Companies need to establish policies regarding data retention and deletion to ensure that data is not held indefinitely.

B. Model Inference and Privacy Leakage

Even when data is anonymized or aggregated, machine learning models can sometimes unintentionally reveal sensitive information. Model inference refers to the process of using a trained model to make predictions or decisions based on new input data. However, the model itself might contain traces of sensitive data learned during the training phase.

- **Membership Inference Attacks**: A membership inference attack occurs when an attacker can determine whether a specific data point was used in the training set of a model. For example, if an ML model was trained on sensitive health data, an attacker could use a trained model to infer whether a specific individual's data was part of the training set, potentially violating their privacy.
- **Model Inversion Attacks**: Model inversion involves using a trained model to infer sensitive information about individuals. Even if data has been anonymized, an attacker may be able to reconstruct individual data points by querying the model repeatedly and observing its outputs.
- **Data Memorization**: In some cases, deep learning models, especially those that are overfitted or poorly trained, may "memorize" the training data. This means that

the model might inadvertently retain and expose private data that was included in the training set, which can compromise privacy.

3. Techniques for Ensuring Privacy in Machine Learning

Given the privacy risks associated with machine learning, several techniques and frameworks have been developed to help mitigate these issues and protect sensitive data. Below are some prominent techniques for enhancing privacy in machine learning:

A. Differential Privacy

Differential privacy is a privacy-preserving technique that ensures that the inclusion or exclusion of any single data point does not significantly affect the output of the machine learning model. This technique introduces noise to the data or the model in such a way that the privacy of individual data points is protected while still allowing the model to learn from the data.

- **Mechanism**: Differential privacy works by adding carefully calibrated random noise to the output of a model or a dataset, making it difficult to identify whether any individual's data was part of the dataset. This ensures that even if an adversary has access to the model or its output, they cannot infer specific details about the data.
- **Applications**: Differential privacy can be applied in various areas, such as data aggregation, statistical analysis, and even training machine learning models. Major tech companies like Google and Apple have implemented differential privacy techniques to collect data while preserving user anonymity.

B. Federated Learning

Federated learning is a decentralized approach to training machine learning models, where the data does not need to leave its original location (e.g., a user's device). Instead of sending raw data to a central server for training, the model is trained locally on each device, and only the model updates (i.e., weights and gradients) are sent to the server.

- **Data Privacy**: Federated learning ensures that sensitive data remains on the local device, minimizing the risk of data breaches and unauthorized access. Only aggregated model updates are shared, making it difficult for external parties to access individual data points.
- **Applications**: Federated learning is particularly useful for applications like mobile devices, where personal data such as health metrics, location, and user behavior

is generated. Examples include Google's use of federated learning for predictive text input and Apple's use of it for improving on-device features like Siri.

C. Homomorphic Encryption

Homomorphic encryption is an encryption technique that allows computations to be performed on encrypted data without decrypting it. This means that sensitive data can be processed and analyzed while it remains encrypted, ensuring privacy is maintained throughout the machine learning process.

- **Applications**: Homomorphic encryption is particularly useful in scenarios where data is sensitive, such as medical records or financial transactions, and where it is necessary to perform machine learning tasks on encrypted data. This allows organizations to analyze data without exposing it to the risk of leaks or unauthorized access.

D. Secure Multi-Party Computation (SMPC)

Secure multi-party computation is a cryptographic technique that allows multiple parties to collaboratively compute a function over their data without sharing the raw data with each other. SMPC enables privacy-preserving machine learning by ensuring that sensitive information is never exposed to any party during the computation process.

- **Use Case**: For example, in a healthcare setting, hospitals can jointly train a machine learning model on patient data without sharing their individual datasets with each other. This allows for collaborative learning while maintaining privacy and data security.

4. Data Security Practices for Machine Learning

In addition to privacy-preserving techniques, ensuring the security of data is crucial for protecting against unauthorized access, data breaches, and attacks. Below are some key data security practices for machine learning systems:

A. Encryption

Data should be encrypted both in transit and at rest to ensure that it is protected from unauthorized access. Encryption prevents third parties from reading or tampering with the data, even if they gain access to the storage or transmission medium.

B. Access Control

Strict access control mechanisms should be implemented to limit who can access the data and model. This includes implementing authentication and authorization processes, such as using multi-factor authentication (MFA) and role-based access controls (RBAC), to ensure that only authorized personnel or systems can interact with sensitive data.

C. Regular Audits and Monitoring

It is essential to regularly audit and monitor machine learning systems for any unusual or suspicious activities. By setting up logs and tracking data access, organizations can detect potential breaches early and take corrective actions to minimize damage.

Privacy and data security are crucial aspects of machine learning, especially as these technologies become increasingly integrated into decision-making processes that directly impact individuals' lives. Protecting sensitive data and ensuring that AI systems are built and deployed with privacy in mind is not only a legal requirement but also a fundamental ethical responsibility. By employing techniques such as differential privacy, federated learning, homomorphic encryption, and secure multi-party computation, organizations can ensure that they respect individuals' privacy while still leveraging the power of machine learning. Additionally, maintaining strong data security practices will help prevent data breaches and unauthorized access, ensuring that ML systems are both effective and trustworthy.

17.4 Ensuring Fairness in AI Applications

As artificial intelligence (AI) and machine learning (ML) technologies become more integrated into decision-making processes across industries, ensuring fairness in these systems is crucial. Whether AI is used for hiring decisions, criminal justice, loan approvals, or healthcare, the decisions it makes can have significant real-world impacts on individuals' lives. If not properly managed, AI models may perpetuate or even exacerbate biases, leading to unfair and discriminatory outcomes. Therefore, ensuring fairness in AI applications is essential for building systems that are equitable, ethical, and trusted.

In this chapter, we will explore the concept of fairness in AI, the challenges that arise in ensuring fairness, and the techniques that can be used to address biases and promote equitable outcomes in AI systems.

1. The Concept of Fairness in AI

Fairness in AI refers to the idea that the outcomes of an AI system should not unfairly disadvantage or discriminate against any particular group of people. Fairness is not a one-size-fits-all concept; it depends on the context and application of the AI model, and different stakeholders may have different ideas of what constitutes fairness.

However, there are several key principles that are generally considered when addressing fairness in AI:

Equal Treatment: AI systems should treat all individuals equally, without bias based on sensitive attributes such as race, gender, age, or socioeconomic status. This principle aims to ensure that people are not unfairly penalized or privileged by the system due to inherent characteristics.

Non-Discrimination: A fair AI system should not systematically disadvantage or exclude specific groups. It should ensure that historically marginalized groups are not disproportionately harmed by the system's predictions or decisions.

Transparency and Accountability: Fairness also implies that AI models are transparent, meaning that stakeholders can understand how decisions are being made. If an AI system's decisions cause harm or unfair outcomes, there should be clear mechanisms for accountability and redress.

Equity of Outcome: In some cases, fairness can be measured by the outcomes the AI system produces. For example, an AI system that is used for hiring should produce outcomes that result in diverse hires across different demographic groups, ensuring that certain groups are not systematically left out.

2. Challenges to Achieving Fairness in AI

Ensuring fairness in AI applications is not a simple task, and there are several challenges that make it difficult to achieve:

A. Bias in Data

Bias in data is one of the most significant barriers to ensuring fairness in AI systems. AI models are only as good as the data they are trained on, and if the training data contains biases, those biases can be learned by the model. There are two main types of biases that can be present in data:

Historical Bias: Historical biases are a result of past societal inequalities or prejudices that have been encoded into data. For example, if an AI system is trained on historical hiring data from a company that has previously discriminated against women or people of color, the model may learn to replicate those discriminatory hiring practices.

Sampling Bias: Sampling bias occurs when the data used to train the model is not representative of the broader population. For example, if a facial recognition system is primarily trained on images of light-skinned individuals, it may struggle to accurately recognize dark-skinned faces, leading to biased results.

B. Lack of Transparency (Black-Box Nature of AI)

Many AI models, especially deep learning models, are often described as "black boxes" because it can be challenging to understand how they arrive at specific decisions. This lack of transparency makes it difficult to assess whether the model is being fair in its decision-making process.

Without transparency, it is nearly impossible to identify and correct biased decision-making. AI systems need to provide explanations for their decisions to enable accountability, detect unfair outcomes, and ensure that biases are addressed.

C. Conflicting Definitions of Fairness

Fairness is a complex and subjective concept. Different people and communities may have different ideas about what fairness means, and these definitions may conflict with each other. For example, one group might define fairness in terms of equal treatment (everyone treated the same), while another might define it in terms of equal outcomes (ensuring equal representation in the outcome).

This conflict can lead to challenges in designing AI systems that satisfy everyone, as optimizing for one fairness definition can sometimes lead to unfairness in another. For example, if an AI system is optimized for equal representation of different demographic groups in its outcomes, it may inadvertently introduce bias elsewhere, such as in terms of how the system treats individuals within those groups.

D. Ethical and Societal Considerations

In addition to technical challenges, ensuring fairness in AI also involves ethical and societal considerations. For instance, the use of AI in sensitive areas such as criminal justice, hiring, or healthcare can raise ethical dilemmas related to the rights and dignity of individuals. The stakes are high, as unfair decisions made by AI systems can have lifelong consequences for individuals, particularly those from marginalized or disadvantaged communities.

3. Techniques for Ensuring Fairness in AI

Despite the challenges, there are several techniques and strategies that can be used to improve fairness in AI applications:

A. Bias Detection and Mitigation

The first step toward ensuring fairness is to identify and address biases in the data. Various methods can be employed to detect and mitigate bias, including:

Bias Audits: Regular audits of data and model outcomes can help identify instances of bias. Audits can involve examining the data for overrepresentation or underrepresentation of certain groups and analyzing model predictions to detect discriminatory patterns.

Preprocessing: Preprocessing techniques can be used to reduce bias in the training data before it is used to train an AI model. This might involve balancing the dataset to ensure equal representation of different demographic groups or applying techniques to remove sensitive attributes (such as race or gender) that may lead to biased outcomes.

Fair Representation Learning: This technique involves training models in such a way that sensitive features, like race or gender, are not used to make predictions or are minimized in the model's decision-making process. This can help prevent the model from relying on unfair correlations between sensitive attributes and the outcome.

Bias Mitigation Algorithms: There are several algorithms designed to reduce bias in machine learning models. These algorithms work by adjusting the model's decision-making process to account for fairness constraints while still maintaining overall model accuracy.

B. Fairness-Aware Model Design

AI practitioners can also design fairness-aware models by incorporating fairness objectives directly into the learning process. This can be done by defining fairness metrics and including them as part of the optimization objective, in addition to the traditional accuracy or performance metrics.

Adversarial Debiasing: This technique uses adversarial networks to ensure that the model's decisions are not influenced by protected attributes, such as race or gender. The adversarial network tries to "trick" the main model into making decisions that are independent of these sensitive attributes.

Fairness Constraints: In some cases, fairness can be ensured by explicitly imposing fairness constraints during training. For example, constraints can be applied to ensure that different demographic groups have equal representation in the outcomes or that the false positive and false negative rates are balanced across different groups.

C. Post-Processing Fairness Adjustments

Even after a model is trained, fairness can be improved through post-processing techniques. These techniques involve adjusting the final predictions or decisions made by the model to ensure fairness across different groups.

Calibration: Calibration techniques ensure that the predicted probabilities of a model are consistent across groups. This can help ensure that the model's predictions are equally reliable for all demographic groups.

Thresholding: Post-processing can also involve adjusting the decision thresholds of a model to ensure that different groups have equal opportunities or outcomes. For example, a hiring algorithm might be adjusted to ensure that applicants from underrepresented groups are given fair consideration.

D. Ensuring Transparency and Explainability

To improve fairness, AI systems need to be transparent and interpretable. This is especially important in high-stakes decision-making areas like criminal justice, healthcare, or finance, where individuals need to understand how decisions are being made and be able to challenge unfair outcomes.

Explainable AI (XAI): Explainable AI techniques can be used to generate human-understandable explanations for model predictions. These techniques help stakeholders understand the rationale behind decisions, increasing trust and ensuring accountability.

Model Interpretability: Models that are easier to interpret, such as decision trees or linear models, can offer greater insights into how decisions are made and which factors are influencing the outcome. While complex models like deep neural networks may offer high accuracy, they may also lack transparency, which can hinder fairness efforts.

Ensuring fairness in AI is a complex and multifaceted challenge that requires both technical solutions and ethical considerations. As AI systems are increasingly used to make decisions that affect people's lives, it is essential to develop models that are transparent, unbiased, and equitable. By identifying and mitigating biases in data, designing fairness-aware models, and ensuring transparency and accountability in AI decision-making processes, we can build systems that are more fair and just. The pursuit of fairness in AI is not only a technological goal but also a moral and societal imperative to ensure that AI systems benefit everyone, without perpetuating harmful disparities.

18. The Future of Machine Learning

What's next in ML? This chapter dives into emerging trends like AutoML, Federated Learning, and Quantum AI, providing insights into the future of machine learning and AI research.

18.1 Trends in ML: AutoML and Meta-Learning

Machine learning (ML) has become one of the most transformative technologies of the 21st century, revolutionizing industries from healthcare to finance, education, and beyond. However, as ML has matured, the need for more accessible, efficient, and adaptive systems has grown. Two prominent trends that have emerged to address these challenges are AutoML (Automated Machine Learning) and Meta-Learning. Both of these approaches aim to streamline and improve the process of building, tuning, and deploying machine learning models, making them more accessible to non-experts and enhancing the capabilities of experts. In this section, we will explore these two trends in detail, focusing on their significance, how they work, and their potential future applications.

1. What is AutoML?

AutoML refers to the automation of the process of applying machine learning to real-world problems. It involves using algorithms and techniques to automate tasks such as model selection, hyperparameter tuning, and feature engineering, which traditionally require deep expertise in machine learning. The goal of AutoML is to make machine learning more accessible to non-experts and improve the efficiency of experts by reducing the time and effort spent on the repetitive and often complex aspects of model development.

A. Components of AutoML

AutoML systems typically consist of several key components:

Data Preprocessing: Data preparation is one of the most time-consuming aspects of machine learning. AutoML systems can automate tasks like data cleaning, missing value imputation, encoding categorical variables, and scaling numerical features.

Model Selection: Instead of manually selecting an appropriate model, AutoML frameworks can automatically evaluate and choose from a wide range of machine learning algorithms (e.g., decision trees, support vector machines, neural networks) based on the problem at hand.

Hyperparameter Tuning: Hyperparameters, such as learning rates and regularization coefficients, significantly affect the performance of machine learning models. AutoML automates the process of tuning these parameters, often using techniques like grid search, random search, or Bayesian optimization.

Model Evaluation: AutoML tools typically include automated processes for model evaluation using metrics such as accuracy, precision, recall, F1-score, and AUC-ROC. These evaluations help select the best-performing model based on the given data.

Deployment and Monitoring: Once the model is built and trained, AutoML platforms often include tools for deploying the model into production environments and monitoring its performance over time.

B. Popular AutoML Tools and Platforms

Several tools and platforms have emerged to make AutoML accessible and powerful. Some of the most well-known include:

Google AutoML: A suite of machine learning tools that includes AutoML Vision, AutoML Natural Language, AutoML Tables, and more. These tools enable users to train models without requiring deep ML knowledge.

H2O.ai: A popular platform that provides AutoML functionality, offering tools for automating model selection, hyperparameter tuning, and deployment.

TPOT and Auto-sklearn: Open-source Python libraries that implement AutoML using genetic algorithms and Bayesian optimization, respectively, to automate model building and hyperparameter tuning.

Microsoft Azure AutoML: A cloud-based service that provides an easy-to-use interface for creating machine learning models, enabling both novices and experts to build models without extensive coding.

C. Benefits of AutoML

Efficiency: AutoML can significantly reduce the time spent on building, testing, and deploying machine learning models. By automating repetitive tasks, data scientists and machine learning practitioners can focus on more high-level problem-solving.

Democratization of ML: AutoML lowers the barrier to entry for using machine learning by enabling non-experts to develop ML models without requiring extensive programming or statistical knowledge.

Improved Model Performance: Automated hyperparameter optimization and model selection techniques often result in models that perform better than those manually crafted, especially when working with large datasets and complex problems.

Cost-Effectiveness: By reducing the need for expert intervention in model creation, AutoML can lower the cost of building and maintaining machine learning systems, making AI more accessible to businesses of all sizes.

2. What is Meta-Learning?

Meta-Learning, also known as "learning to learn," is a branch of machine learning that focuses on developing algorithms that can learn from experience and adapt to new tasks quickly with minimal data. The central idea is that, instead of training models to solve a specific task from scratch, meta-learning algorithms learn how to efficiently solve a variety of tasks and use that experience to generalize to new tasks.

A. Key Concepts in Meta-Learning

Learning Algorithms as Tasks: In meta-learning, tasks are often framed as learning problems themselves. The goal is to design models that can generalize across multiple tasks by leveraging prior knowledge gained from previous experiences. For example, a meta-learning algorithm might learn how to classify images of dogs, cats, and birds, and then quickly adapt to classify images of new animals with very few examples.

Few-Shot Learning: Meta-learning algorithms are typically designed to excel at few-shot learning, which involves learning to perform a task with very limited data. Traditional machine learning algorithms often require large amounts of labeled data, but meta-learning algorithms are able to make good predictions even when only a few labeled examples are available.

Transfer Learning: Meta-learning also involves transfer learning, where knowledge learned from one task is transferred to another task. This is particularly useful in scenarios where there is limited data for a specific task, as a model can transfer knowledge from related tasks to improve its performance.

Optimization-Based Meta-Learning: One approach to meta-learning is using optimization algorithms to learn the best way to update model parameters. Meta-learning algorithms like Model-Agnostic Meta-Learning (MAML) focus on finding an initialization for model parameters that allows rapid adaptation to new tasks.

B. Applications of Meta-Learning

Meta-learning has a wide range of applications, particularly in areas where data is scarce, and the ability to generalize quickly is important. Some of these applications include:

Few-Shot and Zero-Shot Learning: Meta-learning can enable models to make predictions on tasks with very little labeled data. For example, in facial recognition, a meta-learning model might learn to recognize new faces based on only a few images, improving the scalability of AI systems in real-world applications.

Personalized Recommendations: Meta-learning algorithms can be used to adapt models to individual users, learning how to personalize recommendations in real-time based on limited user interactions. This is particularly valuable for applications like personalized content recommendation systems, where users' preferences change over time.

Robotics: In robotics, meta-learning can enable robots to quickly adapt to new environments and tasks, such as learning to manipulate unfamiliar objects or navigate new terrain with minimal data.

Natural Language Processing (NLP): Meta-learning techniques are being explored for NLP tasks, such as machine translation and sentiment analysis, where models need to adapt quickly to new languages or domains with limited annotated data.

3. How AutoML and Meta-Learning Interact

While AutoML and meta-learning are distinct areas of research, there is significant overlap between them. AutoML focuses on automating the end-to-end machine learning process, whereas meta-learning focuses on enabling models to adapt quickly to new tasks. Together, they can complement each other in several ways:

AutoML for Meta-Learning: AutoML tools can be used to automate the process of finding the best meta-learning algorithm or framework for a given problem. This can significantly reduce the time and expertise required to experiment with different meta-learning approaches.

Meta-Learning for AutoML: Meta-learning can enhance AutoML by enabling models to learn from previous tasks and adapt more efficiently to new datasets and problems. For instance, a meta-learning approach could be used to optimize the hyperparameter search process in AutoML, making it more efficient and adaptive.

Improved Performance: By combining the strengths of AutoML's automation and meta-learning's adaptability, it is possible to create systems that not only perform well but also adapt quickly to new tasks or data sources.

4. Conclusion: The Future of AutoML and Meta-Learning

The trends of AutoML and Meta-Learning are reshaping the landscape of machine learning, making it more accessible, adaptable, and efficient. AutoML is lowering the barrier for non-experts to build effective models, while meta-learning is pushing the boundaries of how models can learn and adapt to new tasks. Together, these technologies are accelerating the development and deployment of machine learning systems across various domains.

As these trends continue to evolve, we can expect to see even more powerful and efficient machine learning systems that require less data, less human intervention, and can generalize to new, unforeseen tasks with ease. The convergence of AutoML and meta-learning holds great promise for the future of AI, making it a more versatile, user-friendly, and adaptive tool for solving real-world problems.

18.2 Federated Learning and Decentralized AI

As machine learning (ML) continues to evolve and its applications spread across various industries, two significant trends are emerging in the realm of AI: Federated Learning and Decentralized AI. These approaches are revolutionizing how machine learning models are trained, deployed, and maintained, especially in terms of privacy, security, and efficiency. This section delves into these cutting-edge concepts, exploring their workings, use cases, and the potential impact they could have on the future of AI.

1. What is Federated Learning?

Federated Learning (FL) is a novel approach to machine learning that allows for training models across multiple decentralized devices or servers holding local data, without the need to share the actual data. In traditional machine learning, data is typically centralized on a server for model training, but federated learning distributes the learning process itself, ensuring that data remains private and local to its source.

A. How Federated Learning Works

The core idea behind federated learning is that rather than collecting all the data in one central location, the model is sent to various devices (such as smartphones, IoT devices, or edge servers) that already have access to the data. These devices then train the model locally using their own data and only share the resulting model updates (e.g., weights, gradients) with a central server.

The central server then aggregates these updates, improves the global model, and sends it back to the devices. This process is repeated multiple times, with each iteration improving the global model. The key feature of this approach is that the data remains decentralized, and only model parameters (rather than the raw data itself) are communicated across devices.

Key Steps in Federated Learning

Model Initialization: A central server initializes the machine learning model and sends it to multiple devices or clients.

Local Training: Each device trains the model on its local data. This process may involve multiple rounds of model updates based on local data, improving the model incrementally.

Aggregation: Once the devices complete their local updates, they send only the model updates (weights/gradients) back to the central server, where these updates are aggregated to improve the global model.

Model Distribution: After aggregation, the updated global model is sent back to the devices, and the process repeats for several iterations, gradually improving the accuracy of the model while maintaining the privacy of the data.

B. Advantages of Federated Learning

Data Privacy and Security: Since raw data is never transferred to a central server, federated learning ensures that sensitive information remains secure and private. This is particularly important for applications in healthcare, finance, and other sectors dealing with confidential data.

Reduced Data Transfer: Federated learning reduces the need for large-scale data transfer to central servers, thus minimizing the associated costs and network bandwidth usage. Only model updates (which are typically smaller than raw data) are exchanged.

Compliance with Regulations: Many regions and industries have strict data privacy regulations, such as the General Data Protection Regulation (GDPR) in Europe. Federated learning allows organizations to develop and deploy machine learning models while adhering to these regulations, as no sensitive data leaves the local device.

Edge Computing and Scalability: Federated learning is well-suited for edge devices (like smartphones, wearables, or smart appliances) that can process data locally. As the number of connected devices increases globally, federated learning enables scalable model training across millions of devices without the need for centralized infrastructure.

C. Use Cases of Federated Learning

Healthcare: In medical applications, federated learning can be used to train models on patient data from different hospitals or clinics without compromising patient privacy. This way, hospitals can collaborate to build better predictive models for disease detection while complying with healthcare data regulations.

Finance: Financial institutions can leverage federated learning to develop predictive models for fraud detection, risk assessment, or credit scoring without having to share sensitive customer data. This protects both customer privacy and proprietary financial data.

Mobile Devices: Companies like Google have already implemented federated learning in products like Gboard (Google's keyboard app) to improve predictive text and personalized suggestions based on individual typing patterns. In this case, user data stays on the device, and only aggregated model updates are shared.

IoT Devices: With the growth of Internet of Things (IoT) devices, federated learning enables smart devices to improve their machine learning models based on local data, enhancing their performance in real-time without requiring constant cloud updates.

2. What is Decentralized AI?

Decentralized AI refers to a system where artificial intelligence algorithms and models are deployed across a network of independent devices or nodes, with no central authority controlling the process. In a decentralized AI setup, data processing, model training, and decision-making happen autonomously across multiple decentralized locations or devices. This contrasts with traditional AI, where data and computation are centralized in large data centers.

A. Key Features of Decentralized AI

Distributed Data and Computation: Decentralized AI networks distribute both data storage and computational workloads across multiple devices, eliminating the need for a central server to handle all tasks. This reduces bottlenecks and increases scalability, especially for large datasets or high-demand applications.

Autonomous Decision-Making: Decentralized AI systems are designed to operate without central control, which allows for more responsive and adaptive decision-making. For example, in autonomous vehicles, multiple cars equipped with AI might make decisions based on shared, but decentralized, knowledge of road conditions, traffic, and obstacles.

No Single Point of Failure: Since there is no central server or authority in decentralized AI systems, the network is more resilient to failures. Even if a device or node goes offline, the system can continue functioning by relying on other devices.

Security and Privacy: Much like federated learning, decentralized AI prioritizes privacy and security. Data can be processed locally on devices, meaning it never has to be sent to a central server. This is particularly beneficial for applications involving sensitive or personal data.

B. Advantages of Decentralized AI

Scalability: Decentralized AI systems are inherently more scalable since new nodes or devices can easily join the network and contribute to data processing and model improvement without overloading a central server.

Improved Security: By eliminating the need for centralized data storage, decentralized AI reduces the risk of massive data breaches. The distributed nature of the network makes it harder for attackers to compromise the entire system.

Reduced Latency: Decentralized AI allows for faster decision-making since computation occurs locally on devices rather than waiting for data to be sent to a central server for processing. This is crucial for real-time applications like autonomous vehicles, robotics, or edge computing.

Collaboration: Devices in decentralized AI networks can collaborate without a central authority. For example, in multi-agent systems, devices (or "agents") can work together to solve complex problems or improve system efficiency based on their individual experiences and knowledge.

C. Use Cases of Decentralized AI

Autonomous Vehicles: Self-driving cars can benefit from decentralized AI by sharing information about traffic conditions, road hazards, and nearby vehicles. Each car processes and acts on local data but can also collaborate with other cars in real-time for improved decision-making.

Smart Grids: In energy systems, decentralized AI can help optimize energy distribution by processing data from smart meters and IoT sensors scattered across the grid. Each device can make decisions about energy usage without waiting for instructions from a central authority.

Blockchain and AI: In blockchain applications, decentralized AI is often used to improve consensus mechanisms, detect fraudulent activities, and optimize network operations. By leveraging blockchain's decentralized structure, AI models can be securely and autonomously trained, updated, and deployed without relying on a central entity.

Smart Cities: In the context of smart cities, decentralized AI systems can be used to manage traffic, public transportation, waste management, and other city services. Devices across the city can collaborate to improve efficiency, reduce congestion, and optimize resource allocation.

3. Federated Learning and Decentralized AI: A Synergistic Future

While federated learning and decentralized AI share many similarities, they are distinct in terms of their focus and implementation. Federated learning emphasizes collaborative model training across devices while maintaining data privacy, whereas decentralized AI involves broader autonomy and distribution across various systems.

However, the future of AI likely lies in the integration of both concepts. For example, federated learning can be used to train decentralized AI systems across many devices and platforms without requiring centralized control. This synergy enables the creation of distributed systems that are privacy-preserving, scalable, and adaptive, opening up a wide range of applications in areas like healthcare, IoT, autonomous systems, and finance.

Federated learning and decentralized AI are shaping the future of machine learning by addressing key challenges such as privacy, security, scalability, and autonomy. These trends represent a shift toward more distributed, efficient, and user-centric AI systems that can learn from data without centralizing it. As these technologies mature, we can expect to see further advancements in real-time decision-making, enhanced privacy protections, and innovative applications that were once considered too complex or impractical for traditional, centralized AI models. The combination of federated learning and decentralized AI holds great promise for a more adaptive, secure, and collaborative AI ecosystem.

18.3 Quantum Machine Learning: The Next Frontier

As the field of artificial intelligence (AI) continues to evolve, the rise of quantum computing is opening up new and exciting possibilities. One of the most promising areas where quantum computing is expected to have a transformative impact is Quantum Machine Learning (QML). This emerging field is positioned to revolutionize how machine learning models are trained, optimized, and applied, particularly in solving complex problems that classical computers struggle with.

In this section, we will explore the fundamentals of quantum computing, introduce the concept of quantum machine learning, and examine its potential to reshape AI in the near future.

1. What is Quantum Computing?

Quantum computing is a fundamentally different approach to computation compared to classical computing. At its core, quantum computing exploits the principles of quantum mechanics, which govern the behavior of particles at the atomic and subatomic levels. Unlike classical computers, which use bits to represent data in binary form (either 0 or 1), quantum computers use quantum bits or qubits. These qubits can exist in multiple states simultaneously, thanks to a phenomenon called superposition.

Key Concepts in Quantum Computing

Qubits: Unlike classical bits, qubits can represent both 0 and 1 at the same time due to superposition. This allows quantum computers to process a vast number of possibilities in parallel.

Superposition: This property allows a qubit to be in multiple states at once, enabling quantum computers to solve problems more efficiently than classical computers in some cases.

Entanglement: Qubits can be entangled, meaning the state of one qubit is dependent on the state of another, regardless of distance. This creates a powerful connection between qubits, enabling faster and more efficient processing of complex information.

Quantum Interference: Quantum algorithms leverage interference to amplify correct solutions and diminish incorrect ones. This helps narrow down the range of potential answers, improving the efficiency of quantum computations.

Classical vs. Quantum Computing

Classical computers perform computations based on binary logic and are limited by the processing power of their hardware. Quantum computers, on the other hand, can perform certain types of calculations exponentially faster, thanks to the quantum properties of superposition and entanglement. As quantum computers evolve, they have the potential to outperform classical computers in tasks such as factoring large numbers, simulating quantum systems, and optimizing complex models.

2. What is Quantum Machine Learning?

Quantum Machine Learning (QML) is an interdisciplinary field that combines the principles of quantum computing with the methodologies of machine learning. The goal of QML is to leverage the computational power of quantum computers to accelerate and enhance traditional machine learning tasks, such as data classification, clustering, optimization, and prediction. Quantum machine learning algorithms harness the unique capabilities of quantum computing to solve problems that are currently computationally infeasible for classical machines.

In traditional machine learning, algorithms learn from data by processing and analyzing it through statistical models. Quantum machine learning aims to speed up this process by utilizing quantum algorithms that can handle larger datasets, explore more complex patterns, and solve problems with exponential efficiency.

How Quantum Machine Learning Works

Quantum machine learning can be divided into two main areas:

Quantum-Enhanced Machine Learning: In this approach, quantum algorithms are used to improve the efficiency of classical machine learning tasks. For example, quantum computers can speed up optimization problems, enhance the performance of clustering algorithms, or improve the speed of matrix factorization techniques (a common task in many machine learning models).

Quantum Machine Learning Algorithms: These are completely new algorithms designed to leverage quantum computing's unique properties. These quantum algorithms are designed specifically for machine learning tasks, such as quantum versions of neural networks or quantum support vector machines (SVMs), that could outperform their classical counterparts.

One of the major advantages of QML lies in its ability to process and analyze exponentially larger datasets and more complex problems, as the quantum computer's power grows exponentially with the number of qubits.

3. Potential Applications of Quantum Machine Learning

Quantum machine learning has the potential to significantly transform a wide range of fields and industries. Let's explore some of the key applications where QML could make a profound impact:

A. Optimization Problems

Many machine learning tasks involve solving complex optimization problems, such as minimizing a cost function or finding the best parameters for a model. Quantum computing has the potential to exponentially accelerate optimization tasks by evaluating multiple possibilities simultaneously. This could be especially beneficial in scenarios like:

- Portfolio optimization in finance
- Supply chain optimization in logistics
- Energy grid optimization

Quantum algorithms like Quantum Approximate Optimization Algorithm (QAOA) are designed to tackle combinatorial optimization problems and could offer improvements in terms of both speed and accuracy.

B. Drug Discovery and Healthcare

The field of drug discovery requires enormous computational resources to simulate the behavior of molecules, test potential drug candidates, and predict their effectiveness. Traditional methods are computationally expensive and time-consuming. Quantum machine learning could be a game-changer in this space by enabling more efficient simulations of molecular structures, identifying new drug compounds, and predicting their interactions more effectively.

For example, quantum computers could help researchers model protein folding, which is a crucial problem in biology. Quantum algorithms could also be used to identify biomarkers for diseases, enhancing the predictive capabilities of medical diagnoses.

C. Natural Language Processing (NLP)

Natural language processing involves training models to understand and process human language. Traditional NLP models require substantial computational power and large amounts of data to work effectively. Quantum computing could enable faster training times for NLP models and help handle more complex language structures.

Quantum machine learning could lead to breakthroughs in tasks like:

- Machine translation
- Sentiment analysis
- Text summarization

Quantum computers may help speed up training deep learning models for NLP, improving the accuracy and efficiency of text-based tasks.

D. Machine Learning for Large-Scale Data

As data continues to grow in volume and complexity, classical machine learning algorithms often struggle to handle large datasets efficiently. Quantum machine learning has the potential to significantly enhance the processing of large-scale data by utilizing quantum parallelism. This can lead to improvements in:

Big Data analytics: Quantum computers can process large volumes of data much faster than classical systems, making real-time data analysis more feasible.

Data clustering and classification: Quantum algorithms could find patterns in data more effectively, improving the accuracy of clustering algorithms and classification tasks.

4. Challenges and Limitations of Quantum Machine Learning

While quantum machine learning holds great promise, there are still several challenges and limitations that need to be addressed before it can become widely adopted:

Quantum Hardware: Quantum computers are still in their early stages of development. Many quantum algorithms are theoretical, and the quantum hardware required to run them is not yet mature enough to scale to practical applications.

Error Correction: Quantum computers are highly susceptible to errors due to environmental noise and qubit decoherence. Developing robust error correction methods is a critical step for the realization of practical quantum machine learning.

Integration with Classical Systems: Since quantum computing is still in its infancy, most quantum algorithms need to be integrated with classical systems. This hybrid approach requires seamless communication between quantum and classical computers, which is currently a challenge.

Lack of Expertise: Quantum machine learning is an interdisciplinary field that requires expertise in both quantum mechanics and machine learning. Finding qualified individuals who are proficient in both areas is still a barrier to widespread adoption.

5. The Future of Quantum Machine Learning

Despite the challenges, the potential of quantum machine learning is undeniable. Researchers and organizations around the world are working hard to overcome the technical barriers that currently exist. As quantum computers continue to evolve and quantum algorithms improve, it is likely that we will see a paradigm shift in how machine learning models are developed and deployed.

Quantum machine learning could ultimately lead to:

Faster model training: Quantum-enhanced machine learning algorithms could reduce training times for deep learning models, enabling faster iteration and innovation in AI research.

New model architectures: As quantum machine learning evolves, entirely new types of machine learning models may be developed that exploit quantum properties like superposition and entanglement.

AI breakthroughs: Quantum computing could lead to breakthroughs in AI research, enabling models to solve problems that are currently intractable for classical systems.

Quantum machine learning represents a fusion of two revolutionary technologies: quantum computing and artificial intelligence. By leveraging the power of quantum mechanics, quantum machine learning has the potential to solve some of the most challenging problems faced by AI today. From speeding up optimization and large-scale data processing to improving drug discovery and NLP, the applications of QML are vast and exciting.

As the field of quantum computing matures, the practical applications of quantum machine learning will become more tangible. For now, quantum machine learning remains an emerging area, but it holds the promise of reshaping the landscape of AI in the years to come, heralding a new era of computational power and intelligence.

18.4 The Role of ML in AGI (Artificial General Intelligence)

The field of Artificial Intelligence (AI) has come a long way since its inception, with significant advancements in areas like machine learning (ML), natural language processing (NLP), computer vision, and robotics. However, most of these AI systems are narrow AI—they are designed to excel at a specific task or a narrow range of tasks. While narrow AI has revolutionized industries and improved efficiency in numerous fields, it is far from achieving the ultimate goal of AI researchers: Artificial General Intelligence (AGI).

Artificial General Intelligence (AGI), also known as strong AI, refers to a type of AI that can perform any intellectual task that a human being can do. AGI would be capable of understanding, learning, and applying knowledge across a wide variety of domains, with the flexibility to solve problems in different contexts, just like a human brain. Unlike narrow AI, which excels in specific tasks, AGI would have a broader cognitive capability and adapt to new, unseen tasks.

In this section, we will explore how machine learning (ML) plays a critical role in the pursuit of AGI, the challenges that lie ahead, and how the integration of various ML techniques might bring us closer to building systems that can think, learn, and reason as humans do.

1. What is AGI?

Artificial General Intelligence (AGI) is often described as an AI system that possesses the following characteristics:

- **Adaptability**: AGI can learn and adapt to new situations, tasks, and environments, much like how humans acquire new skills throughout their lives.
- **Autonomy**: AGI can operate independently, making decisions, planning, and taking actions without human intervention.
- **Generalization**: AGI can transfer knowledge from one domain to another, allowing it to apply its understanding to solve problems in a variety of contexts.
- **Consciousness and Understanding**: While this aspect is more speculative and philosophical, AGI may eventually possess some form of consciousness, self-awareness, or understanding of its own existence and the world around it.

In essence, AGI aims to create a system that replicates the general cognitive abilities of the human mind, including reasoning, problem-solving, planning, learning, perception, and decision-making across a wide range of tasks. Achieving AGI requires a level of flexibility and generalization far beyond the capabilities of current narrow AI models, which are typically trained to perform well on a specific set of tasks.

2. How ML Contributes to the Development of AGI

Machine learning (ML) plays a central role in the development of AGI because of its ability to learn from data and improve its performance over time without explicit programming. There are several areas where ML contributes to AGI's pursuit:

A. Learning from Experience

One of the most crucial aspects of AGI is the ability to learn from experience. In contrast to traditional programming, where explicit rules are written for a machine to follow, ML enables systems to learn patterns from data and adjust their behavior accordingly. In the context of AGI, the ability to learn from experience would allow an AGI system to improve and adapt over time.

Reinforcement learning (RL) plays a key role here. RL algorithms enable agents to learn from their environment through trial and error, using feedback from their actions to improve their behavior. This mimics how humans and animals learn from experience and could be an important building block for AGI systems.

Deep learning, particularly neural networks, also contributes by mimicking the structure and functioning of the human brain. Neural networks can identify complex patterns in large datasets, enabling machines to make informed decisions and learn from unstructured data like images, text, and speech.

B. Generalization Across Tasks

For AGI to function in the real world, it must be able to generalize its knowledge across various domains. ML models are often trained for specific tasks, such as image classification or language translation. However, in AGI, a machine needs to perform tasks outside its initial training set, akin to how humans apply knowledge gained in one area to a completely different context.

Some methods that are central to enabling generalization include:

Transfer learning: This technique allows a model trained on one task to apply its learned features to another task. For example, a neural network trained to recognize objects in images can transfer its learning to detect specific objects in a new context.

Meta-learning (learning to learn): Meta-learning algorithms are designed to improve a model's ability to adapt to new tasks with minimal data. This would enable an AGI system to learn quickly in different environments by using prior knowledge from similar tasks.

Few-shot learning: Few-shot learning is an approach that allows a model to generalize from only a small amount of data. This is an important capability for AGI because it mimics human learning, where humans can often learn new tasks with very little prior exposure.

C. Building Cognitive Flexibility

For AGI to exhibit human-like cognition, it must have a level of flexibility that allows it to perform a wide range of tasks. Traditional ML models can be highly specialized but often struggle when confronted with tasks outside their trained domain. AGI, on the other hand, needs the flexibility to switch between different tasks and learn new domains on the fly.

Neuro-symbolic AI: One promising avenue is the combination of neural networks with symbolic reasoning. While deep learning excels at pattern recognition, symbolic AI focuses on high-level reasoning and logic. Combining these methods could help create a more flexible AI capable of both learning from data and reasoning about abstract concepts.

Multimodal learning: Human cognition integrates multiple sensory inputs, such as sight, sound, and touch, to understand and interact with the world. Multimodal learning seeks to combine data from different sources (e.g., images, text, audio) to create a more well-rounded understanding of tasks and concepts.

D. Natural Language Processing (NLP) and Understanding

AGI systems need to comprehend and interact with humans in natural language. This requires an advanced level of language understanding, not just rote translation of words but true comprehension of context, meaning, and intent. Machine learning techniques in NLP, such as transformers and attention mechanisms, allow AI systems to process and generate human language with impressive accuracy.

Language models like GPT (Generative Pretrained Transformer) and BERT (Bidirectional Encoder Representations from Transformers) have demonstrated remarkable abilities in text generation, summarization, translation, and question-answering. These advances are crucial stepping stones towards AGI, as language is a central facet of human intelligence.

E. Emotional and Social Intelligence

AGI systems must also exhibit a level of emotional intelligence—the ability to understand, interpret, and respond appropriately to human emotions. Affective computing, which involves teaching machines to recognize and respond to human emotions, is an area of ML that holds potential for AGI. Social intelligence, or the ability to navigate complex human social interactions, will also be essential for AGI systems to coexist with and function alongside people.

3. Challenges in Achieving AGI with ML

While ML is integral to the development of AGI, there are several challenges that need to be overcome before AGI can be realized:

A. Lack of True Common Sense

Current ML models, including deep learning, excel in narrowly defined tasks but still struggle with common sense reasoning. For instance, a machine may recognize objects in an image but not understand the relationships or context between those objects. Developing common sense knowledge and reasoning is a crucial step toward AGI.

B. Limited Data and Transferability

ML models often require vast amounts of labeled data to learn effectively. For AGI, however, the ability to learn from limited or unsupervised data, generalize across tasks, and apply knowledge to new domains with little data is essential. Methods like unsupervised learning, semi-supervised learning, and reinforcement learning are key to addressing this challenge.

C. Alignment with Human Goals

One of the greatest concerns with AGI is ensuring that it behaves in a manner consistent with human values and goals. Ensuring the alignment of AGI with human ethical standards is a challenging problem in both machine learning and philosophy. We must ensure that AGI is built safely and responsibly, with mechanisms to prevent harmful behavior.

4. Conclusion: The Road Ahead for ML and AGI

Machine learning is one of the most important tools we have in the pursuit of Artificial General Intelligence. By enhancing our ability to learn from experience, generalize across tasks, and understand complex data, ML brings us closer to building systems that can think, learn, and reason like humans.

However, achieving AGI will require more than just advancements in ML; it will also require breakthroughs in areas such as cognitive architecture, symbolic reasoning, common sense reasoning, and ethics. While we are still far from creating AGI, the journey toward it is filled with exciting challenges and opportunities.

Ultimately, the integration of ML techniques with human-like cognitive functions, such as adaptability, generalization, and emotional intelligence, will be key to unlocking the full potential of AGI and shaping the future of intelligent systems.

19. Becoming an ML Hero

Your journey doesn't end here—it's just the beginning! This chapter provides a roadmap for further learning, career paths in ML, certifications, and how to build a strong ML portfolio to land your dream job in AI.

19.1 Learning Resources for Advanced ML

As you progress from beginner to advanced levels in machine learning (ML), it becomes essential to continue your education through the best resources available. Advanced ML topics encompass a wide range of cutting-edge techniques, algorithms, and tools that can be challenging to grasp at first. However, with the right resources, you can deepen your understanding and develop the skills necessary to apply these techniques in real-world problems. In this section, we will explore a variety of learning resources, including books, online courses, research papers, and communities, to help you master advanced machine learning.

1. Books

Books offer a deep dive into theoretical concepts and practical applications of advanced machine learning techniques. Here are some excellent choices:

A. "Deep Learning" by Ian Goodfellow, Yoshua Bengio, and Aaron Courville

This book is one of the most comprehensive and widely recognized resources for learning deep learning. Written by leading researchers in the field, it covers both the theoretical foundations and practical implementations of deep learning techniques, including neural networks, optimization, and unsupervised learning. The book provides a detailed understanding of how deep learning models work and their real-world applications.

- **Topics Covered**: Neural networks, backpropagation, convolutional networks, unsupervised learning, generative models, and more.
- **Best For**: Intermediate to advanced learners with a solid foundation in machine learning.

B. "Pattern Recognition and Machine Learning" by Christopher Bishop

This book is considered a classic in the field of machine learning. It offers a comprehensive introduction to probabilistic graphical models and various machine learning algorithms. It's known for its detailed mathematical explanations, making it an excellent choice for those looking to gain a deeper understanding of the statistical foundations behind ML algorithms.

- **Topics Covered**: Bayesian networks, hidden Markov models, clustering, dimensionality reduction, and more.
- **Best For**: Intermediate to advanced learners with a solid mathematical background.

C. "Hands-On Machine Learning with Scikit-Learn, Keras, and TensorFlow" by Aurélien Géron

This book offers a hands-on approach to machine learning, guiding you through the practical implementation of advanced ML techniques using popular Python libraries like Scikit-Learn, Keras, and TensorFlow. It covers both traditional and deep learning methods, making it a great resource for implementing real-world ML projects.

- **Topics Covered**: Supervised learning, unsupervised learning, deep learning, model evaluation, and more.
- **Best For**: Intermediate learners looking for hands-on experience with modern ML libraries.

D. "Machine Learning: A Probabilistic Perspective" by Kevin P. Murphy

This book provides a comprehensive look at machine learning from a probabilistic viewpoint. It's an excellent resource for understanding the probabilistic models and methods used in advanced ML. The book includes both theoretical aspects and practical algorithms.

- **Topics Covered**: Probabilistic graphical models, inference algorithms, deep learning, Bayesian methods, and more.
- **Best For**: Advanced learners who are comfortable with probability theory and statistics.

2. Online Courses and Tutorials

Online courses are an excellent way to learn advanced machine learning concepts interactively. They often combine video lectures, practical exercises, and projects to reinforce your understanding. Here are some of the top platforms and courses:

A. Coursera – Deep Learning Specialization by Andrew Ng (Stanford University)

Offered by one of the pioneers in machine learning, Andrew Ng, this specialization dives deep into deep learning concepts, including neural networks, convolutional networks, sequence models, and more. The course is structured to build knowledge from foundational to advanced topics.

- **Topics Covered**: Neural networks, CNNs, RNNs, backpropagation, sequence models, and more.
- **Best For**: Intermediate learners looking to specialize in deep learning.

B. edX – Advanced Machine Learning by the Higher School of Economics

This advanced-level course on edX offers a comprehensive study of more advanced machine learning topics, including reinforcement learning, deep learning, and natural language processing (NLP). It is ideal for learners who already have a strong background in machine learning.

- **Topics Covered**: Deep learning, reinforcement learning, NLP, and more.
- **Best For**: Advanced learners with prior experience in machine learning.

C. fast.ai – Practical Deep Learning for Coders

This free course focuses on making deep learning accessible by teaching you how to implement state-of-the-art models without getting bogged down by mathematical complexity. It emphasizes practical applications, making it an excellent choice for learners who want to build real-world projects.

- **Topics Covered**: Convolutional networks, transfer learning, NLP, generative models, and more.
- **Best For**: Intermediate learners who want to quickly apply deep learning techniques to real-world problems.

D. Stanford CS231n – Convolutional Neural Networks for Visual Recognition

Stanford's CS231n course offers an in-depth look at convolutional neural networks (CNNs) and their applications to computer vision. It is a highly regarded course, featuring video lectures, assignments, and projects taught by world-leading experts in computer vision and deep learning.

- **Topics Covered**: CNNs, object detection, image classification, deep learning techniques for vision tasks, and more.
- **Best For**: Advanced learners interested in computer vision and deep learning.

3. Research Papers and Journals

To stay at the cutting edge of machine learning, you must engage with the latest research papers. Journals and conferences often publish groundbreaking work on new algorithms and methodologies.

A. ArXiv

ArXiv is a free preprint repository where researchers publish their papers before they are peer-reviewed. You can find a vast collection of research papers on machine learning, including the latest advancements in deep learning, reinforcement learning, and more. Staying updated with papers on ArXiv will give you insights into the current state of ML research.

Website: https://arxiv.org/

Best For: Learners who want to explore the latest developments in ML research.

B. NeurIPS (Conference on Neural Information Processing Systems)

NeurIPS is one of the premier conferences for machine learning research, and it covers a wide range of topics, including deep learning, reinforcement learning, and artificial intelligence. You can find some of the most cutting-edge research papers and presentations from experts in the field.

Website: https://nips.cc/

Best For: Advanced learners who want to stay up-to-date with the latest ML research.

C. Machine Learning Journal (Springer)

The Machine Learning Journal is a peer-reviewed journal that publishes articles on the theory, algorithms, and applications of machine learning. It covers both traditional machine learning methods and emerging techniques.

Website: https://www.springer.com/journal/10994

Best For: Advanced learners interested in theoretical and applied ML research.

4. Communities and Forums

Engaging with machine learning communities can significantly enhance your learning experience. These platforms offer a space to share ideas, ask questions, and get feedback from other learners and professionals in the field.

A. Kaggle

Kaggle is the most popular platform for data science and machine learning competitions. It offers a large selection of datasets, challenges, and community-contributed notebooks. Participating in Kaggle competitions or collaborating with others on machine learning projects can help you gain practical experience in applying advanced techniques to real-world problems.

Website: https://www.kaggle.com/

Best For: Learners looking to apply machine learning skills to real-world projects and competitions.

B. Stack Overflow

Stack Overflow is a widely-used platform for asking and answering programming-related questions. Many ML practitioners and researchers contribute to the platform, making it an excellent resource for troubleshooting and solving problems related to machine learning algorithms and programming.

Website: https://stackoverflow.com/

Best For: General programming and ML-related questions.

C. Reddit - r/MachineLearning

The r/MachineLearning subreddit is one of the largest communities for discussing machine learning news, research, and tutorials. It's a great place to keep up with the latest trends in ML, share projects, and learn from other researchers and practitioners in the field.

Website: https://www.reddit.com/r/MachineLearning/

Best For: Learners who want to engage in discussions on machine learning theory, research, and applications.

As you continue on your journey toward mastering advanced machine learning, the resources listed above can guide you in expanding your knowledge and skills. Whether you prefer books, online courses, research papers, or engaging with the ML community, there is a wealth of material available to help you advance your understanding of complex algorithms and techniques.

By combining theory with practical applications and continuously staying updated with the latest research, you will be well-equipped to tackle challenging machine learning problems and contribute to the future of AI and ML.

19.2 Certifications and ML Career Paths

As machine learning (ML) continues to reshape industries, the demand for skilled professionals in this field is growing rapidly. With the right certifications, hands-on experience, and a clear understanding of career paths, you can position yourself for success in the fast-evolving world of ML. In this section, we will explore some of the most respected certifications available in ML, as well as the various career paths that individuals can pursue after gaining expertise in this area.

1. Machine Learning Certifications

Certifications can help demonstrate your expertise and commitment to potential employers. Here are some of the best machine learning certifications that will enhance your credibility and improve your career prospects.

A. Google Cloud Professional Machine Learning Engineer

The Google Cloud Professional Machine Learning Engineer certification is one of the most sought-after credentials in the industry. It validates the skills needed to design, build, and productionize ML models using Google Cloud technologies. This certification focuses on key ML concepts, such as model training, hyperparameter tuning, data processing, and deploying ML solutions on the cloud.

- **Topics Covered**: Data engineering, machine learning pipelines, model deployment, Google Cloud tools (TensorFlow, BigQuery, etc.).
- **Best For**: ML professionals looking to specialize in cloud-based machine learning environments and tools.

B. Microsoft Certified: Azure AI Engineer Associate

Microsoft's Azure AI Engineer Associate certification focuses on AI and machine learning solutions built on the Azure platform. The certification covers key areas like using Azure Machine Learning services, deploying AI models, and integrating AI into business applications. This certification is ideal for those working with Microsoft Azure tools and services.

- **Topics Covered**: Data preprocessing, model training and evaluation, Azure Machine Learning Studio, deploying models, using AI solutions for business.
- **Best For:** Professionals interested in integrating ML models with business applications and working in cloud computing environments.

C. IBM Data Science Professional Certificate

Offered by IBM on platforms like Coursera, the IBM Data Science Professional Certificate provides a comprehensive introduction to data science and machine learning. Although it starts with foundational topics, the program gradually covers more advanced ML techniques. It includes hands-on projects using Python, Jupyter Notebooks, and libraries such as Scikit-Learn, making it an excellent entry point for those aiming to build practical ML skills.

- **Topics Covered**: Python programming, data visualization, machine learning algorithms, data analysis, and statistics.
- **Best For**: Beginners looking to enter the field of data science and machine learning with a structured learning path.

D. TensorFlow Developer Certificate

The TensorFlow Developer Certificate is for individuals who want to demonstrate their proficiency in using TensorFlow, one of the most widely-used machine learning frameworks. The certification exam focuses on practical machine learning concepts like neural networks, model optimization, and deploying models using TensorFlow.

- **Topics Covered**: Neural networks, deep learning, model evaluation, TensorFlow tools (Keras, TensorFlow.js, TensorFlow Lite), and deployment strategies.
- **Best For**: Learners with a basic understanding of machine learning looking to specialize in deep learning using TensorFlow.

E. AWS Certified Machine Learning – Specialty

Amazon Web Services (AWS) offers a Certified Machine Learning – Specialty exam that assesses the skills required to design, implement, and maintain ML solutions on the AWS cloud platform. This certification covers the entire ML lifecycle, from data exploration and modeling to deploying and optimizing models.

- **Topics Covered**: Data engineering, exploratory data analysis, model training, deployment, and optimization using AWS tools.
- **Best For**: Professionals who want to work in cloud-based ML environments and specialize in AWS tools and services.

F. Coursera – Deep Learning Specialization by Andrew Ng

Offered by Andrew Ng and Stanford University, the Deep Learning Specialization is a widely recognized course that covers deep learning techniques in detail. It consists of several courses that provide hands-on projects and cover concepts such as neural networks, CNNs, RNNs, and generative adversarial networks (GANs). This specialization is ideal for learners who want to specialize in deep learning and neural networks.

- **Topics Covered**: Neural networks, deep learning, CNNs, RNNs, GANs, sequence models, and more.
- **Best For**: Individuals interested in specializing in deep learning or AI applications that rely heavily on neural networks.

2. Career Paths in Machine Learning

Machine learning offers a broad range of career paths depending on your interests, skillset, and specialization. Here are some of the most common career paths in ML:

A. Machine Learning Engineer

Role: Machine learning engineers are responsible for building and deploying machine learning models into production environments. They work with data scientists to develop algorithms and implement them at scale. ML engineers focus on ensuring that models perform well and can handle large-scale, real-world data.

- **Key Skills**: Programming (Python, Java, C++), deep learning, algorithms, software engineering, cloud services (AWS, Azure, GCP).
- **Key Tools**: TensorFlow, Keras, PyTorch, Scikit-Learn, Apache Spark, cloud platforms.
- **Salary**: $100,000 - $160,000+ per year (depending on experience and location).
- **Best For**: Those with a strong background in software engineering who enjoy building and optimizing models for real-world applications.

B. Data Scientist

Role: Data scientists analyze large datasets and use machine learning algorithms to extract valuable insights. They are responsible for building predictive models, performing exploratory data analysis (EDA), and communicating findings to stakeholders. Data scientists often work on a variety of projects, from improving business operations to developing recommendation systems.

- **Key Skills**: Data analysis, statistical modeling, machine learning, data visualization, programming (Python, R).
- **Key Tools**: Scikit-Learn, Pandas, Matplotlib, Jupyter Notebooks, SQL.
- **Salary**: $90,000 - $140,000+ per year.
- **Best For**: Individuals who enjoy working with data, solving complex problems, and communicating insights from data analysis.

C. Deep Learning Specialist

Role: Deep learning specialists focus on designing and implementing deep neural networks, including CNNs, RNNs, and transformers. They typically work in fields like computer vision, natural language processing (NLP), and autonomous systems. This role requires specialized knowledge of neural network architectures and frameworks.

- **Key Skills**: Deep learning algorithms, neural networks, GPU computing, model optimization.
- **Key Tools**: TensorFlow, Keras, PyTorch, CUDA.
- **Salary**: $110,000 - $160,000+ per year.

- **Best For**: Professionals with an interest in neural networks, AI, and cutting-edge deep learning research.

D. Research Scientist (Machine Learning)

Role: Research scientists in ML focus on advancing the field by developing new algorithms, models, and techniques. They work in academic institutions, research labs, and large tech companies, contributing to the state of the art in machine learning. Research scientists often publish their findings in journals or present at conferences.

- **Key Skills**: Machine learning theory, statistical modeling, research methodology, programming.
- **Key Tools**: Python, MATLAB, TensorFlow, PyTorch, Git.
- **Salary**: $90,000 - $150,000+ per year.
- **Best For**: Individuals with a passion for conducting research, solving theoretical problems, and pushing the boundaries of ML technology.

E. AI Product Manager

Role: AI product managers oversee the development of AI-powered products. They bridge the gap between technical teams (engineers and data scientists) and business stakeholders. Their role involves understanding both customer needs and the technical feasibility of implementing AI solutions.

- **Key Skills**: Product management, AI/ML concepts, project management, business strategy.
- **Key Tools**: Jira, Trello, Agile methodology.
- **Salary**: $100,000 - $170,000+ per year.
- **Best For**: Those with a combination of technical knowledge and business acumen who enjoy managing AI-driven products.

F. AI/ML Consultant

Role: AI and ML consultants advise businesses on how to integrate machine learning solutions into their operations. They provide guidance on model selection, deployment strategies, and scaling solutions. Consultants often work with multiple clients, offering their expertise across a variety of industries.

- **Key Skills**: Problem-solving, client communication, machine learning algorithms, business strategy.

- **Key Tools**: Python, SQL, cloud services.
- **Salary**: $90,000 - $150,000+ per year.
- **Best For**: Experienced professionals who enjoy working on diverse projects and providing strategic advice to businesses.

Machine learning is a rapidly evolving field with vast career opportunities across industries. Earning certifications can help solidify your knowledge and demonstrate your proficiency to employers. Whether you are just starting or are looking to deepen your expertise, the right certifications will set you apart in a competitive job market.

As the demand for machine learning professionals continues to rise, it's important to choose a career path that aligns with your interests and strengths. Whether you're drawn to engineering, research, product management, or consultancy, the world of machine learning offers exciting and lucrative career opportunities.

19.3 Building an ML Portfolio & Contributing to Open Source

As you advance in your machine learning (ML journey, one of the most important aspects of showcasing your expertise is building a strong portfolio. A well-curated portfolio not only demonstrates your technical skills but also highlights your problem-solving ability and your capacity to handle real-world challenges. Alongside this, contributing to open-source projects is another powerful way to gain visibility, develop practical skills, and network within the ML community. In this section, we'll discuss strategies for building an ML portfolio and how contributing to open-source projects can accelerate your career in machine learning.

1. Building an ML Portfolio

A portfolio serves as a tangible representation of your abilities, and it allows potential employers or collaborators to see your practical experience in the field of machine learning. Here's how to build an impressive and effective ML portfolio:

A. Showcase a Diverse Range of Projects

To make your portfolio stand out, it's important to showcase a variety of projects that demonstrate the breadth of your machine learning skills. Here are a few project ideas that will help you display your versatility:

Supervised Learning Models: Build classification or regression models, such as predicting house prices (linear regression) or classifying images of animals (decision trees, random forests, etc.). These projects demonstrate your understanding of common ML algorithms.

Unsupervised Learning: Implement clustering algorithms like K-means or hierarchical clustering to analyze customer data, or use dimensionality reduction techniques like PCA or t-SNE to explore high-dimensional data sets. These projects show your ability to work with data where labels are unavailable.

Deep Learning: Implement deep neural networks for tasks like image classification using Convolutional Neural Networks (CNNs) or time series forecasting using Recurrent Neural Networks (RNNs). Working with popular frameworks like TensorFlow or PyTorch will show your skills in the latest ML technologies.

Reinforcement Learning: Work on projects where you can apply reinforcement learning algorithms, such as training an AI agent to play a game or optimize a business process.

Natural Language Processing (NLP): Implement text classification, sentiment analysis, or language translation using NLP libraries like NLTK, SpaCy, or Hugging Face's Transformers. Projects like these demonstrate your ability to work with unstructured data.

Time Series Forecasting: Build models that predict future data points using time series techniques. This can be applied to financial forecasting, sales prediction, or even weather forecasting.

Anomaly Detection: Detect anomalies in data (e.g., fraud detection or network intrusion). This kind of project showcases your ability to work with imbalanced datasets and unsupervised learning.

End-to-End Machine Learning Projects: Instead of just building a model, show that you can go from data collection to data preprocessing, feature engineering, model building, evaluation, and deployment. This is essential to demonstrate your ability to handle the full machine learning pipeline.

B. Publish Your Work on GitHub

GitHub has become the gold standard for sharing code and collaborating with others in the data science and ML communities. It provides you with an excellent platform to showcase your projects, collaborate with others, and get feedback on your work. Here's how to make the most out of GitHub:

Organize Your Repositories: For each project, make sure your repository is organized in a way that makes it easy for others (or potential employers) to understand. Include a detailed README file that explains the purpose of the project, the data used, the models implemented, the results achieved, and any challenges you faced.

Include Jupyter Notebooks: Many data science and machine learning projects are shared in Jupyter Notebooks. They allow you to present both the code and the results (visualizations, model accuracy) in an easy-to-read format. This makes it easy for others to follow your thought process.

Document Your Code: Good documentation helps others understand your code, making your repository more appealing to potential collaborators and employers. Use inline comments, docstrings, and markdown cells in your notebooks to explain the steps and the logic behind the code.

Create Project Descriptions: Include well-written descriptions and outlines for each project. Add visuals like plots, graphs, and model evaluations to illustrate your results. This not only shows your technical ability but also your communication skills.

Showcase Challenges and Solutions: Don't hesitate to share the challenges you faced during the project and the steps you took to overcome them. Employers love candidates who can demonstrate problem-solving skills, as these are essential for working with real-world data.

Share Model Performance: Include performance metrics (accuracy, precision, recall, etc.) and visualizations of your model's results, such as confusion matrices, ROC curves, or learning curves. This shows your ability to evaluate and fine-tune models effectively.

Collaborate with Others: Contributing to others' projects or collaborating on open-source ML projects is a great way to demonstrate teamwork, as well as your willingness to learn from others.

C. Create Personal Projects that Reflect Your Interests

One of the best ways to make your portfolio stand out is by creating projects that align with your personal interests. When you're passionate about the problem you're solving, the quality of your work will naturally be higher, and it will also be more engaging to potential employers. Examples include:

- **Sports Analytics**: Analyzing game data to predict outcomes or optimize team strategies.
- **Healthcare**: Building models to predict disease outcomes or analyze medical images.
- **Music or Art**: Developing machine learning algorithms that generate new music or artwork.

These personal projects not only demonstrate your ML expertise but also highlight your passion and creativity.

2. Contributing to Open Source

Contributing to open-source projects is one of the best ways to gain exposure, work on real-world problems, and collaborate with experienced ML practitioners. Here's how to get started with open-source contributions and why they can benefit your career:

A. Why Contribute to Open Source?

Hands-On Experience: Contributing to open-source projects allows you to gain practical experience working on large-scale projects. You can contribute code, bug fixes, documentation, and testing, all of which build your ML and software engineering skills.

Exposure to Real-World Problems: Many open-source projects involve working on real-world problems that can range from NLP to computer vision, data cleaning, and more. You'll get exposure to challenges that arise in industry settings.

Networking: Open-source communities are vibrant and collaborative. By contributing, you'll have the opportunity to network with professionals, learn from experienced contributors, and even find mentors who can guide you in your career.

Building Your Reputation: Active participation in open-source projects can boost your reputation within the ML community. It allows you to demonstrate your skills to potential employers, collaborators, and peers.

Portfolio Building: Contributions to popular open-source projects are a great addition to your portfolio. They show that you can work within a collaborative environment and contribute to impactful work.

B. How to Contribute to Open Source

Start Small: Find beginner-friendly open-source ML projects on platforms like GitHub and start with small contributions. You could fix minor bugs, write documentation, or improve code comments. Many repositories label issues with "good first issue," which are great starting points.

Pick Projects that Align with Your Interests: Choose open-source projects that align with your learning goals. If you're interested in NLP, for example, contribute to projects focused on text processing. Working on projects that interest you will make your contributions more engaging.

Learn the Tools: Familiarize yourself with Git, GitHub workflows, and pull requests. These tools are essential when collaborating on open-source projects. Learning how to properly contribute, review, and merge code is crucial in a professional setting.

Engage with the Community: Don't just contribute code. Participate in community discussions, ask questions, and help others by reviewing pull requests. By building relationships with other contributors, you can grow your knowledge and make your mark in the community.

Contribute to Libraries and Frameworks: Many popular machine learning libraries and frameworks (like TensorFlow, PyTorch, Scikit-Learn, etc.) are open-source and welcome contributions. Contributing to such libraries can help you learn best practices and gain exposure in the ML community.

C. Finding Open Source Projects to Contribute To

Some popular open-source machine learning projects where you can contribute include:

- **Scikit-Learn**: A popular Python library for machine learning. The project welcomes contributions ranging from bug fixes to adding new features.
- **TensorFlow**: A widely-used framework for deep learning. Contributing to TensorFlow helps you work on cutting-edge deep learning technologies.
- **Keras**: A high-level neural networks API. Keras is another excellent project to contribute to, especially if you're interested in deep learning.
- **Hugging Face Transformers**: A popular NLP library. Hugging Face welcomes contributions related to improving models, documentation, or adding new features.

By contributing to such projects, you'll not only improve your skills but also gain credibility within the ML community.

Building a strong ML portfolio and contributing to open-source projects are two of the best ways to develop your skills, gain practical experience, and make meaningful contributions to the ML community. A well-curated portfolio allows you to showcase your expertise, while open-source contributions can connect you with like-minded individuals and help you grow in your career. Both of these activities will give you the credibility and visibility you need to succeed in the exciting and rapidly growing field of machine learning.

19.4 The Road Ahead: Continuing Your ML Journey

Machine learning (ML) is an incredibly dynamic and rapidly evolving field. As you progress through this journey, you'll realize that there's always more to learn, explore, and experiment with. The road ahead is both exciting and challenging, as new advancements and methodologies continue to emerge. In this section, we'll explore how you can continue your ML journey, further enhance your expertise, and stay at the forefront of this ever-changing field.

1. Embrace Lifelong Learning

The field of machine learning is vast and constantly evolving. What you learn today may be surpassed by newer algorithms, techniques, and frameworks tomorrow. As an ML practitioner, it's essential to adopt a mindset of lifelong learning. Here's how you can keep growing:

A. Stay Updated with the Latest Research

Machine learning research is advancing at an unprecedented rate, with new papers and breakthroughs being published regularly. To stay at the cutting edge, it's crucial to keep up with the latest research and trends. Some ways to do this include:

- **Reading Research Papers**: Websites like arXiv offer access to preprints of the latest machine learning papers. Reading papers can give you insights into new methodologies, algorithms, and trends in the field.
- **Following Key Conferences**: Major conferences such as NeurIPS (Conference on Neural Information Processing Systems), ICML (International Conference on Machine Learning), and CVPR (Computer Vision and Pattern Recognition) are great places to discover the latest developments in ML and deep learning.

- **Engaging with Research Blogs**: Many ML researchers and companies publish insightful blogs summarizing recent papers, trends, and emerging topics. Blogs from organizations like Google AI, OpenAI, and DeepMind are excellent resources.

B. Learn Advanced Topics

As you become more comfortable with the basics of machine learning, you can explore more advanced topics. Some areas to dive deeper into include:

- **Deep Learning**: Understand the intricacies of neural networks, including advanced topics such as generative models (GANs), attention mechanisms, transformers, and reinforcement learning. Exploring the inner workings of these algorithms will give you a deeper understanding of state-of-the-art ML models.
- **Natural Language Processing (NLP):** With the growing importance of text and language in today's data landscape, exploring NLP topics such as transformers (BERT, GPT), semantic embeddings, and neural machine translation will expand your capabilities.
- **Graph Neural Networks (GNNs):** GNNs are an exciting area for modeling graph-structured data, with applications in social networks, biology, and recommendation systems.
- **Explainable AI (XAI):** As ML models become more complex, there's an increasing need for explainability. Exploring techniques in XAI will allow you to make ML models more interpretable, a key consideration in high-stakes fields like healthcare and finance.
- **Quantum Machine Learning**: Although still an emerging area, quantum computing has the potential to revolutionize machine learning. Exploring this frontier will open new doors to understanding how quantum mechanics can accelerate ML.

C. Online Courses and Certifications

Taking online courses is a great way to deepen your knowledge. Many top universities and organizations offer specialized courses that dive into advanced ML topics. Some recommended platforms for continuing education include:

- **Coursera**: Offering a wide range of ML courses, from basic to advanced levels, including deep learning and reinforcement learning.
- **edX**: Home to several university-level courses in AI, ML, and related fields, including MIT's renowned "Deep Learning for Self-Driving Cars" course.

- **Udacity**: Offering nano-degree programs in machine learning, artificial intelligence, and deep learning, tailored for both beginners and advanced practitioners.
- **Fast.ai:** Known for its deep learning courses that emphasize hands-on practice and rapid deployment of models, Fast.ai is a great resource for learning modern ML techniques.

Certifications from well-known institutions like Google, Microsoft, and IBM can also be beneficial in demonstrating your expertise to employers.

2. Build a Strong Network

Networking is an essential part of your journey in machine learning. Being part of a community allows you to collaborate, exchange ideas, and stay motivated. Here's how to build and maintain a strong professional network:

A. Attend Conferences and Meetups

Machine learning conferences are ideal for learning about new research and connecting with others in the field. These events allow you to:

- Learn from experts in the field.
- Participate in workshops and tutorials.
- Meet potential mentors, collaborators, and employers.

If attending conferences in person isn't feasible, many events are held virtually. Additionally, ML meetups and workshops in your area or online offer more casual settings to connect with like-minded individuals.

B. Join Online Communities

The machine learning community thrives on collaboration. Joining online communities can help you stay informed about new trends, get feedback on your work, and contribute to discussions. Consider joining:

- **Reddit**: Subreddits like r/MachineLearning, r/learnmachinelearning, and r/datascience are great for sharing resources, asking questions, and staying updated on ML news.

- **Kaggle**: Kaggle is not only a platform for data science competitions but also a vibrant community of ML enthusiasts. Engaging in Kaggle kernels (notebooks) and competitions will help you learn from others and improve your skills.
- **GitHub**: Contributing to open-source projects and collaborating with other ML practitioners on GitHub will help you build your network and credibility.

C. Mentorship and Collaboration

Seek out mentors who can guide you in your ML journey. Whether through formal mentorship programs or informal collaborations, learning from someone with more experience is invaluable. A mentor can help you avoid common pitfalls, suggest resources, and offer career advice.

Collaborating on projects is another great way to learn. Working with others on real-world ML projects will help you expand your skill set and gain exposure to new tools and techniques.

3. Build Real-World Experience

The best way to learn is through hands-on experience. As you continue your ML journey, applying your knowledge to real-world problems will help you solidify your understanding and prepare you for challenges in the professional world.

A. Freelance or Work on Projects

Freelancing or taking on part-time work related to ML can be a great way to gain real-world experience. Websites like Upwork, Freelancer, and Fiverr allow you to find clients who need ML expertise. Additionally, you can offer services to startups or NGOs that are looking for data-driven insights but may not have a dedicated team.

Alternatively, you can continue working on personal or collaborative projects that tackle real-world problems. For example, you can build ML models for local businesses, non-profits, or social causes, which will help you expand your portfolio.

B. Build Industry-Specific Expertise

If you're interested in a particular industry—finance, healthcare, retail, or gaming—specializing in ML for that industry can give you a unique edge. By understanding both the domain and the technology, you can apply ML in more targeted and impactful ways. For instance:

- **Finance**: Work on fraud detection, risk analysis, and algorithmic trading.
- **Healthcare**: Focus on medical image analysis, drug discovery, or patient outcome prediction.
- **E-Commerce**: Develop recommendation systems or predictive customer behavior models.

Building domain-specific expertise can help you stand out to employers and provide unique value.

4. Contribute to the Growth of ML

As you gain more experience, you may find that you want to give back to the ML community. Here are a few ways you can contribute:

A. Share Your Knowledge

Writing blog posts, creating tutorials, or teaching others in online courses can help you solidify your knowledge while also giving back to the community. Sharing your experiences and insights allows others to learn from your journey and builds your reputation as an expert.

B. Develop Open-Source Tools

If you identify a gap or a need in the ML community, consider developing open-source tools or libraries. This will not only help others but also position you as an innovator in the field.

C. Engage in Ethical AI Initiatives

As ML grows, so does its societal impact. Getting involved in initiatives related to ethical AI, fairness, bias, and transparency will contribute to ensuring that ML models benefit society in positive and inclusive ways. You can help promote responsible AI practices by engaging in debates, writing papers, and participating in relevant groups or organizations.

5. Conclusion: Stay Curious, Stay Passionate

The road ahead in machine learning is filled with limitless possibilities. By committing to lifelong learning, building real-world experience, staying connected with the community, and contributing to the growth of the field, you will not only advance your own career but also help shape the future of ML. Stay curious, keep experimenting, and always be open to new ideas and technologies. Your journey is just beginning, and the best is yet to come!

Machine Learning is revolutionizing the way we interact with technology, making data-driven decision-making more powerful than ever before. Machine Learning 101: From Zero to Hero is your comprehensive guide to understanding and applying machine learning concepts from scratch. Whether you're a complete beginner or looking to refine your ML skills, this book takes you step by step through the fundamentals, key algorithms, real-world applications, and advanced deep learning techniques.

Starting with the basics of data, models, and mathematical foundations, this book gradually builds up to more complex topics, including supervised and unsupervised learning, neural networks, and deep learning architectures like CNNs and RNNs. With hands-on coding exercises in Python, practical examples, and industry case studies, you'll gain both theoretical knowledge and real-world experience.

By the end of this journey, you will be able to build, train, and optimize your own ML models, apply them to real-world problems, and take your first steps toward a career in AI. The road from zero to hero in machine learning starts here—your adventure into the future of AI begins now!

Dear Reader,

From the very first page to the last, you have been on an incredible journey into the world of machine learning. Whether you are a complete beginner or an aspiring expert, I am truly grateful that you chose Machine Learning 101: From Zero to Hero as your guide. Your time, curiosity, and dedication to learning mean the world to me.

Writing this book has been a labor of love, fueled by the belief that knowledge should be accessible to all. If even one concept in these pages has helped you take a step forward, then this journey has been worthwhile. Machine learning is a vast and ever-evolving field, and I encourage you to keep exploring, experimenting, and pushing the boundaries of what is possible.

I also want to extend my deepest gratitude to my readers, supporters, and the entire AI community for inspiring me to continue sharing knowledge. If this book has helped you in any way, I would love to hear your thoughts. Your feedback, questions, and ideas not only help me grow as a writer but also shape future editions and projects.

Thank you for being a part of this learning experience. Keep challenging yourself, keep building, and never stop learning—because the future of AI needs thinkers, creators, and innovators like you.

With appreciation and best wishes,

Gilbert Gutiérrez

www.ingramcontent.com/pod-product-compliance
Lightning Source LLC
Chambersburg PA
CBHW080548060326

40689CB00021B/4780